AF540239

COOPERATIVE PRINCIPLES AND PRACTICE

By

Dr. M.Karthikeyan
Assistant Professor
Department of Cooperatives
Institute of Cooperatives & Development Studies
Ambo University
P.B. No. 511
Ambo, West Shoa
Ethiopia

DISCOVERY PUBLISHING HOUSE PVT. LTD.
NEW DELHI-110 002

Published by:
Tilak Wasan
DISCOVERY PUBLISHING HOUSE PVT. LTD.
4383/4A, Ansari Road, Darya Ganj
New Delhi-110 002 (India)
Phone : +91-11-23279245, 43596064-65
Fax : +91-11-23253475
E-mail : parul.wasan@gmail.com
discoverypublishinghouse@gmail.com
web : www.discoverypublishinggroup.com

***First Edition:* 2012**
ISBN: 978-93-5056-000-6

Cooperative Principles and Practice

Printed at:
Shree Balaji Art Press
Delhi

Preface

Dear Readers! It is my pleasure to introduce the text book on 'Cooperative Principles and Practice' to you. It has been designed in a detailed manner so as to help you understand the basic concepts of cooperation, principles and practice of cooperation. This textbook is like compendium on cooperative principles and practices world over. I have tried to dovetail everything inline with cooperative basics, concepts, principles, contributions made by cooperators from various countries and cooperative practices.

This work is based on my experience as teacher, practitioner, trainer and researcher in the field of cooperatives for more than 15 years. The present work is based on Under Graduate programme curriculum and outcome of my teaching and research experience, articles published in reputed journals, and discussions with cooperative officials. This book will be very much useful to the students of under graduate, to professionals in cooperatives, and the trainers who are working in various training establishments. I have drawn the inputs from various materials; papers, journals, books and I have consulted several of my friends, colleagues and field experts. I am ever grateful and thankful to them for their immense support and healthy criticism. I hope that the readers of this book will get knowledge on Cooperative principles and practices. Any useful comments, suggestions to improve the present version are welcome and solicited from the readers. I am thankful and grateful to Parul Wasan, Discovery Publishing House Pvt. Ltd., New Delhi for publishing this book neatly under his renowned label for the cooperative knowledge community.

M. Karthikeyan

Contents

Contents

Chapter 1 Economic Systems and Cooperatives

Meaning

The word 'system' refers to any set of objects which together form a functioning whole, as well as the relationships between these objects or their characteristics which link them up in to that whole. The objects are to be understood very broadly, not necessary as material things. An economic system's objects are people, their institutions, their resources and productive assets, their wealth of consumables, their skills, and others.

The adjective 'economic' refers to on particular aspect of human behaviour. All human activities involve the use of some resources: material assets, persons' aptitudes, and time. All human activities also involve choice between alternative courses of action and their combinations. Choice involves the consideration of available alternatives from the point of view of the intended purpose, i.e., the benefit value of the outcome, and the associated costs. Thus, activities appear as economic if the accompanying allocation of resources is considered from the point view of costs and benefits.

Every activity has its resources—allocation and cost-benefit side. Therefore, every activity has its economic angle, besides having plenty of other characteristics. If every activity has its economic aspect, then 'economy' is coextensive with society, and the 'economic system,' too, spreads out across the social space. Its location is the entire span of the social system of which it is an aspect a sub system.

Elements of Economic System

There are four major classes of elements, which constitute an economic system: resources, participants, process elements, and institutions. There is no special difficulty in sorting out into these 'boxes' all the basic familiar concepts one encounters in discussing things economic.

Resources

These include, first of all, portions of the nature-given environment, selected by people as suitable for their purpose. These are the raw natural resources — land, water, air, gravity, as well as physical, chemical, and biological properties of inorganic and organic things. Processed natural resources become materials and fixed producer durables, i.e., 'tools' in the broadest sense, not just plows or machine tools but also structures, means of transportation and communication, computers, books, records of information, etc. The stock of money and other assets of social use belong here too. Finally, there is labour—the so-called human capital: a reservoir of physical and mental services, a stock of capacity to work, skills, and accumulated knowledge attached to human beings. Technology and entrepreneurship are other resources of economic system.

Participants

These are naturally people. They may be considered as individuals, but it is more useful to think of them as aggregated into groups or units organized for define purposes. Also, one and the same individual will, as a rule, appear in different participating groups, simultaneously or in succession. We all play different roles as members of a consuming household, citizens, producers (workers, entrepreneurs, hobbyists, or government agents), etc.

The standard way is to subdivide participants of the economic system into firms (mainly transforming inputs into outputs), households (mainly transforming outputs into final satisfaction, i.e., consuming, plus supplying human resources), and the government (transforming inputs into outputs which have the character of public or collective goods).

Process Elements

The process elements form a logical sequence. The list starts with information, which underlies decisions. Decisions are followed by their implementation, i.e., the use of real inputs, and their transformation into various outcomes. Among outcomes we count not only outputs in the narrow sense, but also income distribution, price changes, inventory accumulation, degree of unemployment, environmental disruption, new inventions and discoveries, and ultimately the level of satisfactions, the state of 'social welfare,' which includes the impact upon the social structure and its various non-economic aspects.

Institutions

By 'institutions' (in the sense of elements of the economic system) we mean certain stabilized patterns of relationships, which tie the participants together, or particular forms and patterns of the process elements inaction. 'Institutions' in this sense are analytic abstractions. Needless to say, they must not be confused with the buildings (such as offices, factories, or stock and commodity exchanges) in which some of these stabilized patens of behaviour occur. Market is an economic institution in that sense: stabilized patterns of buying or selling. Slavery is an institution: behaviour of human beings such that one class is treated as property of another class. Private property is an institution: it stabilizes the access to the use of certain objects and narrows it down to specified individuals while excluding the rest.

Cooperation and Capitalism

Capitalism is a system of economic organization in which business and industries are organized and carried on for profit by private enterprises with a minimum of government interference. The essential features of capitalism are:

- Individualism and personal gain as primary motives.
- The private ownership of the means of production.
- Private property and inheritance.
- Competition in the market as the regulator of price and business activity.
- Freedom of contract and enterprise.
- Class conflict between labor and capital.
- Freedom from state interference.

Cooperation and Capitalism have been viewed as same on account of the following points of similarity:

- Like capitalism, cooperatives also accept the right of private property, the right of contract, inheritance and right of private enterprise.
- The cooperatives also use capital to carry on the activities and pay interest for its use.
- Like a capitalistic enterprise they also employ managers and compensate them on the basis of the quality of service they render.
- Cooperatives also depend upon business efficiency for their success just as capitalistic enterprises do.
- Cooperatives also lay emphasized on profits.
- Both capitalists and cooperators generally oppose the encroachment of government in business.

The following are the main points of difference between cooperation and capitalism:

- In capitalistic economy a clique of shareholders predominates and plays the pivotal role, but in cooperatives it is each member who is its foundation and occupies an equal position.
- In capitalistic economy capital occupies the most important position while in a cooperative economy capital is reduced to a secondary position.
- Capitalistic economy is dominated by profit motive while cooperative exists for service and profit is only a byproduct of the services rendered.
- In capitalistic economy voting is done on the basis of share holdings while in a cooperative enterprise every man has only one vote irrespective of the number of shares held by him.
- Capitalism is built upon the exploitation of man, whereas cooperation seeks to end exploitation of man by man.
- Capitalist believe in competition and spirit of rivalry which leads to clash of interests whereas cooperation works on the principle of self-help through mutual help and adopts peaceful methods in a spirit of service.
- In a capitalistic organization money rules men while in cooperative organization men rule money.
- Capitalistic organizations are association of capital, while cooperatives are association of human beings.
- Capitalism leads to concentration of wealth and inequalities but cooperation tends to bring about equalities, and dispersal of wealth.
- A capitalistic organization is a combination of the strong to exploit the weak, whereas a cooperative is a combination of the weak, whereas a cooperative is a combination of the weak, whereas a cooperative is a combination of the weak to grow strong.
- In the capitalistic system the capitalists employ the workers and undertake the risk, while in the cooperative system of association, the workers employ capital and undertake the risk of business.

- The evolution of capitalism is towards monopoly, while the evolution cooperation is towards decentralization.
- Under capitalism there is no joint ownership, equal control or equitable sharing of the returns, while under cooperation all are owners, all are equal in control, all shares equitably on the returns of their joint efforts.
- Capitalism leads to booms and slumps, but cooperation leads to steady production as it prevents speculation and stabilizes prices.
- Capitalism exalts materialism, while cooperation strives for the development of cultural and spiritual values of individuals.

Cooperation and Socialism

Socialism is a socio-economic system in which public authority or the community owns material means of production and operates not for profit but for the services of the community. Under this system the state owns, operates and distributes all the productive resources of a community. The essential features of an economy are as follows:

- All means of production and distribution are to be owned by the state.
- No private enterprise is permitted.
- The state takes the responsibility of employment.
- Central planning is the chief instrument of bringing about socialism.
- All social services like education; medical facilities and other welfare services get top priority and become responsibility of the state.
- Each individual gets fixed wages.
- Profits go to the state.
- Remuneration is made on the basis of each according to his ability and each according to his need.

The following are the points of similarity between cooperation and socialism:

- Both the systems lay emphasis on distribution of wealth.
- Both the systems have a common origin.
- Both lay emphasis on service and not for profits.
- Both lay emphasis on improved use of resources.
- Both lay emphasis on collective action as opposed to individualism of capitalism.
- Both systems are democratic in character.
- Both system desires to eliminate the evil effects of competition.
- The cardinal principles of both these systems are equality, equity and liberty.
- Both the systems are based on moral foundation and believe in human brotherhood.

The following are the main points of distinction between cooperation and state socialism:

- Sate socialism stands for the abolition of private property, while cooperation favors extension of private property.
- The object of state socialism is public welfare, while the object of a cooperative enterprise is service to members.
- In state socialism there is the element of compulsion, whereas cooperative movement is a voluntary association in which compulsion does not find any place.
- In state socialism a central authority takes the decisions, while in cooperative enterprise members take decisions'.
- Capital does not find an important place in a socialist economy but cooperatives do not recognize the place of capital in the production of wealth.
- Socialist economy is basically a workers' economy, based on state help, while in cooperative economy the consumer is the foundation.

- In socialist economy the surplus or profit goes to the state, in cooperatives it goes to the members on the basis of patronage dividend.
- In socialist economy state officials exercise control, while in cooperative members do it democratically.
- Politics finds a top place in socialism, but the creed of cooperativism is political neutrality.

Socialist advocates the use of force and violence to attain the objectives, whereas cooperators desire to achieve the goal by education and propaganda.

Cooperative Commonwealth

So far we talked about different kinds of business organization and compared them with a cooperative organization. These organizations work under two broad types of economic systems, namely, capitalistic and socialistic, or in other words, systems of private enterprise and public enterprise. In the former, the production as well as distribution are owned and controlled by individuals while in the latter they are under the ownership and control of the state.

The latter system was initiated with the chief objectives of augmenting social welfare and of providing equality of opportunities. However, lack of personal touch and incentive for workers, curtailment of individual freedom and lack of proper use of individual talents have been responsible for the slow growth of the system.

Cooperation acts as a balancing factor between these diverse economic systems. It combines the maximum of both. It fulfils the needs of individuals without harming or exploiting others. It assures higher standard of living for its members without deteriorating the standard of others. It honours ethical values as well as efficient business. In the distribution of profits it treats the entire members equal. All members are equally the owners of the instruments of production. There is no difference between the workers and employer and consumers and producers. This harmonious blending of interests does not only provide economic and social benefits to individuals but to the society as a whole. Cooperation is a method of business, but it does not undermine human welfare. It believes in character building and in inculcating moral values among its members. Cooperation is, thus, an equalizing factor, between, capitalistic and socialistic forms of organizations. It mitigates the voracious profiteering of the capitalistic enterprisers and reduces social tensions between the social classes. It safeguards the interest of the weaker sections within capitalism and is also socialist in its nature. In a capitalist economy it plays an equalizing role as a welfare factor.

Charles Gide, one of the cooperative pioneers aimed at establishing a cooperative republic in which the cooperatives would rule the entire economic life. In other words, he wanted to establish a cooperative world through cooperation. The idea of a 'cooperative commonwealth' has gained quite a good deal of currency in various quarters. According to the International Cooperative Alliance, "it should replace the present day system of private enterprise base on competition with a cooperative system supporting the interests of the whole community and based on the principles of mutual self-help".

The concept of national economy based entirely on cooperatives has not been supported on the following grounds:

- Owing to the rapid changes in the field of science and technology the development of heavy industries, mining, power etc., has reached such a stage that a few enterprisers control their supply. These gigantic enterprises cannot be run on a cooperative basis, and if that were done, it would lead to the establishment of cooperative monopolies, which would not serve the best interest of the society.
- The modern industrial sources require large capital, which cannot be supplied by a cooperative system since cooperatives are essentially an organization of the weak.

- Foreign trade with a large volume of turnover cannot be organized on a cooperative basis.
- The existing industrial enterprises operating with huge capital cannot be liquidated since small people cannot purchase them.
- The big financial institutions like the banks cannot run efficiently and smoothly on a cooperative basis.

Cooperation, thus, has its own role to play. It has wide scope of operation both in capitalistic and socialized economies. It can function effectively in every sphere wherever the direct interest of the members is involved. It has wide scope in the supply of goods and services to the consumers, in agricultural production and construction and maintenance of houses, production of consumer goods etc. A strong cooperative sector can and must exist within the capitalistic as well as the socialistic system.

Cooperatives and other forms of Enterprises

All non-government operated business is private business including that of cooperatives. Through common usage, the term private business often refers to non-cooperative, non-governmental business and is considered the opposite of cooperative business. However, it should be apparent that cooperatives are also private businesses—but with cooperative ownership.

From the standpoint of legal organization, there are three basic types of private business organizations in our free enterprise system: individually owned businesses: partnership of two or more persons: and corporations. Corporations may be either profit-type (standard investor-oriented) or non-profit type (patron-oriented or cooperative). Since these two differ in many respects, it may be just as well to classify the forms of business organizations as:

- Individually owned businesses or sole proprietorships.
- Partnerships.
- Standard or regular corporations.
- Cooperatives.

The following table summarizes the differences in methods of operation of these four types of business. (*See Table 1.1 on next page*)

Individually-owned

One person owns and controls the operations. He assumes the risk of ownership keeps all profits, and bears any losses. The owner's decisions are final. He is personally responsible for the investment in the business, the actions of his firm, and for any growth or expansion of his company.

There are advantages to this method of doing business. The owner is his own boss-he does not take orders from anyone. Any net profits belong to him and need not be shared with anyone. (This does not preclude a profit-sharing plan with employees.) Individually owned businesses are easy to set up-on incorporation papers need to be drawn, no incorporation fee need be paid; no bylaws need to be adopted. Personal talents and initiative are personally rewarded and, thus, the incentive to achieve is compensated.

Individually owned businesses also have handicaps. The available capital is limited to what the owner has or can small. As a result, many of these firms are small. Business losses are borne by the owner and not unlimited liability of the owner. Decision making rests in one individual, so it is limited to the business ability of the owner. Also, unless otherwise provided for, the business ceases with the death of owner.

Partnership

When two or more persons mutually agree to own and operate a business jointly, without the formality of incorporating, then a partnership is formed. Each person in the combine is a partner but not necessarily on an equal basis. Together they pool their resources, borrow on the strength of all the partners, share in the decision-making process and collectively bear the debts. They divide the net earnings of the business as well as its losses according to

Table 1.1: Methods of Doing Business under Private Enterprise

Features Compared	Types of Business		Corporation	
	Individual	Partnership	Investor Oriented	Cooperative
Who uses the Services?	Non-owner Customers	Non-owner Customers	Non-owner Customers	Chiefly the Owner Patrons
Who owns the business?	The individual	The partners	The Stockholders	The member Patrons
Who votes?	Not Necessary	The partners	Common Stockholders	The member patrons
How is voting done?	Not Necessary	Usually by partner's share in capital. The partners	By shares of common stock	Usually one member one vote
Who determines policies?	The individual	The partners	Common Stockholders and directors	The member Patrons and directors
Are returns on ownership capital limited?	No	No	No	No
Who gets the Operating proceed?	The individual	The partners in proportion to interest in business	The Stockholders in proportion to Stocks held.	The Patrons on a patronage basis

their contractual agreement. The additional capital and skills, training and experience that the several partners can provide strengthen the organization.

There are some disadvantages too. Each partner is personally liable for any and all debts of the business and commitments made any partner (so called unlimited liability. There are also 'limited partnerships' in which partners' liability is limited.). The partnership ends with the death or withdrawal of any partner. Also, the partners need a high degree of 'give and take' if the arrangement is to last.

Corporation

A corporation is a legal entity created by law. Its owners hold shares of common voting stock. The powers of corporation are derived from the corporation laws under which the organization look place. Business firms are incorporated or charted under law.

The advantages to incorporating a business are:

- Stockholders have limited legal liability. In the event of losses or bankruptcy each stockholder can only lose the amount represented by the stocks he owns (assuming he is not a creditor of the corporation).
- The corporation can go on indefinitely unless it is purposefully dissolved or was incorporated for a specific number of years-the death of a stockholder or the sale of his stock does not terminate the corporation.
- Investment in the corporation through the purchase of shares of stock can be made easy for large and small investors since share values can be kept low enough to attract many investors-savings of many people can be used by business undertakings as a result.
- Transfer of ownership rights through the sale of stock is accomplished relatively easily.
- Since the corporation is separate and distinct from any of its stockholders (except in the case of a corporation held tightly by one or a few persons), its ability to

borrow money is generally greater than that of its individual owners-hence; greater business activity may be undertaken.

- A corporation operating profitably can generate capital for business growth and expansion. Such capital can be more easily acquired than through additional sales of shares of stock.

The major disadvantages are:

- Each stockholder has limited, and oftentimes very little, if any control of the business, Proxy voting (where one person is authorized to their stockholdings) and cumulative voting (where a holder does not vote on certain issues but is permitted to cast correspondingly more votes an another issue) may give more control to some stockholders than to others.
- Many corporations are impersonal, 'cold' and 'soulless'. Directors and stockholders frequently condone actions in the name of a corporation, which would never be permitted if identified with any particular person.
- There are costs involved in forming corporations, incorporating them, distributing dividends, paying corporate taxes, reorganizing their structure and dissolving them.
- Profits of a corporation are subject to double income taxation-first, at the corporation level, again, at the stockholder or dividend recipient level.

The above comments pertain to corporations generally. From a legal standpoint, there are two kinds of corporations-the investor-oriented Corporation; and he patron-oriented or Cooperative Corporation. (Since very few cooperatives are not incorporated, the term cooperative refers to an incorporated organization unless otherwise specified. Cooperatives, therefore, are special types of corporation.)

Cooperatives and Self-help Groups

Self-help Groups are considered to be informal cooperatives. As the cooperative organizations get more formalized and institutionalized, rigidity and bureaucracy has set into the system, which has given rise to the alternative models of organizing people at grassroots level. Formulation of self-help group is a natural response to the growing realization among people that participatory, self-help approach is more amenable for economic betterment marginalized people.

Self-help group has been defined as "A group of association of individuals with common economic needs who undertake a systematic economic activity participating directly in decision-making and sharing benefits on an equitable basis".

Basically self-help groups are inherently cooperative and incorporate its basic tenets.

- They are voluntary
- They are democratically managed on the basis of equality
- Even though primarily exist for their members, are often closely tied to their communities.
- They have to ensure the sustainable development of the community in all aspects — economical, social, cultural, ecological, etc.
- The mandate for the development of the community should be approved by their members.
- They promote common economic interests through self-help
- They share the benefits among the members equitably.

Yet self-help groups are distinct entities and differ from the formal cooperative organizations in certain respects.

- Cooperatives are formal, registered corporate bodies, while the SHGs are informal and unregistered.
- Cooperatives often include large heterogeneous membership while the SHGs are homogenous and small.

- Cooperatives are governed by Act, Rules and Bylaws while SHGs are governed by their own bylaws.
- Cooperatives often rely outside finance for its operation while SHGs generate internal finance through thrift and self-help.
- Formal Cooperatives make decisions by means of a well designed democratic structure while SHGs provide greater scope for participatory decision making.

In recent years SHGs, which adopt the principles stated above have come to e recognized as informal cooperatives.

The nature and purpose of an ideal cooperative association cannot find better expression than in George Jacob Holyoake's following words:

> Cooperation touches no man's fortune, it seeks no plunder, it gives no trouble to statesmen, it enters into no secret association, it contemplates no violence, it subverts no order, it envies no dignity, it asks no favour, it keeps no terms with the idle and it will break no faith with the industrious. It means self-help, self-dependence and such share of the competence as labor, skills or thought can win and this it intends to have.

The above analysis reveals the distinct associative nature of cooperatives, which differentiates it from other associations. It is a system of social relationship built around values. The social relationship is characterized by values like participation, self-regulation, leadership development and member development. It is these normative and value considerations, which make the cooperative association unique.

Self-learning Activity

Try to answer the following questions on your own.

1. What are the elements of an economic system?

2. Differentiate cooperation from socialism.
3. What do you understand from cooperative commonwealth?

Summary

- The adjective 'economic' refers to on particular aspect of human behaviour. All human activities involve the use of some resources: material assets, persons' aptitudes, and time. Resources, participants, process, and institutions are elements of an economic system.
- In economic organizational settings we have capitalism, socialism and cooperativism. There are similarities and differences between these systems. Cooperativism is a golden mean between the capitalism and socialism, which takes the merits of both.
- Charles Gide, one of the cooperative pioneers aimed at establishing a cooperative republic in which the cooperatives would rule the entire economic life. In other words, he wanted to establish a cooperative world through cooperation. The idea of a 'cooperative commonwealth' has gained quite a good deal of currency in various quarters.
- There are different forms of business enterprises: individually owned, partnership, and corporations.
- The analysis made in this chapter reveals the distinct associative nature of cooperatives, which differentiates it from other associations. It is a system of social relationship built around values.

Chapter 2

Cooperative Models, Traditional and Modern Cooperatives

The Origin of the Idea of Cooperation

Cooperation is the very basis of human civilization. The interdependence and mutual help among human beings have been the essentials of social life. History tells us that man cannot successfully live by himself and for himself alone. He is dependent on others. The spirit of association is essential to human progress. Therefore, working together is as old as human society. Since the beginning of the human society, men have co-operated first in foraging and then in hunting, later in agriculture and still in manufacture. There is practically nothing, which a man by himself alone can achieve. Cooperation is therefore, the basis and essence of human life.

Concept of Co-operation

Everybody is familiar with the word Co-operation. It is the basis of our social life. So it has been said that man is a social animal because he cannot live in isolation. He depends on others. Co-operation is the basis of human development. In society we all depend on each other for different work.

Co-operation consists of two words co-operation. 'Co' means jointly and 'operation' means functions mean to work jointly for a common purpose. It is a process of collecting work for a common cause, In other words we can say co-operation is form of economic organization which people joint deliberately to fulfill an objective. It is an essence of life as 'In Rigveda' has been described, "May you all have a common purpose, May your hearts be in Unison, May you all be of the same mind, May you all co-exist together, so that you may obtain you objectives efficiently well"

Everybody is supposed to work for each other. This is only possible if one has feeling of sacrifice and one feels happy because other is happy. If we have common purpose we can be more co-operative and that common purpose can be fulfilled efficiently. This is the feeling behind concept of co-operation.

Co-operation can be understood form different point of view. Co-operation is a philosophy of life where people associate voluntarily as the basis of equality for achieving the common objectives. Although money is of great importance in life but it is not everything. Money-minded people are not near to God. Money creates moral degradation and help is the real aim of life. Co-operative can only succeed on the basis of equality, honesty and service motive. Man is important than money. Live and let live is now old quotation. Now we can say *Not only live and let live but live and help live.*

We live here not only for ourselves but to help the needy person. It is the real co-operation and it is the real philosophy of life.

Cooperative Idea in Ancient Times

It is very interesting to trace the origin of cooperative activities in the early period of civilization. Instances of cooperative efforts were found in the ancient Egyptian Era. Cooperatives or quasi-cooperative systems were in existence. The craftsmen and artisans during the reign of pharaohs developed a system of trade, which led to the constitution of associations, charged with the regulation of the entire trade system during 3100 to 1150 B.C.

Cooperative associations existed in ancient Babylonia where the agricultural leases had cooperative features. Large estates were managed by farmers on a cooperative basis. The cooperative tenant farming was popular during this period. In Babylonia trade and commerce also, cooperative method of business was practiced. In order to protect and assist the small farmers and craft men the loan societies were also created.

Instances of cooperative societies were found among the ancient Greeks. There were some burial benefit societies, which had legal entity. Assured there members of a burial place and decent funeral and which was aimed at promotion of mutual assistance. There were the religious and cultural associations, which rendered valuable services to their members by undertaking bulk purchase of fuel and beverages and extending aid to the poor. The associations followed open membership policy and admitted all free citizens, slaves, strangers and even women. the principle of democracy was practiced the members themselves managed the affairs of the associations and the membership meetings were held frequently. It was found that the workers organized themselves into clubs or stone masons, marble cutters, wood workers, ivory workers, potters, fishermen etc. They made payments to sick members and contracted collectively for specific enterprises.

The first moneylending society and savings associations bearing cooperative features flourished in China during the Hon Dynasty 200 year before the Christian Era. the main characteristic feature of these ancient Chinese associations was that they were limited to a small group of members in a community. The important service rendered by these associations was provision of loan facilities to members. They used to conduct frequent meetings to discuss their problems. All the members had to attend the meeting compulsorily. The principles of equality and equity were strictly followed by all those associations.

In the Roman Era, Collegial, a type of cooperative craftsmen organizations came into prominence. Such organizations were formed for shoe makers, pot makers, dyers, carpenters, coppersmiths, goldsmiths and flute players. There were separate guilds of trumpeters, classic players etc. In the collegiums all the men were brothers and all the women, sisters and in some of them the slave could sit at table or council with freeborn men. Further, burial Benefit and craftsmen societies were also very popular during 510 BC to 475 A.D.

In the early Christian Era also there were some in stances of cooperative experiments. There were number of artisan societies which extended burial benefits to its members. These societies raised funds by way of common subscription. It was said that the artisan societies were the forerunners of the modern consumer cooperatives. It was found that due to the impact of the teachings of Christ, people began to enjoy personal freedom.

Another type of cooperative effort was found in the barbaric age (476 to 700 A D); people lived in communities for self protection form robbery which was rampant in those days, since the main occupation was farming, mostly the farming operations were also conducted cooperatively.

History tells us that in 600 A.D. the Islamic Faith emphasized the relative significance of cooperation; and aid to poor persons formed a matter of the faith. The Islamic Bible thus supported strongly the idea of cooperation to better the socio-economic and political conditions of the community.

In the middle ages (5000 to 1,400 A.D.) the cooperative idea took more concrete shape. The first notion of a self-supporting community, within a state, of which the members would live together in amity. Substituting cooperation for competition in the business of getting a living was probably the monastic idea of early middle ages'. It is during this age the guilds developed Europe. These guilds were nothing but craftsmen associations, mostly organised to render specific services to their members. They raised common funds, which were utilized to pay funeral expenses, allowances to physically handicapped and grants to widows. Later agricultural cooperatives began to develop particularly in the field of dairy. Stewart c. Eastern writes in 'the Heritage of the past' that the strips system was found during the middle Ages. In this strips system, the cultivation was done on a cooperative basis.

The mutual fire insurance cooperatives prevalent in London and Paris in between 1,400 and 1750 A.D. Provide further instances of cooperative activities.

The idea of cooperation is not in any way new to India. Cooperation had been practiced in various forms since ancient times. In the Vedic literature there were references to the existence of guilds. V.D. Mahajan writes in Ancient India', that there were guild system for-wood workers, weavers. Metal workers, stone workers, leather workers, potters, dyers, fishermen, hunters, butchers, cooks, basket makers, barbers, garland makers etc. The joint family system is another example of ancient form of cooperation in India. In this system the lands were commonly owned and cultivated and benefits were shared by the members equitably. The system was based on self-help and mutual help. Another form of cooperation was the chit fund, which was based on mutual confidence and honest dealings. The Nidhis is south India is another form of mutual credit associations.

It is thus clear that the germs of cooperative ideas had prevailed ever since the dawn of civilization; and history throughout its course has witnessed myriad forms of cooperative activities. But the modern concept of cooperation is in no way the continuation of the ancient and mediaeval cooperative ideas and efforts, which were ad hoc, less cohesive and less scientific and limited in scope. There is no historical link between the ancient cooperative ideas and the modern concept of cooperation, which originated in the nineteenth century.

Nevertheless, the roots of cooperation as a formal organisation should be carefully traced. In the opinion of Prof. Namjoshi, there are three important sources, which inspired the modern cooperatives. Firstly, they are indirect decedents of the mutual self-help associations typical of early industrialization. The third and most interesting root is the active social experimentation of the utopian socialists and other cooperative leaders.

The Genesis of Modern Cooperative Doctrines

History records that the modern cooperative movement is the by-product of industrial Revolution which took place in about 1750 A.D. the development of capitalism and the modern factory system were the noted features of the industrial Revolution. The Industrial Revolution brought many radical changes in the techniques and organisation of production, both in the field of agriculture and industry. The production shot up and wealth and riches were in abundance. At the same time the increased wealth was concentrated in the hands of few capitalists, which led to the division of the society into two hostile camps, namely have and have-nots. Moreover factory system led to exploitation of the poor workers and created several social evils. Jack Bailey rightly remarked that "developing capitalistic system devoured greedily and indiscriminately the lives of men and women, boys and girls" The evils and miseries of the oppressive system led to commotions and upheavals in the society and resulted in far-reaching changes in the socio-economic life of the people. The Industrial Revolution, as its peripheral impact unleashed a knowledge revolution. Several scientific inventions were made and new organizational innovations were tried.

Isolated Experiments

It must be noted that from the very early stages of Industrial Revolution several isolated cooperative efforts were tried and experimented by the consumers and producers to protect their interests. The people belonging to different occupations had attempted to conduct business on cooperative basis as early as 1752 in different parts of the world. The following were some of the earliest attempts: the Corn Mills at Chatham and woolwich in 1760; the Fenwich weavers' store society at Ayrshire, Scotland in 1769; the Govan Victual city in 1777; The Oldham Cooperative supply company in 1795; the corn Mill at Hall in 1797; the Lennox own cooperative society in 1812: the sheerness Economical society's Bakery in 1816 which was later developed into a general cooperative store. The Lennox town society was also credited with the adoption of the system of dividend on purchases. Early records also indicate the formation of cooperatives for the benefits of the farming community in different parts of the world. For example, as early as in 1752, mutual insurance society was organized in Philadelphia by Benjamin Franklin and attempts were made to start Dairy Cooperatives at Goshen, Connectient and Trenton, New York. Ewell Paul Roy says that the Mutual savings banks and workers productive Cooperatives were also organised in the United States in 1816. Another Excellent example was the origin of the land schaften system of Germany in 1767. In Russia, the first attempt to create a cooperative institution was made by the Decembrists on 14th December 1825 in the cells of the Petrovsky prison where the rules of that cooperative were hammered out. It was the first consumer cooperative that country formed, 13 years before the foundation of the famous Rochdale pioneers'.

The Decembrists' common prison life and the cruel exploitation of local merchants and shopkeepers, who charged exorbitant prices for the bare necessaries of food urged them towards self, help action. The tremendous part played by the Decembrists' wives, the great deprivation of their lives and their intelligent use of their connections in high places to ease the hardship of the prisoners, played a significant role in the formation of a 'self-help association' and 'Artel'. Infact, the activities of the Decembrist Artel played an important role in the creation of an extremely well organised consumer cooperative society structure. In 1831 nine people were elected to form a committee and the Rules of the society were announced on 2nd march 1831. A Board of Management was elected and historically this date marks the foundation of Russian Cooperative, with a set of statutes binding all members. It was called Artel (association) because at this time, the term consumer society was not known either in Russia or anywhere else.

It was a multipurpose society whose activities included shoe-making book binding, a barber shop and pharmacy and also engaged in trade production, kitchen gardening, pig breeding, fattening of livestock, sale of surplus flour, sale of market garden produce to the community outside the prison and also thrift and credit activities, sale of surplus flour, sale of market garden produce to the community outside the prison and also thrift and credit activities. the Artel remained viable for 13 years. It is interesting to note that the rules of an Artel are almost identical with those of the Rochdale pioneers. (*Source:* I Rubashow, "Against All Odds— the Decembrist— Foundation of the First Russian pre cooperative Institution," Review of International cooperation, 1975, p.180). Equitable society in Britain, similar sporadic cooperative experiments could also be noticed in other parts of the world.

Though the germs of good many cooperative ideas are to be found in these schemes, they had no ulterior purpose and were not linked together in any wider movement. Most of the cooperatives started in the earlier periods collapsed, and therefore these schemes had only little practical effect. It must also be noted that these societies were isolated experiments mainly concerned with the problem of subsistence and they do not at this stage aspire to present an alternative to the prevailing industrial systems and these sporadic cooperative actions remained as historical curiosities the modern cooperative movement in an organised form as a world movement emerged in the middle of the 19th century, when men and women combined to find out an alternative to replace the exploitative tendencies and cut throat competition unleashed by industrial Revolution. But 'what is important about these ventures is that they were undertaken by people who pooled their small resources to help themselves and regain some of the. Independence they had lost'.

Dreams Coming to Birth

As a revolt against the new capitalistic order based on the doctrine of individualism, socialist ideas began to develop. Cooperative leaders like Robert Owen opposed capitalism and the competitive system. Owenite cooperators opposed capitalism not only on the grounds of its injustice and inefficiency, but also because of its ill-effects on human character and happiness. They sought to create a new social order, a New Moral world—favourable to the promotion of good character and human happiness. Thus, the long series of changes initiated by industrial revolution in human conditions and human relations gave birth to a galaxy of social thinkers and reformists to evolve a perfect alternative system which would serve as a 'powerful influence in the remolding of thought, and culture and in the re-organisation of economic life in the modern world'. the social thinkers visualized an ideal form of system based on cooperation and mutual help instead of competition and exploitation. Corporatism thus emerged as distinct doctrine in opposition to the doctrine of individualism. E.R. Bowen one of the authorities on cooperation said that 'at least man has invented a new economic order in which every citizen has opportunity to get riches without making the other man poor: a way to abandon poverty and strife and turn towards the road of happiness through abundance and cooperation'.

Cooperative ideology contains itself elements of vision and realism. it combines within its fold the most enduring principles of democracy and liberal socialism. Therefore, the doctrine attracted the attention of many social scientists and it has been accepted the attention of many social scientists and it has been accepted as an instrument of social and economic reform. Dr. Namjoshi was of the opinion that among the variety of socialist Doctrines which have emerged to deal with social and economic ills, no doctrine has received so much attention, thought and experimentation as the Cooperative Doctrine. Cooperatism thus appeared as one of the best economic miracles. It was recognized that the Cooperative model based on democratic principles can remove many of the evils of capitalistic systems. Appreciating the merits of cooperatism, Alfred Marshall, the eminent Economist in a speech in 1889 said that' some movements have a high social aim; other movements have a broad business basis; cooperation alone has both".

All those who advocated the supremacy of cooperative system to other systems belong to cooperative school of thought. Economic writers had classified these cooperative thinkers as Associationists. Barring this one common heritage cooperative thinkers differ vastly in their ideologies plans and strategies for cooperative development. there are among them utopian socialists like Robert Owen and Charles Fourier; Christian socialists like Maurice Kingsely; Edward Van Sittard- Neale, Charles Gide, Raiffeisen, Bishor Gruntving, Philippe Buchez; protagonists of cooperative common wealth like Earnest Poisson, T.W. Mercer, George W. Russell, Sidney and Beatrice Webb, Dr. James Peter Warbasse, Gevaret, Leonard Woolf, Anders Orne; Cooperative pace makers or those who belong to competitive yard-stick school like Dr. Georges Fauquet and Loon Walras. Such classifications are not of course, free from imperfections. As Mr. Louis smith say; "all these categories overlap, and they are an arbitrary division of personal opinions". whatever may be their ideological differences; nevertheless, they have all contributed to the richness and variety of cooperative thought and added new dimensions in the realm of cooperative doctrines.

Thus, the twentieth century witnessed a break-through in the evolution of cooperative thought. The doctrines hitherto propounded by previous century cooperative thinkers, have been classified on systematic basis. The objectives, scope, potentialities and limitation of cooperatives in that competitive setting is debated and discussed threadbare. This provided ample scope for the evaluation of different cooperative doctrines, ideologies and cooperative growth models.

Important Personalities in the Development of Cooperatives

There are very many contributors as for cooperative movement in the world. They were classified into Contributors of Pre-Rochdale Era and Contributors of Post-Rochdale Era. Some of the early thinkers and their contributions made for the promotion and development of cooperative idea and concept are discussed in this unit to understand and know their contributions.

Edward Vansittart Neale, (1810-1892)

Edward Vansittart Neale, a Christian socialist and cooperative idealist was born at bath as son of the Rev. E. Neale family home Bisham Abbey. He was one of the key promoters of cooperative movement in Britain and international cooperative Movement. As a Christian socialist he was busy promoting working Men's Associations during 1850.

Neale, a cooperative idealist served the cooperative movement longer and more continuously than any others. The term Christian socialist is generally applied to a group of clergymen and lawyers which existed form 1848 to 1854 and who so called themselves. The notable Christian socialists were J.M Ludlow (Barrister), Rev. R.D Maurice (Professor of Theology at King's College, London), Rev. Charles Kingsley (a poet and Novelist) and Thomas Houghes (a close friend of Neale) of the circle, had a more comprehensive view and a better understanding of its potentialities.

Neale's Cooperative Plans and Schemes

As a person belonged to the Christian socialist school, Neale believed that the evils of the day arise from the neglect of the Christian obligations of man to man, especially in their economic relations with each other. Joined with other Christian socialists Neale condemned selfishness and competition and encouraged mutual love and fellowship. He, therefore, desired that the existing system to be replaced by a cooperative system.

Cooperative distribution was the first step towards this better system; it would be followed by developments into wholesaling, production, importing. Shipping and thus he saw the way opening to the quite, gradual introduction of that world of cooperative union.

To him "cooperation is essentially a voluntary system. Its root has been traced back to that deepest of all principles known to us— free, that is self-governing, reasonable, will; only by free self-help can cooperation procure for man the good claimed as being capable of being produced by it". He was one of the chief legal advisors of cooperatives. He was instrumental in drafting the Industrial and Provident Societies Act of 1852 and its amendments in 1876.

Wholesale Society

Neale is said to be the originator of the wholesale society. He realised that a cooperative wholesale society of a truly federal nature was necessary if the movement was to continue. Neale had preached this idea continuously from 1850 and helped Rochdale pioneers like Greenwood. Hooson and Edwards to initiate a demand for amendments to the Industrial and Provident Societies Act, which would remove the legal obstacles to a federal wholesale society. Neale also prepared rules for registration of the National organization and model rules for cooperatives published by the cooperative union.

Two Schools of Thought

It is interesting to note that with the development of productive activities by the wholesale societies, two schools of thought emerged, one favouring ownership and control by producers i.e., by the work people-engaged in production, the other favouring the ownership and control by the consumers of the product.) The first is known as producer cooperation and the second consumer cooperation.

When the struggle between the favourites of producers and consumers cooperation was going on, Neale introduced the idea of National and International Cooperation. Neale recognised that a cooperative economic system would need an organisation for exchange a role which he thought might be discharged by a federal wholesale society serving both consumers and producers.

Cooperative Education

Neale influenced the creation of a national organisation for cooperative education, viz., cooperative union. He drafted rules for the registration of the cooperative union. He served as the General Secretary of the union in 1873 at a nominal salary. The cooperative union had form the beginning been intensively concerned with education in cooperation.

International Cooperation

A principle cooperative thinker, Neale was one of the founders of International cooperative organisations. He gave advisory, legal and administrative assistance to form a national federation of French societies in 1885. He also took steps to develop international trading between cooperatives in USA and Britain in 1876. The establishment of an ICA was expressed earlier in 1886 at a cooperative congress. In 1892, Neale met De Boye (French Cooperator) at the Rochdale Congress and sought his help to revive the idea. Accordingly a provisional committee was formed consisting of Neale, Holyoake, Greening, Albert Grey, Mrs. Lawrenson and Miss Tournier. It was also decided to hold the first International congress in 1893, but unfortunately, Neale died on September 16th, which was a great loss to his friends and admirers.

Neale chaired, attended and addressed many cooperative congresses and conferences. He served on the Board of Cooperative League, the Central Cooperative Agency, the Cooperative Insurance Company (1867), the Cooperative Newspaper Society (1871), the Cooperative Productive Federation (1882), the Agricultural and Horticultural Association (1867) and General Secretary cooperative Union (1873).

Neale's Writings

With Houghes, he wrote a 'Manual for Cooperators' which was a classic in cooperative ethics and economics.

Sincerity of Service

Neale proved himself not only a sincere idealist but also one who took practical actions to achieve his goals. He not only framed principles but also applied them. He had been associated with the cooperative movement over twenty years and was personally acquainted with many cooperative pioneers and thinkers in European countries.

Louis Blanc

Louis Blanc was an outstanding French socialist thinker. He secured a distinguished place in history owing to the part he played in the revolution of 1848. through his writings he had been expressing the grievances of the working class. His famous work, Organization du travail, appeared in 1840 four years before Rochdale experiment. He condemned the existing individual and competitive rivalry and thus came to be regarded as the best qualified exponent of the views of the proletariat'.

Social Workshop

In 1848 at the age of 37, Louis Blanc proposed that industrial cooperatives be organized to alleviate the evils of factory type system in France and elsewhere. The idea of producers' cooperative society was his distinct contribution to cooperative and socialist thought. According to Louis Blanc competition was the main cause of economic evils and he proposed to satisfy all the needs of the society by means of voluntary associations. He deviated from the 'utopian', agrarian schemes of Fourier and Owen and insisted that workers should own and control the tools, machinery and other instruments of production. For this he proposed 'Social workshops' which simply means .a cooperative producers society. The social workshop was intended to combine the members of the same trade, similar to Butchez's plan of combining together of carpenters. Masons, shoe-makers etc, The social workshop is distinguished from ordinary workshop by being more democratic and equalitarian. He also favoured the application of the principle of association to agriculture which he thought could be organized along cooperative line.

Blanc's Plan: Collectivization

In many respects Blanc's plan was similar to Butchez, who in turn drew inspiration from the great Christian socialist Saint Simon. He developed a social workshop plan on the basis of the principles evolved by Butchez.

The Phillippe Buchez. Set up in 1931 the following basis of autonomous producers' cooperatives:

1. The members of the Association will elect among themselves one or two representatives who would have the signature of the firm-democratic principle.
2. The Surplus would be distributed among the associates proportional to their work.
3. In the case of dissolution of their society, cooperators donate the net assets or reserves to another society, a philanthropic institution or state.

4. The association would not be allowed to employ non-affiliated labour; all hands working in cooperatives must become member of it.

He believed in the democratic management of the workshops and workers would elect their leaders among themselves and the administrative hierarchy will be established. To make the system work, a new system of education with improved morality and new ideas would be implemented.

His plan was simple and practical which every one can understand. His passion for concrete attracted the attention of everybody. Though Blanc opposed the capitalism and competition, he was opposed to the idea of class war. "the social workshop in his conception was just a cell out of which complete collectivization of society would some day emerge".

State Intervention

Blanc believed that state intervention or helps is necessary to organize producers cooperatives. Realizing that workers would have difficulty in organizing those cooperatives, he advocated that Government intervene and set up cooperatives and withdraw when the workers become able to manage them. blanc therefore, was father of 'Government aid to cooperative' idea which has become widely prevalent throughout the world.

Blanc's Influence

In many respects Louis Blanc's plan has been carried out today. For instance Blanc's thesis on state aid has been applied in the United States, especially in the Agricultural credit and Rural Electric cooperatives. His plan has been carried and Rural Electric cooperatives. His plan has been carried out in Yugoslavia and Israel. His cogent superiority over numerous other socialist theoreticians is that he believed that even in a completely socialist society, the state must still act as a coordinator of economic activities.

Nikolai Frederick Sevorin Grundtvig (1783-1872)

Nikolai Frederick Sevorin Grundtvig was born in Denmark, as the son of a clergyman. He comprehended two factors viz, spiritual freedom and liberal education, which in his opinion contributed for social development of that country. These impressions had great deal of influence when he started his work among his own people.

Grundtvig's Folk High School Concept

Grundtvig's contribution to cooperative movement and the advancement of cooperative idea was very much original Modern Denmark owes more to him than to any body else. his main contribution to cooperation was his inspiration for folk high school which supply the enthusiasm for the cooperatives.

For Grundtvig, education about life was always a prime factor and they placed much stress on individual development. Many folk high schools have special departments for the teaching of agriculture, domestic science, nursing gymnastic and cooperative methods.

Adult Education

Grundtvig was an advocate of adult education also, which he felt could be imparted through folk high schools, The clergymen who were also the followers of Grundtvig, also performed great deal of work in adult education.

The adult education was generally imparted through the medium of lectures, songs, readings and discussions and only a minor extent by means of books and journals.

Grundtvigians

Inspired by Grundtvig's ideologies several priests and educationists started experimenting the Grundtvig's ideologies In fact, Grundtvig himself did not organize Danish Folk high schools; he inspired persons like Christian Flor, Sofus Hogsbro, Christisn Kold etc.

Charles Gide (1847-1932)

Charles Gide (1847-1932) was an eminent French economist and a cooperator. His advent was a great moment in the history of cooperative thinking. Even as a student Charles Gide was attracted by the ideas of Fourier; and the pioneers' solution to socio-economic problems.

His Contributions

Charles Gide had a reputation as a theorist and expositor of cooperative doctrines. He coined for cooperative education, several phrases and terminologies. He had brought out several publications. Principles of political Economy, Institution of social progress, consumers' cooperative societies, selected works of Fourier, History of Economic Doctrines and Lectures on political Economy were his chief works. It was he who designed the flag of the international Cooperative Alliance, with seven colours of the prism, which denotes unity in diversity; so also the symbol with 'two joint hands' was his contribution.

Gide's Views on Liberalism and Competition

Charles Gide clearly distinguished between liberalists and associationist (Cooperators). He fought against the liberal school and the ideas like profit and competition, it stood for cooperation according to him, aims at creating a new social milieu.

Gide's ' Fair Price Doctrine'

He was the greatest respondent of fair price doctrine which remained as the focal point of his theory. To him the aim as cooperation was the suppression of profit and free competition. He held the view that "the cooperators can not believe that the law of supply and demand is sufficient to ensure fair price, nor that competition even if it were free can cut down price to a normal rate".

Consumers' Socialism

Professor Charles Gide belonged to a small group of intellectuals, who joined together under his leadership to form what is commonly known as 'Nimes school' It was a socialistic school, which aimed at establishing Democratic socialism based on voluntary association of consumers quite contrast to the socialism based on enterprises managed by employees for their benefit.

Andes Orne on Co-operatism

Andes Orne was the great cooperative Theorist of Sweden, the first to develop a logically coherent cooperative philosophy.

Economic Cooperation

Andes Orne, had neither faith in nor time for the utopian schemes of Robert owen. He held the view that cooperation arose out of the direct economic interests in goods and services of those participating. He found that the driving power of cooperative undertakings to be simply economic interest.

Consumerism

Andes Orne's views on the cooperative movement were influenced by French cooperator and economist Charles Gide who was a protagonist of 'consumer societies'.

Cooperatism

Cooperation according to him represents something much more that simply a type of business. In its full realization it constitutes a social system. Andes Orne in his book 'cooperatism' (1921) has given a logical and clear account of this social system.

Cooperation and State Aid

Andes Orne felt that the cooperative movement should develop by its own force. He rejected every thought of letting the state grant the cooperative type of enterprise any special privileges, let alone a monopoly position. according to him, cooperation cannot, without betraying its very mission, place itself under the guardianship of the state or allow itself transformed into an instrument of state's general policy.

But, cooperation is no way hostile to the state. It subordinates itself loyally and readily to the authority of the state.

G.D, H. Cole

G.D, H. Cole was one of the well-known British cooperators. He belonged to the socialistic school of cooperators, who placed faith in producers' cooperation. they implemented the ideas of Buchez and Louis Blanc by forming self-governing producers' Associations and urging the Government to accept Blanc's plan of 'National workshop'.

Guild Socialist

As a socialist Cole was greatly attracted towards Guild socialism. Guild socialism was in the essence a plan for transferring industries and services to public ownership and delegating their management, under charter, to guilds including all workers by hand and brain engaged in them.

Cooperation and Trade Union Movement

Cole maintained that the cooperative movement was a product of trade union movement; and the former owned very much to the latter for its success.

Democratic Practices

Cole is an earnest believer of democracy. But democracy, according to him, is rendered meaningless when the membership grows larger. To preserve the cooperative character and to ensure genuine democracy he demanded the preservation of cooperatives at an optimum level.

Horrace Plunkett (1854-1932)

Horrace Plunkett was a pioneer of agricultural cooperation. He was born in Gloucestershire as the third son of Lord Donstang in 1854.

In 1894 he promoted the Irish Agricultural Organization society and was its president until 1899. only with his efforts the Department of Agriculture and Technical Instruction for Ireland was established in 1895; and Plunkett was its vice president until 1907.

His Organizational Strategy

Plunkett first came into contact with the cooperative movement in England while he was at Oxford University. When he returned to Ireland he thought that cooperative store would benefit the peasant community as it had benefited the weavers and industrial workers elsewhere.

Due to their organizing ability' Plunkett and his followers were able to persuade the farmers to combine to build their own creameries rather than form joint-stock companies or allow this vital this vital section of their industry to fall into the hands of middlemen

Plunkett's Integrated Philosophy

Plunkett never meant cooperation to stand-alone. The idea is well represented in the phrase "Better farming, better business and better living".

Plunkett's Contribution

Sir Horrace Plunkett's contributions are more significant in practical sphere than in theoretical plane. The credit of organizing the peasants successfully for the first time on cooperative basis goes to Sir Horrace Plunkett. As stated by George W. Russel: the true significance of the movement promoted by Sir Horrace Plunkett is that it is an attempt to build up a new social order in Ireland, which will bring men into mutually beneficial relationship with each other; which will create or draw out the highest economic, political and human qualities in the people and remind them that they are the units of a society. Besides contributing to the socio-economic betterment of Irish Society, he provided a workable model for the economies which are predominantly agricultural. The cooperative development model evolved by Plunkett is eminently suited to countries with similar socio-economic setting even today. Following are some of his specific contributions:

Firstly Plunkett's organization work started from the above. This growth model is a pragmatic approach to cooperative development.

Secondly, the state aid is another special feature of Irish cooperative movement. The state aid never affected the self-reliance of cooperatives as they never desperately depended on state aid. thus the ideas of state partnered cooperation was first mooted and successfully demonstrated by Horrace Plunkett.

When cooperative movement is in its infancy and the private interests are powerful a closer collaboration between government department and cooperatives will yield positive results. Such a collaboration between government departments and cooperatives is yet another contribution of Sir Horrace Plunkett to cooperative theory.

J.P. Warbasse (1866-1957)

Dr. Warbasse was one of the pace-makers in the American Cooperative movement. Born in Newton, New Jercy, he graduated 1889 from Columbia University's college of physicians and surgeons.

Concept of Consumer Supremacy

Dr. J.P. Warbasse was an ardent believer in the doctrine of consumer supremacy and hence belonged to the school of consumer socialism enunciated by Charles Gide, Mitchell, Beatrice Webb and Pission, quite contrast to guild socialism and 'workers control' of cooperative advocated by G.D.H. Cole. According to him: "Cooperative organization begins best with the people as consumers. It is for the individual user and absorber of things. ... The basic idea of cooperation is that the consumers are everybody and that all the machinery of industry and the organization society should be for them.

Labour and Co-operatives

He visualized a close cooperation between cooperatives and the labourers. He declared that one aim of cooperation was to abolish exploitation and parasitism to harmonize capital and labour.

State and Cooperatives

Warbasse acknowledged the supremacy and authority of state. To him "the cooperative way is a kind of business and social action which may go on side by side with profit business and political government, using their currencies supplementing each of them and expanding as its efficiency proves its justification".

Cooperative Democracy

Warbasse declared his profound faith in democracy and his conception of democracy in the context of cooperative movement is an economic democracy. To his "democracy as a political ideal is not enough. Democracy must dominate as well as political affairs or it comes to nothing."

Dr. G. Fauquet (1873-1953)

Dr. G. Fauquet was a great cooperator who had made significant contribution for the advancement of cooperative thoughts in modern times. He was closely associated with I.C.A and I.L.O., and such other international bodies representing the cooperative movement. Since 1924 he had been continuously contributing movement. Since 1924 he had been continuously contributing to the cooperative studies.

Double Origin of Cooperatives

According to Dr. Fauquet, cooperation originates as a joint group. expression against individualistic economic system. It institutes common action. But this common action should be based on the free accord of individuals. Cooperative action, in his opinion, pre-supposes free and responsible persons who have voluntarily joined together.

Cooperative Sector

The place accorded for cooperation in and economy in subject to constant change, as the economic environment in which the cooperatives have to function varies. The cooperatives, within the over-all economic framework must decide what place it means to claim in the economy. The place accorded to cooperatives depends upon the economic policies and plans adopted to mould the economic edifice. Fauquet classified the major sub -divisions of an economy into public sector, capitalistic sector. Among these various sectors he visualized a close relationship between cooperatives and private sector proper, which comprehended the non-capitalist units of the household economy.

State and Cooperatives

Fauquet acknowledged the supremacy of the state He stated that once cooperators accept mixed type of economic development public authorities have every right for the over all regulation of economic life.

Cooperative Integration

Fauquet believed in the unity of the cooperative movement. According to him, "it is a peculiar characteristic of cooperative integration that it groups together economic units which are very numerous but at the same time very small".

Concepts of Undertaking and Association

Another significant contribution of Fauquet to cooperative thought is his classification of the cooperative organization into two viz., undertaking and association. By undertaking or enterprise he meant the economic characteristics of cooperative institutions.

Father Moses M. Coady

Father Moses M. Coady was an outstanding figure in the field of Canadian cooperation. He was called high priest of learning and knowledge, as his contribution to social and cooperative education was great.

The Antigonish Movement

Dr. Coady was one of the principal spokesmen of the Antagonism Movement. It was developed at Antagonist Nova Scotia, one of the Atlantic provinces of Canada. This area had a challenging climate and much of the area was covered with national forests. Farming, inshore fishing and small scale lumbering were the principal occupation of the rural people. people lived in small farms and followed traditional techniques in their activities and innovations were accepted very slowly.

The Principles of Antigonish Movement

Dr. Coady's Antagonism Movement had six fundamental principles as follows:

- Dignity of Man
- Education—the Bases of Social Reform
- Education Must Be Through Group Action
- Education Must Meet Economic Needs
- Fundamental Changes in Social and Economic institutions:

A Full and Abundant Life: the ultimate object of the Antagonism Movement is full development of and abundant life for everyone in the community. Every individual is given an opportunity to develop his capacities.

Techniques of Adult Education

Many new techniques were followed for adult education. The principal techniques were the mass meeting and the discussion group. In addition, a number of methods were used to the special needs of the people.

- The Mass Meeting
- The Discussion Group
- The short Course
- The Leadership school
- Radio Listening Groups
- Industrial Study Classes

The Coady International Institute

In December 1959 St. Francis Xavier University founded the Coady international Institute as a special department within the university to coordinate, direct and expand, the international phase of the Antagonism Movement in response to the increasing demand by governments, agencies and individuals.

Prof. Paul Lambert

Prof. Paul Lambert was a great Belgian cooperator who has made notable contributions to the advancement of cooperative thought. He started his career as Professor of Economics at the University of Liege and was drawn towards the cooperative movement later on.

Cooperation—A Social Philosophy

Prof. Lambert regarded cooperation as essentially a social philosophy far from being a mere science. According to him: "Science explains the real, but social philosophy judges the real and proposes several changes in order to improve it. Science at the most, does not go beyond the strict and pure intelligence of the real, when it attempts to seek and coordinate adequate means in order to reach the aims that are given to it by social philosophy or policy".

Concept of Economic Democracy

Prof. Lambert considered economic democracy as the cardinal principle of cooperation. In his view it distinguishes cooperative business most sharply from capitalist business and it can be applied uniformly to any type of cooperative.

Fair Price Doctrine

The Fair price doctrine' advocated by the economists like Charles Gide, as a tool for price determination attracted Prof. Lambert in his view the fair price doctrine is a weapon in the hands of cooperators which allows them to denounce the present system of price formation.

Concept of Consumers' Supremacy

Consumers are the sovereigns of modern market economy. Several economists have considered that the capitalistic system and market economy was based on demand which was a resultant factor of consumers' preferences.

Cooperatives and Trade Unionism

Prof. Lambert advocated closer relationship between cooperatives and trade unions. He was in full agreement, in this respect, with English theorist G.D.H. Cole who believed that cooperation would develop in collaboration with trade unionism.

Cooperation and State

The relationship between cooperatives and the state, in the opinion of Paul Lambert, was complementary and reciprocal. The state, through legislative measures extend certain special favour to cooperatives, in the larger interest of the society.

Dominate Cooperative Sector

Prof. Lambert visualized the large expansion of cooperatives in future, as the cooperative trade expands, the cooperative ideas spread and when the cooperatives are called upon to solve number of problems.

Robert Owen

The cooperative movement in a real sense began with Robert Owen—a factory manager, a Utopian Socialist, a pioneer of industrial cooperation and trade unionism, and an advocate of communal living. Owen (1771-1858) envisaged villages including farmlands and small-scale industry, all operated cooperatively by the citizens of the villages who would live communally.

Owen's communities were originally conceived as a cure for unemployment but later as a way to replace private capitalism and completion with self-employment and with conditions that should provide universal happiness. He planned that such communities would consist of about 100 people, 1500 acres of land, with common buildings and apartments for individual families; and would cost between $200,000 and $250,000. Wealthy sympathizers of Owen's schemes were to finance such projects rather than the inhabitants of the communal villages. Such villages were attempted at New Harmony, Indiana (1825-27); and at Orbinston, Scotland; Ralahine, Ireland; and Queenswood, England. All failed.

This failure, however, did not keep Owen from preaching cooperation as the best solution to mankind's problems. Because of the stimulus of his teachings cooperative societies, labour exchanges (where handicrafts were exchanges presumably on the basis of the amount of labour involved in their making), trade unions, and magazines for workingmen started about 1820 and afterwards. Most lasted only a short time, but the seeds were sown for a later harvest of cooperatives.

Owen was an idealist more than a realist, visionary rather practical and an advocate of industrial cooperation, not of consumer distributive cooperation. Owen declared, "Profit-making was necessarily the exploitation of man by man. Profit upon price for individual gain and the accumulation of useless and unnecessary individual wealth brought into action the lower passions of human nature; and a false estimate of all things ensured and everything became valued by its cost instead of its intrinsic worth. Cunningness and deception usurped the place of wisdom and sincerity".

As already stated, the schemes of Owen undoubtedly ended in failure; his principles and ideas have continued to inspire the cooperative movement. These principles are:

1. abolition of private profit
2. voluntary association
3. common ownership of the means of production
4. the utilization of the wealth of the community for increasing the happiness of mankind

Owen had more grandiose ideas, encompassing agricultural and industrial production, education, housing, and commercial distribution — the whole gamut economic activity on a cooperative basis. No doubt, Owen (called by some the Father of Cooperation) believed it far more important for persons to increase their incomes, to improve their living conditions, and to free children from debilitating factory employment than to save a few pennies on retail buying.

Robert Owen, the son of a saddler and ironmonger from Newton in Wales, was born on 14th May 1771. Robert was an intelligent boy who did very well at his local school, but at the age of ten, his father sent him to work in a large draper in Stamford, Lincolnshire. After spending three years in Stamford, Robert moved to a draper in London. This job lasted until 1787 and now aged sixteen; Robert found work at a large wholesale and retail drapery business in Manchester.

It was while Owen was working in Manchester that he heard about the success of Richard Ark Wright was having with his textile factory in Cromford. Richard was quick to see the potential of this way of manufacturing cloth and although he was only nineteen years old, borrowed £100 and set up a business as a manufacturer of spinning mules with John Jones, an engineer. In 1792 the partnership with Jones came to an end and Owen found work as a manager of Peter Drink water's large spinning factory in Manchester.

As a manger of Drink water's factory, Owen met a lot of businessmen involved in the textile industry. This included David Dale, the owner of Chorton Twist Company in New Lanark, Scotland, the largest cotton-spinning business in Britain. The two men became close friends and in 1799 Robert married Dale's daughter, Caroline.

With the financial support of several businessmen from Manchester, Owen purchased Dale's four textile factories in New Lanark for £600,000. Under Owen's control, the Chorton Twist Company expanded rapidly. However, Robert Owen was not only concerned with making money; he was also interested in creating a new type of community at New Lanark. Owen believed that the effects of their environment form person's character. Owen was convinced that if he created the right environment, he could produce rational, good and humane people. Owen argued that people were naturally good but they were corrupted by the harsh way they were treated. For example, Owen was a strong opponent of physical punishment in schools and factories and immediately banned its use in New Lanark.

David Dale had originally built a large number of houses close to his factories in New Lanark. By the time Owen arrived, over 2,000 people lived in New Lanark village. One of the first decisions took when he became owner of New Lanark was to order the building of school. Owen was convinced that education was crucially important in developing the type of person he wanted.

When Owen arrived in New Lanark, children from as young as five were working for thirteen hours a day in the textile mills. He stopped employing children under ten and reduced their labours to ten hours a day. The young children went to the nursery and infant schools that Owen had built. Older children worked in the factory but also had to attend his secondary school for part of the day.

Owen's partners were concerned that these reforms would reduce profits. Unable to convince them of the wisdom of these reforms, Owen decided to borrow money from Archibald Campbell, a local banker, in order to buy their share of the business. Later, Owen sold shares in the business to men who agreed with the way he ran his factory.

Robert Owen hoped that the way he treated children at his New Lanark would encourage other factory owners to follow his example. It was therefore important for him to publicize his activities. He wrote several books including *The Formation of Character* (1813) and *A New View of Society* (1814). In 1815 Robert Owen sent detailed proposals to Parliament about his ideas on factory reform. This resulted in Owen appearing before Robert Peel and his House of Commons committee in April, 1816. Robert Owen toured the country making speeches on his experiments at New Lanark. He also publishing his speeches as pamphlets and sent free copies to influential people in Britain. In his speeches, Owen argued that he was creating a "new moral world, a world from which the bitterness of divisive sectarian religion would be banished". His criticisms of the Church of England upset many people; including reformers such as William Wilberforce and William Cobbett.

Disappointed with the response he received in Britain, Owen decided in 1825 to establish a new community in America based on the socialist ideas that he had developed over the years. Owen purchased an area of Indiana for £30,000 and called the community he established there, New Harmony. One of Owen's sons, Robert Dale Owen became the leader of the new community in America.

By 1827 Owen had lost interest in his New Lanark textile mills and decided to sell the business. His four sons and one of his daughter, Jane, moved to New Harmony and made it their permanent home but Owen decided to stay in England where he spent the rest of his life helping different reform groups. This included supporting organizations attempting to obtain factory reform, adult suffrage and the development of successful trade unions. He expressed his views in his journals, *The Crisis* and *The New Moral World.*

Owen also played an important role in establishing the Grand National Consolidated Trade Union in 1834 and the Association of All Classes and All Nations in 1835. Owen also attempted to form a new community at East Tytherly in Hampshire. However, like New Harmony in America, this experiment came to an end after disputes between of the community. Although disillusioned with the failure of these communities and most of his political campaigns, Robert Owen continued to work for his 'new moral order' until his death on 17th November 1858.

Dr. William King — Father of Distributive Cooperation

Dr. William King (1786-1865) of Brighton, England was a social reformer and a realistic advocate of consumer cooperation. He learned about Robert Owen and accepted much of Owen's philosophy although he differed with him as to how to achieve its ends. King was a physician and soon became interested in improving the welfare of the working people of Brighton. To this end he became involved in organizing an Infants' School (1823), the Brighton Provident and District Society (1825), a Subscription Library (1826), the Cooperative Benevolent Fund Association, and the Brighton Cooperative Trading Association (1827). Some of this lasted only short time.

Beginning in May 1828 and continuing for two years, Dr. King published at his own expense a small magazine called 'The Cooperator'. Its 28 issues contained King's important contribution to cooperative thought and were a source of inspiration, information, and instructions on cooperation in general and cooperative shop keeping in particular.

King was much more realistic and far more understandable about cooperation than Owen. His plan was relatively simple. He urged the workers to:

- Save their money;
- Invest their money in their cooperative retail store;
- Pay cash for merchandise;
- Operate democratically;
- Publicize the cooperative movement so it might grow and become effective;
- Reinvest the 'profit' or net earnings in the store to enable the store to employ its own members who would make things to be sold in the store or to other buyers.

King taught that cooperatives should start small with members supplying the original capital (Owen relied on wealthy outside investors to supply the funds for large-scale operations). He also believed that cooperatives should not pay a patronage refund but the net earnings should be put in a reserve fund and used for the good of all the members so as to enlarge the cooperative's activities in production, crafts, and provide employment. He did not object to Owenite self-sustaining cooperative communities provided they were set up with the members' own capital and restricted to Christians. (King was a deeply religious man who believed that the spirit and ethics of the Gospel were those of cooperation also).

In many respects Dr. King was more responsible for the extension of the cooperative idea and for the organization of many cooperatives than Robert Owen ever was. King was truly the 'Father of Distributive Cooperation', the inspirer of consumers' cooperative stores in England where as Owen encouraged self-employment and communal living and started no stores. King's little periodicals were distributed throughout England. It advocated the king of cooperation within reach of the common man in its realistic, albeit optimistic, proposals. His was a grassroots bottom-up, simple scheme of organization contrasted with the far more expensive top-down plan of Robert Owen. As a result, the movement grows from a few societies in 1826 to around 300 shops in 1830 — many patterned after King's Brighton Cooperative Trading Association. (King's ideas may also have influenced American cooperation — a Mr. William Bryan, treasurer of a cooperative at Brighton, England came to New York in 1829 and helped organized a consumers' cooperative store in that city in 1830).

Pioneers of the French Cooperative Movement

Among the pioneers of the French cooperative movement mention may be made of Charles Fourier, Louis Blanc, Andragodin, and Leclaire. Charles Fourier conceived of a unique scheme of establishing communistic colonies, known as 'Phalanstere' through which he desired to establish a new economic and social order. He detailed out his scheme in his book, The New Industrial and Social World, which was published in 1892. Louis Blanc and Buchez made efforts to start a movement for the establishment of 'social workers'. There was a difference between the schemes of Blanc and Buchez. Buchez wanted to establish cooperative societies for the organization of small industries whereas Blanc was in favour of organizing large-scale industries on a collective basis. Andragoding and a Hamilistire in 1879 on a guidelines provided by Charles Fourier. Leclaire started a 'Mutual Aid Society' in 1838. The experiments of Andragodin and Leclaire proved that the industrial concern could be successfully operated and managed by the workers having neither education nor experience of business organization.

France has been the torchbearer for other countries of the world in the fields of 'producers cooperatives'. The French cooperatives movement have been essentially a workers' movement. In no other country of the world, workers' societies have attained those heights of success, which have been attained in France. Charles Fourier, a great Utopian socialist, sowed the seed of the cooperative movement as early as the beginning of the 19th century the world has ever known. The cooperative movement in its present form could only be started after the Revolution of 1848 and it gained movement after passage of the Act of 1863. Although the cooperative movement has diversified its activities, like are counterparts in other countries, the workers' cooperatives still occupy a dominant position?

Charles Fourier (1772-1837) and the Phalanstere

Charles Fourier was born in 1772 at Besancon. He was the son of a coffee merchant. At the time of his father's death Fourier was quite young. He inherited a good fortune, which he invested in trade. After an unsuccessful career as a businessman he devoted himself to thinking and writing and acquired fame for his schemes of social reform. He felt very much distressed by the prevailing social and economic conditions of France. He wanted to re-build the social system which "forces children to lie and men to allow food needed by hungry people to rot".

According to Fourier, the existing social system did not allow a free play of the twelve major passions of mankind, viz., seeing, hearing, smelling, feeling, tasting, enmity, love fraternity, ambition, desire for intrigue, love of change and desire for union. When these twelve passions are combined together, the result is brotherly love. He calculated that these passions could be combined in different individuals in 820 ways. It was, therefore, necessary that in an ideal social system all these combinations should be possible and there should be sufficient number of persons to ensure the result. His estimate was that in one combine there should not be less than 500 and not more than 2,000 persons, roughly speaking, about 400 families. He, therefore, suggested that people should form themselves into voluntary associations, which, he called 'Phalanxes' or 'phalansteries'. Each Phalastery was to be organized like a modern hotel, containing a large and magnificent building, divided into apartments of all kinds to suit the tastes of different people with common dining hall, theatre and concert room, and library and all other accessories of a comfortable life. Each Phalanstery was to be sub-divided into units. Larger units were to be called as groups while smaller units as series. Individuals were free to join any series or groups. For the production of food and raw materials required, each Phalanstery would have land of 400 acres all around it. Goods, needed by the members were to be produced and manufactured by them. Each member could join any occupation he liked. The Phalanstery was, thus a combination of producers and consumers, a self-sufficient world in miniature. It was to be organized on a joint stock basis. Each person could own as many shares as he liked. The profits were to be divided among the members on the principle: capital 1/3, labour 5/12, and management 3/12.

These Phalanxes were to be organized on purely democratic basis. All officers and directors were to be elected. The organization was to be like this: Each phalanx was to be managed by a director known as 'Unarch'. Groups of Phalanxes comprising three or four were to be managed by an officer known as 'Durach'. There could be even bigger federations having their own chiefs. His aim was to organize the entire world into Phalanxes and the highest officer would be known as 'Omniarch'. The capital of the world would be located at Constantinople. He believed that these reforms would enhance the productivity of the people owing to the economies of associated efforts and the increased efficiency of labour. Another great advantage of such an organization would be the elimination of superficial classes and the disappearance of hatred and prejudices among men. He declared: "In the new society, there would be no soldiers of distress, no policemen, agents of discordant social regime, no criminals and lawyers, both products of civilization of disharmony, finally no metaphysician and no economist".

In Fourier's scheme, Phalanxes were to be connected with each other by a good communication system, and the goods produce by on Phalanx were to be exchanged with the goods produced by other Phalanxes. Thus, Phalanxes were to be set up according to the principle of 'social attraction'. The work was to be undertaken on a cooperative basis and there was to be complete harmony. Competition had no place in his scheme. Cooking, heating, lighting and living were all to be common. Such an arrangement would enable the people to enjoy maximum of comfort at minimum of cost. People would have brotherly feelings and lead a common life based on mutual sympathy, harmony affection and love.

Fourier's scheme was, thus, an ideal arrangement of things based on integrated from of cooperation. Consumers' cooperation, producers' cooperation, cooperative labour and cooperative living, were all integrated in his scheme and the entire life of the people in the Phalanxes was to be organized on a cooperative basis. Under his scheme, work was to be done with pleasure and every one was free to choose the occupation he liked. He wanted to establish Phalanxes without introducing any radical change in the existing framework of the society. Further, with a view to removing all possibilities of clash of interest between capital and labour, he suggested that labourers would not only be the wage earners but also, cooperative owners in the cooperative production societies. Thus, the workers were to get their share of profits. The members of a Phalanx were to be the members of the producers' as well as consumers' cooperatives. In this way, he wanted to bring the consumers and producers together.

Fourier and his disciples made efforts to establish Phalanxes but owing to the paucity of funds they ended into failure. Members did not take much interest and lacked discipline as well. He could not realize his dream in his lifetime and even after his death the efforts made to organize Phalanxes in France, Holland, and America, did not succeed. Despite his failure, Foureir has been regarded as the intellectual godfather of modern profit-sharing schemes since he wanted to transform wage earner into cooperative owner.

The Rochdale Pioneers

During the early period of cooperative development, one of the societies, which had sprung up in 1830s, was at Rochdale (Rochdale Friendly Cooperative Society), England. Dr. King's writings might have influence this early Rochdalian cooperative because James Smithies, one of the leaders among the 28 Rochdalians, was inspired by King's 'The Cooperator' and showed it to eth Rochdalians. A nucleus of this determined group continued to work actively for social reform. From the work of his nucleus, the cooperative movement in Great Britain was able to achieve outstanding success. The foundation of this success was not new. It was based upon the intelligent combination of various ideas, which had been tried by previous cooperatives. The failures of the past became the warning signals of later years so that firmer foundations could be laid.

A Consumers' Cooperative Store, started in Toad Lane, Rochdale, England on 21-12-1844, and continued to this very day, provided the organizational and operating pattern that became the prototype for other consumers' cooperatives, both at the retail and wholesale levels, the world over.

These 28 Rochdalians had high hopes and aspirations. They hoped not only to establish a store for the sale of provisions but also to acquire homes in which their members might live; to manufacture articles that the society's members might need as well as to provide employment; to acquire land on which to produce products needed by members; and to employ those members out of work or those whose wages were very low. They wanted to "establish a self-supporting home colony of united interests" and to "arrange the powers of production, distribution, education and government" in the interest of its members. And finally, "for the promotion of sobriety a temperance hotel (was) to be opened in one of the Society's houses as soon as convenient". This was, indeed, an ambitious programme, and how different it was from the purposes which cooperatives today state as their reasons for organizing.

The business practices (later called as Rochdalian Principles), which these pioneers laid down for operating their store on Toad Lane were not individually novel but the combination of all them are essentially new. These practices were:

- Capital should be of members own providing and bear a fixed rate of interest. (Limited interest on equity capital).

- Only the purest provisions procurable should be supplied to members (to do away abominable adulteration of food).
- Full weight and measures should be given. (Provide honesty in weighing).
- Market prices should be charged, and no credit neither given nor asked. (Cash trading; no charge accounts; charge prevailing prices).
- profits should be divided in proportion to the amount of purchases made by each member (Patronage refunds).
- The principles of 'One-member-one-vote' should prevail in government, and the equality of the sexes in membership (Democratic control).
- Management should be in the hands of officers and a committee elected periodically by the members. (Representative government and control of the cooperative).
- A definite percentage of profit should be allotted to education. (Provision for education in cooperation)
- Frequent statements and balance sheets should be presented to the members (Member information).
- No inquiry should be made into the political and religious opinions of those who apply for membership. (Political and religious neutrality).

Note that these Rochdalian rules were devised to run a small grocery store and although they have wide application, they are not necessarily appropriate for all types of cooperatives. Such principles as democratic control by member users, limited dividends on equity capital, and operations at cost (with its corollary that if gross margins or incomes exceeds costs, refunds will be made on a patronage basis) are almost universally followed. But cash trading, charging prices that other dealers charge, sending out frequent statements and balance sheets, or even setting aside a part of the new savings in an education fund are not adhered to by all associations. The success — one might add, the phenomenal success — of the Rochdalians was by all means the shot in the arm that the cooperative movement needed in its doldrums days of the mid forties (Hungry Forties). Rochdale became the beacon for other to follow.

The Christian Socialists

During the doldrums days Christian Socialists (churchmen who criticized the then existing economic system on religious grounds), advocated the establishment of self-governing workshops. Several associations were organized but few of them had a long life. The main cause of their failure was lack of cooperative knowledge, purpose and will among the members. In 1854, Christian Socialists started a workmen's college where the noted economists, philosophers and cooperators delivered lectures to the workmen in the night classes. Although the associations promoted by the Christian Socialists did not proved to be a success, definitely proved that the success of an association lied in the strength of character of members. The chief contribution of Christian Socialists lies in their efforts for getting the Industrial Provident Societies' Act passed for the cooperative, in 1852. It may be mentioned that prior to this Act, the cooperative were recognized under the Friendly Societies' Act, 1846. The Cooperative Act recognized the cooperative organizations for trade and work, permitted rising of funds by voluntary subscription of members, the payment of interest at 5 per cent, distribution of dividends on purchases and the auditing of accounts twice a year.

Herr F.W. Raiffeisen

Germany was the first country in the world to apply the principles of cooperation in the field of credit. The cooperative credit movement was started in Germany in the middle of the 19th century. At that time the economic condition of Germany was extremely deplorable and the peasantry and artisans felt crushed under the heavy weight of indebtedness. Famines were common phenomena. Usury was the order of the day. The Jews ruled over the market and the poor labourers and farmers had no way out to buy articles of their requirements from them and sell their products to them. The Jews were not only buyers and sellers but moneylenders as well. German peasantry and labourers were thus passing bad times and were almost broken.

Herr F.W. Raiffeisen (1818-1888) and Herr Franz Schulze (1809-1883) the two pioneers in the field took initiative and started introducing various measures of relief. They started their schemes at about the same time but their field of operation was entirely different. Raiffeisen tried to reduce the sufferings of the people living in the rural areas; while Schultz adopted the new measure for giving relief to the people living in the urban areas. Both were convinced that the lot of people could be improved only if they were taken out of the clutches of the 'Jews'. They had realized that providing monetary help was not a permanent solution, and any time, in adverse circumstances, the people could fall a prey to the Jews. Hence, they thought that people should be made to take part effectively in any step aimed at ameliorating their condition. Self-help was considered to be the only way out.

It was Raiffeisen who contributed the maximum to the spread of the cooperative movement n Germany. He was the Mayor of Weyerbusch. He had witnessed how dishonest moneylenders created poverty-stricken farmers. His commune was in the grip of famine. He sought the support of the Government and got some grain. He appealed to the people for help. He employed bakers on wage basis for preparing breads. He also organized a 'Poor People's Committee', which provided food to the poor and recovered the loan after the expiry of the specific period. In 1849, he was transferred to Flammersfield where he organized 'Union in Aid of Impoverished Farmers'. The funds for this union were raised on the security of the rich persons of the locality.

This union achieved great success and rescued a number of farmers from the jaws of greedy Jews. Raiffeisen was then transferred to Heddesdorf where he set up the 'Hoddrsdorf Beneficent Society' whose members were also well-to-do people. These people deposited money with the society on interest. Loans were given to deserving farmers and artisans for productive purposes. Although the society was a grand success, Raiffeisen did not like the idea that the poor people should be at the mercy of the rich. He therefore, enrolled as members of the society. Accordingly, a new society was constituted under the name of 'Heddesdorf Credit Union'. The memorable phrase, *'Each for all and all for each'* was coined there. The movement gained momentum and in a short time many credit unions were organized. The Grand Union of Rural Cooperatives also known as 'Raiffeisen Union' was set up in 1877.

Characteristic Features of the Raiffeisen Societies:

- Membership was limited to the rural masses, especially farmers and cultivators.
- Unlimited liability of the members.
- Small area of operation.
- Small loans were given to the members, which were recovered over a long period.
- Loans were given on the basis of personal security of the members and only for productive purposes. Emphasis was on the *personal character* of the borrower.
- Nominal share capital.
- Profit earning was not the motive and even under the cooperative law only a small portion of profits was distributed to the members as dividend.
- Losses and profits were transferred to the reserve fund and endowment fund. The endowment fund was indivisible.
- The management was honorary.

- Emphasis was given to moral as well as material well- being.

Herr Frank Schulz

Schulze was a judge in his native town of Delitzsch. He had seen the miserable condition of the people, especially of low means, with his own eyes. In 1846, he organized an association with his friend Dr. Bernhardi, a friendly society for Relief in sickness and later established an association of shoemakers for the purchase of raw material. In 1850, he founded the first credit association with the funds provided those who were well-off and who did not require any financial help. Schulze was conscious of this situation and, therefore, he emphasized that no one could obtain loan from the association unless he was its member. Two years later, in 1852, Schulze founded a society at Delitzsch, which was based on cooperative principles. He obtained the required capital through the sale shares. He was a wonderful propagandist and his efforts bore fruits quickly. He published book in 1856, which contained the principles of cooperative banking as formulated by him. The number of banks started by him increased rapidly, and in 1859 organized a congress of these banks. The congress decided to set up 'The General Union of German Industrial Societies'. He was its director till his death in 1883. He was also responsible for securing from Prussia the first cooperative law in 1867, which later on was made applicable to the entire country.

Characteristic Features of the Schulze-Delitzsch Societies:

- Membership was limited to artisans, industrial workers and middle class people living in cities and towns.
- Limited liability of the members.
- Large area of operation.
- The amount of loans advanced was bigger and the period of the repayment was short.

- Loans were given on eth security of tangible assets. Although loans were advanced for productive purposes, no supervision over the utilization of the loan was made.
- A strong share capital.
- Profit earning was the chief motive and rate of divident was quite high.
- Not much emphasis was given to the reserve fund. Reserve fund was used for making up losses, but it was required to be made good as soon as possible.
- The management was paid.
- The chief concern was with the material well-being of the members.

Cooperative Schools of Thought

Cooperative Commonwealth School

Cooperative commonwealth has been variously described as Cooperative system. Cooperative Republic or cooperative order. The cooperative commonwealth school believes in complete cooperativsation of an economy. in other words, cooperation would be the dominant institution in an economy. According to this school, cooperative process is an end itself and as much economic activities as possible be brought within the ambit of cooperation. the protagonists of this school were Morgan John Minter (1782-1854), Edward Vansittart Neale (1810-1892),T.W. Mercer (1885-1947) Beatrice Webb (1858-1943) and Sydney Webb (1859-1947), Leonard Woold in Britain; Charles Gide (1847-1932) and Earnest Poisson (1882-1942) in France; Sir Horrace Curzon Plunkett (1854-1932) and George W. Russel in Ireland; Anders Orne (1881-1956) in Sweden; Dr.James Peter Warbasse (1866-1957) in USA: Dr. Alexander Laid Law (1908-1980) and Gevaret Keen in Canada; Fobes Burnham in Guyana; V.L Mehta, Dr.D.G. Karve and Prof. Gadgil in India.

It is interesting to note that the idea of establishing cooperative Commonwealth had been in the air. Robert Owen, and his ardent supporters desired to establish cooperative village communities as the means to create a New Moral world by placing all within arrangements of surroundings as will form the character. Create the wealth and cordially unite all in one interest and feeling all over the world. The Rochdale pioneers the Owenite idealists whose objective was the creation of a self-supporting home colony of united interests which paved the way for the establishment of cooperative commonwealth.

Edward V. Neale and Thomas Houge who were connected with the British cooperative movement and supporters of cooperative commonwealth condemned the system of competition, as not merely wasteful but injurious to character. They desired such a system should be replaced by a cooperative system. To them cooperative distribution was the first step towards this better system and which would be followed by cooperative developments into wholesaling, production, importing, exporting, transporting and banking. Thus their theories were based on the evolution of cooperation into a state within the state. The cooperative congress of 1925 approved the inclusion in the objects of the cooperative union as stated in its rules "the ultimate establishment of a cooperative commonwealth".

Professor Charles Gide the great French Cooperator suggested three steps to achieve the cooperative common wealth. Firstly to group the local societies and withhold as much surplus as possible, so as to found huge wholesale societies, secondly, with the capital so obtained to produce everything necessary for the members benefits. Thirdly, acquire estates, farmers' produces, the oil, the milk and milk products, poultry products and other necessaries of life, which are the bases of consumption.

Earnest Poisson another distinguished member of cooperative commonwealth who introduced the idea of 'cooperative Republic', expounded how if certain hypotheses were fulfilled or realized, a cooperative commonwealth could be achieved. He detailed his theory of the evolution of the cooperative movement into a commonwealth in his famous book entitled 'the cooperative Republic'.

Earnest Poisson explained his theory in the following words: 'supposing the consumers' societies began to spread successfully in all places without leaving even a single town or district and all these societies were affiliated to wholesale organization; if the wholesale organisations organised their production and reached the stage of controlling industry from the sources of raw materials to the final stage of processing, if these wholesale societies took in hand all phases of distribution and organised their own transport, acquiring railways and ships; if they have established banks and providing all the credit needs of all cooperators; supposing they acquired all the land, so that trade, industry, finance and agriculture were organised, owned and managed by consumers' societies; if these hypotheses were realised, a new economic society would be created which we shall call the cooperative Republic". Earnest Poisson further stated that "The Cooperative Republic is not a mechanical result of the existence and evolution of the present industrial system. it is the work of men. Its development and progress also become determinants of the action of cooperators".

Further, the Webbs stressed consumer cooperation as the practicable alternative to capitalism, i.e., "a means by which the operations of industry must be carried on under democratic control without the incentive of profit-making and they theorized on the place of cooperation in a socialist state. In their constitution for a socialist commonwealth 1920, the Webbs discussed the place of voluntary consumer cooperation in such a commonwealth and gave it a prominent place. There would be no limits on its expansion, although its primary field would be production and distribution of goods for domestic consumption.

George W. Russel, a noted poet and a practical organizer of cooperative associations of Ireland expressed that the fourth alternative to capitalism, Fascism and communism was the cooperative commonwealth. "The cooperative commonwealth alone of all these systems allows freedom and solidarity". He further elaborated that a social order should provide for three things—for economic development, for political stability and a desirable social life which are our most pressing national necessaries".

Anders Orne, a great admirer and upholder of Rochdale pioneers and one of the foremost theoretician of the Swedish Cooperative movement held that the cooperative commonwealth is a new socio-economic order, which could be created by cooperative evolution. The development of cooperation was, to Orne the only means of creating a better economic and social order, free from the defects of capitalism and state absolutism.

Dr. James Peter Warbasse, anther distinguished member of cooperative commonwealth school was of the opinion that when complete cooperation takes place, it would replace the political state. He expressed his ideas of cooperative commonwealth in his elaborated treatise on cooperative Democracy. He wrote: "when the people in their cooperative societies provide old age pensions and houses to take care of the poor, when they create their own parks, recreations, bands and orchestras, when they maintain their own hospitals, and schools, when they build roads, carry on postal services, and provide themselves with electric power and light when they drain swamps to eliminate malaria, when they own and conduct life saving stations on the ocean coast with full time life savers and up-to-date boat equipments when they maintain fire-extinguishing apparatus with automobile engines and everything modern in its design, when they put up blocks of houses in crowded cities to remove congestion, when they maintain medical clinics for protecting their members' health, when they conduct courts for the trying of cases of disagreement of litigation among members with higher courts for appeals, when in short, the people themselves do the useful things that Governments are supposed to do. Warbasse expected the functions of the state to fade or contract, when cooperation expands. Sir. Horrace Plunkett in Ireland, pointed out that state action even in advisory services, would do more harm than good if it took the form of direct intervention. The state should act through the local cooperative which handled all produce credit and even the flow of ideas through its educational activity.

According to V.L. Mehta, the establishment of cooperative commonwealth and a welfare state would mean the abolition of unemployment, the production of wealth on a much larger scale and its equitable distribution among all sections of the community. the present individual acquisitive economy should be changed into a socialized economy and cooperation according to him provides the socially controlled economy which is to replace the individualistic economy and at the same time assures, the dignity of the individual.

Prof. D.R. Gadgil, another Indian Cooperator who believed in cooperative commonwealth was of the opinion that for establishing cooperative commonwealth the transformation of individual cooperative organisations into cooperative sector and finally into a cooperative social order are the essential steps. His concept of cooperative commonwealth is a moral economy based on certain ethical principles.

Thus leading cooperators at various times and in various countries have expressed their faith in the creation of a cooperative commonwealth and for which the activities of the cooperative movement were directed.

Among the developed countries only in Finland and Iceland where cooperation occupied a commanding place. In recent years in a number of developing countries also the concept of a cooperative system or cooperative commonwealth has received official recognition. In India, the Planning Commission described the concept in the following words in a country whose economic life has its roots in the villages, cooperation is something more than a series of activities organised on cooperative lines, basically its purpose is to evolve a system of cooperative community organisation which touches upon all aspects of life.

Guyana was another country, which attempted to create cooperative republic. In 1970, the prime Minister Forbes Burnham who is a strong crusader for the concept of a cooperative republic, formally declared Guyana to be Cooperative Republic, In a statement, he said "the cooperation is the means through which the small man can become a real man, the means through which the small man can participate fully in the economic life of the nation and the means through which the small man can play a predominant part in the working of the economy." Thus the cooperative order is envisaged to take its place in every form of human activity in Guyana. Cooperation is the dominant institution — not a periphery to any other sector or system, but the system.

Whether such a cooperative commonwealth can be achieved or not depends upon the policy of the Government, and the united interest and will of the people.

As Ernest Poisson has pointed out "the cooperative Republic is not a mechanical result of the existence and evolution of the present industrial system. It is the work of men. Its development and progress also become determinants of the action of cooperators. "Arnold Bonner further remarked. "The cooperative commonwealth cannot be forced upon people, it can only grow as, how, when, where people desire it. But it is growth which each individual can directly assist day by day, without having to wait for general elections and revolutionary situations".

The School of Modified Capitalism

Casselman designated this school as moderate school or the competitive Yardstick school. Cooperative thinkers belonging to this school look on cooperatives as having a 'balance wheel' or 'Yardstick' role in the economy. They say cooperatives are essentially capitalism but with a different set of rules. Cooperatives would be treated as a means of keeping the deficiencies and excesses of the capitalistic economy in check. This school also believes that in no country can cooperatives be expected to become a dominant factor in the economy. The followers of this school hold that cooperatives can co-exist with economic enterprises which promote and practice the principles of social justice and equitable distribution and which eliminate profit making as their motive. The sectors like private, public and cooperative of the economy would function simultaneously to attain a kind of economic balance between them. Thus the constructive role of cooperatives in a capitalistic economy is that of competitive pacemaker.

Sometimes this school is referred to as 'the school of modified capitalism'. Dr. E.Fred Koller a well - known authority on cooperation at land- grant colleges says that cooperative business accepts the fundamental institutions of capitalism including the right of private property, the right of contract, inheritance and the right of private property, the right of contract, inheritance, and the right of private enterprise with its emphasis on the dignity and importance of the individual.

Even in the matter of motivation the differences are a matter of form rather than basic principles. Dr.Fred Koller after reviewing the basic concepts of capitalism and cooperation stated that there is maximum agreement in their underlying principles and foundations. They are an integral part of the capitalistic economy just as are ordinary corporations partnerships, and individual proprietorship. Cooperation is a phase of the capitalistic free enterprise system and not foreign or antagonistic to it. Thus, cooperation according to school is nothing but a modified application of capitalism.

The Co-operative Socialist School

Of the different schools of cooperative thought, only the socialistic school is based on ideological foundation. To the founder of modern cooperation Robert Owen, the two terms cooperation and socialism were apparently synonymous. The Cooperative movement and socialist movement had a common origin and both these ideologies are nothing but two streams of thought generated by the post-industrial revolution milieu. The social and economic upheavals and the exploitative and oppressive methods of capitalism motivated Some social minded thinkers to evolve solutions to set right the malfunctioning of capitalism. Both cooperative movement and socialist movement are the consequences of the continuous process of seeking alternative methods of production and distribution and a new economic and social order based on equality and justice. According to G.D.H. Cole both these movements have identical aims, namely elimination of the profit motive and democratic control.

The socialists of varying shades of opinion and ideologies emerged in the scene during the post-industrial era such as Utopian socialists, Christian socialists, Fabians and Guild socialists, each proclaiming their own means of achieving socialism. A few among them were the advocates of cooperative Associations for achieving socialism, who had come to be called as Associative socialists or cooperative socialists. Yet, none of these different brands of socialism were strong enough to make an impact of the socio-economic relation between man and man and between factors of production. The advent of Karl Marx and his scientific socialism and the efforts to establish proletariat state, marked the beginning of revolutionary thrust to socialistic ideology, which has brought about fundamental changes in the socio-political scene and the socialists usurped political power. In the post Marxian era the cooperators who are committed to the socialistic political ideology believed that cooperatives are essentially a socialist institution. They considered cooperative institution as a public rather than private institution, and a junior partner in the state in a centrally planned socialist economy. State and public enterprises will be at the commanding heights of the economy and cooperatives will be subsidiary to the state enterprises. Under such arrangement, in some spheres the ownership and control rest in the state as a whole, while in others they rest in groups of individuals who are participants in and beneficiaries from those particular enterprises. the socialist cooperators believed that it is possible to bring about a synthesis between cooperative movement and socialism in practice.

Lenin applied the principles of Marxian socialism to the building up of a new social order in Russia. A number of countries followed suit, though the pattern of socialism varies from state to state. Though the predominant pattern of economic action in these socialistic states is that of state enterprises, there remains sectors of economic life where the form of organisation is cooperative, in which the small groups of organisation can enjoy the opportunities for democratic action in their economic life. These cooperative enterprises help to prevent socialism from degenerating into bureaucracy.

James A. Yunker defines Cooperative socialism as the type of economic system combining the public ownership of the non-human factor of production with a situation of relatively limited control of the economy by the central Government. The socialistic cooperators were convinced that the peaceful expansion of cooperation would not be sufficient of cooperation would not be sufficient of cooperation would not be sufficient of cooperation would not be sufficient of cooperation would not be sufficient of cooperation would not be sufficient to solve the social problems and the political power would have to proceed to nationalization. According to them cooperation is not an end in itself. It is only a means. The socialistic cooperators placed faith on collectivism in the production process. the cooperatives' policy will be guided by direction from central authority and to that extent the cooperatives will have to forfeit their autonomy, the characteristic feature of capitalistic cooperatives. In a socialistic system the general social interests are not opposed to socially motivated interests of groups and society. Every cooperative satisfies groups of interests; the personal interest of every one of the members, the group interest of the members and general interests in socialism all the three interests supplement each other and depend on each other, though they are not fully identical cooperative socialists conceive a socialist society in which both the consumers cooperatives as well as producers cooperatives play a significant role in the economic affairs. the self managed enterprises of producers as well as consumers will grow and expand under the cooperative socialism. Yet, the usefulness of public sector in the collective economy is recognised and hence it is accorded an important place.

Prof. Oscar Lange and Lezso Nyers considered cooperatives as instruments of decentralized socialist model. This decentralized model will make the distinction between ownership by group and ownership by society as a whole disappear. According to Oscar Lange, "If progress is towards a decentralized socialist model, the difference between cooperative ownership and public ownership is organised on the principles of democratic participation in management. Under decentralized Socialist regime, the cooperatives thus assume an optimal role under state direction". In the opinion of Nyers, socialism and cooperative ideology may differ in content but, they are not alien and contradictory to each other. Both these concepts embody community aspirations as opposed to individuals or capitalists seeking profit. In socialist construction the cooperatives become the representatives of community interests. They thus become one of the sectors of the socialist economy and a revolutionary decentralized sector.

Cooperative Sector School

Cooperative Sector School has been an influential school of cooperative thought. Fauquet, the well-known French cooperator was the chief exponent of this school of thought. Fauquet divided the entire economy into four sectors: Public sector, capitalistic private sector, non-capitalistic private sector and cooperative sector. According to him cooperatives constitute a distinct economic sector in their own right, essentially different from both capitalist and public enterprises, but with some features of one and certain features of other. Fauquet thought that cooperative sector is closely related to private sector, since the former is essentially a structure arising out of small units of the family and peasants and handicrafts economy.

Those who subscribe to sector school consider that no single sector will be able to fulfill all the needs of the citizens and all the three sectors must be complementary to each other. Every sector must be encouraged to operate in those activities and spheres in which it is best suited. Fauquet divided the economy into three zones- the initial one, consisting of primary production including agricultural production and final zone consisting of retail trade and service i.e., the non-capitalistic private sector. the intermediate zone consisting of large industries is left to private and public sectors. According to him the cooperative sector suited is for initial and final zones.

The adherents of this school also believe in a mixed economy and they see Cooperatives as Co-existing with both Private and public enterprises and all the three playing as complementary role in the national economy. The political state is neutral to all the sectors and provides encouragement and opportunities for all of them. Mixed economy aims at combining political liberty with economic equality. it prefers institutions which best combine growth with economy or middle way. Under the mixed economy the ownership of means of production is kept in optimal proportion by private, public and cooperative sectors. It is a system more suited to properly handle the trade-offs between general interest and sectional interest than Capitalism and socialism. A mixed economy implies a fair balance between social goals and individual goals. There is a strong government, which exercises a coordinating influence and intervenes in the market without distorting the market mechanism.

The Economy Theory of 'Optimum Regime' is of central importance to mixed economy. On the basis of this it is possible to develop a combination of different instruments of policy and different economic institutions in consistent manner, combining administrative and market segments in the best proportions. the full potentials and interests of the cooperative form becomes even more apparent than is the case when we assume a purely capitalist or a purely communist model.

Cooperatives are appropriate organisations in mixed economy situation and in fact they are the representatives of mixed economy. The aggregate of all the cooperative enterprises in any non-cooperative system would constitute the cooperative sector. the cooperative sector in the mixed economy has the potential to transfer the urban-rural relation and more fundamentally the property and work relations. It keeps the initiative out of state hands while evolving at least some of the institutions of mixed economy. It helps by-pass and reform public and private sectors. it represents an evolved form of public participation and an attempt to solve the problems with social and political initiative at the micro-level.

There were several staunch supporters of this school of thought among the cooperators, of whom Warbasse and

Laidlaw are prominent. While expressing firmly in favour of this school, Laidlaw has stated thus: to imagine the economy according to school we have to see it as a circle with three fairly distinct sectors, but with boundaries shifting from time to time as economic circumstances changes.

P.R. Dubhashi rationalizes the sector school as follows:

"Realism requires that the operators must lower their sight and remain content at least for the time being with the successful demonstration of the cooperative form of organisation in at lest a few sectors of economic activity." the protagonists of This School are more influenced by pragmatism than idealism, the dominant feature of cooperative commonwealth school of thought. Those who support the cooperative sector school rest their case on a number of cogent arguments. Prof. Laidlaw has put forward his arguments as follows:

- No one system alone can build a perfect socialist order. Certainly capitalism has not been able to do it; neither has monolithic State. A suitable mixture of all three can bring us as near as we can get to the ideal economic system.
- If the three methods of business are allowed to operate simultaneously and independently—but of course under general regulations of Government applying to all business—they will tend to supplement one another, each one specializing in the particular economic function, for which it is best suited.
- With all three—public enterprises, Cooperative and private business operating in some sort of balanced Co-existence, there will be provision for the widest possible range of conditions:
    - ➢ Universal coverage and protection by state where necessary, for example through public utilities

- ➢ The direct participation of citizens in their own economic affairs wherever possible; and
- ➢ The progress that flows from individual initiative and reward for personal effort.

Self-learning Activity

Try to answer the following questions on your own.

1. Clarify the concept of cooperation?
2. Write short notes on Neale's School of Thought.
3. What is the Blanc's view on State and Cooperatives?
4. Charles Gide and Consumer Socialism—comment?
5. What do you understand by Fair Price Doctrine of Paul Lambert?
6. Cooperative Communities—Whose experiment? Explain.
7. Discuss about Phalansteres?
8. List out the business practices laid down by Rochdale pioneers.
9. Describe the Cooperative Sector School?

Summary

- Cooperation means "working together for a common cause. We live here not only for ourselves but to help the needy person. It is the real co-operation and it is the real philosophy of life.
- Cooperative models had been evolved through traditional and modern doctrines by several experiments. During ancient times: Egyptian, Babylonian, Greek Era, in China Hon Dynasty, Roman, Christian Era, Islamic faith, and during middle ages there are evidences of associations, guilds, societies of cooperative nature. Modern cooperative doctrines are after the Industrial Revolution (1750).
- The major contributors of cooperative movement in the world are: Edward Neale (wholesale society, cooperative

education, international cooperation); Louis Blanc (social workshop, state aid); Grundtvig (folk school, adult education); Charles Gide (liberalism and competition, fair price doctrine, consumer socialism); Andes Orne (consumerism, economic cooperation, state aid); GDH Cole (Guild socialism, cooperatives and trade unions, democracy); Horrace Plunkett (pioneer of agricultural cooperation, social order, contributions on practical sphere); J.P Warbasse (consumer supremacy, labour and cooperatives, state and cooperatives, cooperative democracy); G.Fauquet (double origin of cooperatives, cooperative sector, state and cooperatives, cooperative integration); father Moses M.Coady (antigonish movement, techniques of adult education); Paul Lambert (economic democracy, fair price doctrines, consumer supremacy, cooperatives and trade unionism); Robert Owen (experiments on cooperative communities, human relations); Dr.William King (distributive cooperation); Charles Fourier (Phalanstere); Rochdale pioneers (business practices-base for cooperative principles, 1844 consumer coop); Christian Societies (self-governing workshops); Raiffeisen (rural credit); Schulze (urban credit).

- Schools of Cooperative Thought are: Cooperative common wealth school, school of modified capitalism, cooperative socialist school and cooperative sector school.

Chapter 3

Definition and Principles of Cooperation

Cooperation—Meaning

Various economists, cooperators, thinkers and leaders in the specific context of the circumstances prevalent in their respective countries have attributed a number of meanings and definitions to the term 'Cooperation'. Cooperation in its ordinary sense would mean 'Working together'. Whereas in its technical sense the term would denote a special mode of doing business, which gives rise to the formal organisation and the methods and techniques associated with it *(Krishnaswami 2000).* C.R. Fay viewed cooperation as an association for undertaking joint trade and emphasised the principle of Patronage Dividend *(Quoted in Calvert 1959).* Herric stressed the principle of Voluntary Membership *(Quoted in Jalal 1990).* Prof. Paul Lambert emphasized democratic control and social aspects of Cooperation *(Paul Lambert 1963).* Verhagen has defined cooperation as "an association of persons (or households), usually of limited means, who have agreed to work together on a continuing basis to pursue one or more common interests and who for that purpose have formed an economic organisation which is jointly controlled and whose costs, risks and benefits are equitably shared among the members" *(Verhagen 1984).* O.R. Krishnaswami defines cooperation as a voluntary and democratic association of human beings based on equality (of opportunity and control) and equity (of distribution and mutuality) for the promotion of their common interests as producers and consumers *(Krishnaswami 2000).* The International Cooperative Alliance (ICA) Statement on the Cooperative Identity (1995) defines a Cooperative as `an autonomous association of persons united voluntarily to meet their common economic, social and cultural needs and aspirations through a jointly owned and democratically controlled enterprise' *(ICA 1995).*

Definitions of Co-operation

The term co-operation as generally understood today is a term, which like philosophy and religion defies exact definition and description. Almost every writer has tried to define this term in his own way. No two definitions are identical and no single definition has so far succeeded in including within a single unassailable formula all the ingredients of co-operative ideology. One important reason as to why the definitions differ so widely is that co-operative movement developed in different countries in different forms under different social environment. The difficulty in defining the term co-operation also arises because of the fact that in some countries they are aided and controlled by the state; in some they are used as instrument of state planning, in some they are state partnered while in some they are state organs, and in some they are voluntary organizations. Because of this difficulty, Dr. Laszlovalke of the U.S.A. distinguishes between welfare co-operatives and 'economic cooperatives'. By the former he means societies, which are largely state aided.

The concept and meaning of co-operation has been given by utopian socialists, religious thinkers, sociologists, economists and reformists in their own way in the context of the circumstances prevalent in their respective countries. Some of the definitions of co-operation and their critical analysis are given below:

Holyoake defined co-operation "as a voluntary concert, with equitable participation and control among all concerned in any enterprise".

It is worthwhile mentioning that Holyoake and his contemporaries. Had their attention fixed on the evils resulting from the early and rapid rise of capitalism. In those days, the onrush of the Industrial Revolution had necessitated the accumulation of the capital of many people in joint stock enterprise. as liability was still unlimited it was but natural that those who bore the risk should retain the control and take all the profits. During those days money was all-powerful and the human element was at its mercy. Thus, Holyoake's definition repeats the cry of men ground down in poverty, who thought their way of escape lay in securing fair dealing, fair opportunity, freedom to choose their own lives and emancipation from the capitalist and middleman.

According to *Mr. C.R. Fay,* "A co-operative society is an association for the purpose of joint trading, originating among the weak, and conducted always in an unselfish spirit, on such terms that all who are prepared to assume the duties of membership way share in its rewards, in proportion to the degree in which they make use of their association".

An analysis of this definition shows that:

- a co-operative society is an association;
- originates among the weak;
- its aim is joint trading;
- its business is conducted in an unselfish spirit; and
- the rewards are shared by members in proportion to the degree in which the association is used.

While drafting this definition, Fay had in his mind only the consumers' movement, which had developed in England after the Rochdale pioneers. 'Trading' is too narrow a term to cover all the activities which can be carried on by co-operatives. Thus, definition is very narrow as it is largely confined to societies formed for joint trading. The definition also does not say anything about the voluntary aspect of the co-operative movement, which is considered to be of considerable importance.

Sir Horace Plunkett's definition of co-operation is 'self help made effective by organization'. He summed up theory and practice of co-operation in their famous maxims, "Better Farming, Better Business and Better Living." This definition reflects the spirit of the co-operative enterprises. It, however, lays over-emphasis on the principle of self-help, which is, no doubt, an important principle of co-operation but the only one.

Dr. R. Philips has given the following definition of co-operation.

The co-operative association is an association of firms or households for business purposes—an economic institution through which economic activity is conducted in the pursuit of economic objectives.

The definition has number of limitations. It regards co-operative enterprise as an association of either firms or households while co-operation is always regarded as association of people and not capital. this definition also assumes that economic motive is the sole inducement of co-operative undertaking. In other words it assumes that co-operator in his role as a member of an association functions as an economic man. Another weakness of this definition is that it considers the co-operative association as an economic institution. But it is difficult to regard co-operative undertaking as purely a firm or an economic undertaking as it does not pursue profit maximization for its own sake. This definition also does not give any idea of the basic principles for which co-operation stands.

A pure economic concept of co-operation as envisaged by Dr. R. Philips is unthinkable as our economic affairs have to be re-aligned in a manner consistent with morality and spiritual values. *Prof. P.H. Casselman* has stated: "co-operation is an economic system with a social content." It may be mentioned that co-operation is not simply another way of doing business. The root of the co-operative idea is that there is a relation between business and ethics, which is greater than the necessary commercial honesty of our present industrial system. It has an idealism which in the words of Dr. smith, "in some cases is almost religious".

Mr. Rrank Robotka of the U.S.A., defines co-operation "as an association of autonomous units (farm or other business units, or households) whose purpose it is to conduct jointly some activity which is an integral part of the operations of the participating units, as a means of increasing incomes, reducing costs or otherwise enhancing the economic interests of the participating units".

This definition is most defective as it can perfectly well apply to a capitalist cartel. It makes no reference to any of the co-operative principles. it has to be borne in mind that the mere fact of uniting for the furtherance of one's own interests is not a co-operative activity. If people unite purely with the intention of fostering their own interests as far as possible. Come what may, they form a cartel but not a cooperative.

Mr. H. Calvert defined co-operation "as a form of organization, wherein persons voluntarily associate together as human beings, on a basis of equality for the promotion of the economic interests of themselves".

The essentials of this definition are that:

- a co-operative is a voluntary form of organization;
- it is an association of human beings;
- it is organized on the basis of equality; and
- its objective is the economic interests of its members Calvert's definition is.

Most widely quoted and is generally accepted as the best definition of co-operation but its main weakness is that it does not recognize co-operative organizations for the promotion of interests other than economic. Again, a co-operative society is not entirely formed for the promotion of the economic interest of its members only. it has a social philosophy of serving the interest of the community which is conspicuous by its absence in this definition.

Prof. Paul Lambert who is a leading authority on co-operation and is the editor of the famous journal, "annals of public and co-operative Economy" in his renowned book, "Studies in the social philosophy of co-operation" has given the following definition of a co-operative undertaking.

"A Co-operative society is an enterprise formed and directed by an association of users, applying itself the rules of democracy and directly intended to serve both its own members and the community as a whole." The term user in this definition has been used in the broad sense—not as consumer.

The essentials of this definition are that:

- a co-operative enterprise;
- it is an association of users;
- it applies the rules of democracy; and
- it is intended to serve both:
  - its own members; and
  - the community as a whole.

Prof. Lambert's definition has attracted considerable attention in the co-operative world. It has found favour with many commentators. It has been considered as pertinent by Mr. C. Vinney and has been explicitly approved by Mr. Rezsohazy. The greatest merit of this definition is that for the first time it has been made clear that a co-operative society is to serve not only the interests of its members but must also serve the interests of the whole community.

Mr. Lambert has stated, "A co-operative society does not aim only at furthering the interest of its members, but in so far as it may legitimately do so and only in so far as this is compatible with the general interest." In this respect Lambert's definition is certainly an improvement over Calvert's definition.

Other Definitions

According to *Talmaki*, "Co-operation is an organization where a person voluntarily associates together with others on a basis of equality for the promotion of their economic interest by honest means".

Dr. Louis P.F. Smith defines a co-operative as "an association belonging to economic units (whether of producers or consumers) controlled by them for service to themselves in which the risk of profit or loss is borne by a variable price of goods and services rather than the profit on capital.

Mr. W.P. Watkins, a former director of the international co-operative alliance, defines co-operative as "a system of social organization based on the principles of unity, economy, democracy, equity and liberty".

A good definition of organized co-operation is found in the report of the inquiry on cooperative Enterprise in Europe published by the Government of the United States. It states, "A Co-operative enterprise is one which belongs to the people who use its service, the control of which rests equally with all its members and the gains of which are distributed in proportion to the use they make of its services.

According to *Co-operative Independent Commission*," A co-operative society. in its economic aspects, is a voluntary organization set up by consumers or producers to serve their own needs."

Mr. V.L. Mehta, the veteran co-operator of India has described co-operation as follows:

"Co-operation is a vast movement which promotes voluntary associations of individuals having common needs who combine towards the achievement of common economic ends."

Dr. E.M Hough defines it as follows:

"In its broadest sense, co-operation may be defined simply as voluntary association in a joint undertaking for mutual benefit."

Dr. L.P. Jacks has called co-operation "the most difficult and beautiful art in the world". Two things are indispensable to any art—vision and technique. As in all arts, the effective expression of co-operation depends even more upon vision than upon technique, important, as are the forms of organization and the operating methods.

Legal Definitions

In some countries a co-operative society is defined by law as an organization which has as its object" the promotion of the economic interest of its members" or "the promotion of thrift, self-help and mutual aid among agriculturists and other persons with common economic needs, so as to bring about better living, better business and better methods of production". Sometimes a co-operative is defined as a body formed and working under the 'co-operative Act' of the country concerned.

Under the Austrian Act, a co-operative society is an association with unlimited number of persons, the object of which is the promotion of industry or trades of their members by means of common action or credit.

Under the Japanese Law of 1921, a co-operative society is an association having legal existence, formed by persons of modest means in order to promote and develop, according to the principles of mutuality, the exercise of their occupations and the improvement of their economic condition.

Under the British Columbia Agricultural association Act of 1911: an association shall be deemed to have been organized on a co-operative basis of its constitution and bye-laws provide for securing to all producers who are its members a share in the profits of association in proportion to the value of the produce supplied by them after payment of a dividend upon the capital stock not exceeding a statutory maximum.

The German Law while placing emphasis on open membership and furtherance of the commercial interest of members by means of a common business undertaking, has defined it as an association of persons varying in number and grappling with the same economic difficulties and voluntarily associating on a basis of equal rights and obligation and endeavouring to solve these difficulties mainly by conducting at their own risk the undertaking to which they have transferred one or more of such of their economic functions as correspond to their economic needs, and by utilising their undertaking in joint co-operation for their common material and moral benefits.

The Indian Co-operative Societies Act or 1912 has not given any definition of co-operation. Section 4 (c) considers a co-operative society as "a society, which has its object the promotion of the economic interests of its members in accordance with co-operative principles." the Act, has, however, not precisely defined what is cooperation; nor has it attempted to define economic interests or co-operative principle an attempt to define these terms precisely was avoided deliberately in the interest of elasticity and simplicity.

Characteristics of Co-operation

On the basis of above description following are the main characteristics of Co-operation:

1. Co-operation is an undertaking or enterprise

    (i) It is an institution

(ii) It is based on service motive
(iii) It is not based on pure sacrifice
(iv) It fulfils special objectives
(v) Profit and loss is divided into members
(vi) It traders on the basis of co-operative principles

2. Association of persons
   (i) It is organization of human beings
   (ii) Money is important than capital
   (iii) Membership can be irrespective of caste, creed, sex or business

3. Voluntary Organization
   (i) It is not a forced organization
   (ii) Members are free to decide
   (iii) Members may come and go on their own will

4. An Organization of the needy
   (i) It is basically an organization of needy poor persons
   (ii) They solve their mutual problems
   (iii) Poor cannot save their interest due to lack of resources so they unite
   (iv) Now-a-days medium class persons are also interested in co-operative movement

5. Open Membership
   (i) Membership is not seasoned
   (ii) It is always open
   (iii) Every person who can be benefited by society can be the member of society
   (iv) But a person living in a city cannot be the member of rural co-operative credit society

6. More importance to man than capital
   (i) It is based on the principle that man should dominant capital not capital should dominate man

(ii) Capital is means not end
(iii) End is human welfare
(iv) Profit is distributed among men on equality basis

7. Service motive
(i) It is a philosophy of life
(ii) Profit is secondary motive
(iii) Primary motive is service
(iv) It is not merely a business

8. Democratic Decentralization
(i) It is democratic institution
(ii) Its management and organization on democratic basis
(iii) Equal right and duties to each member
(iv) Member with more share cannot dominate
(v) Man is important than capital

9. Decentralized Management
(i) Division of duties and right on equality basis
(ii) No concentration of powers
(iii) One man one vote

10. Basis of Equality
(i) It includes equality
(ii) It does not differentiate rich and poor, literate or illiterate
(iii) It is irrespective of caste, creed and sex

11. Based on equality
(i) It is based on justice
(ii) Distribution of profit on equality is justified based
(iii) Profit distribution is in ratio of share purchased by its members

12. Mutual Co-operation
(i) Self help through mutual help

(ii) All works for each and each work for all

(iii) Have not can take help from haves

13. Check on Exploitation

(i) It is exploitation free organization

(ii) Member are owners

(iii) No exploitation as in capitalization

14. A Universal Movement

(i) Its area is not limited

(ii) It is movement for social re-structure

(iii) Its principle are true in capitalism socialism as well as in fixed economy

15. A middle path

(i) It is a via media between capitalism and socialism

(ii) It adopts the qualities of socialism and capitalism

(iii) It is a via media for checking the drawbacks of capitalism and socialism

16. No Discrimination

(i) It believes in no discrimination on basis of caste, creed, sex, wealth etc.

(ii) It considers all equal

(iii) It believes that everyone is for all and all are for every one.

17. Federal Base

(i) Co-operation is based on federalism

(ii) Primary Co-operative societies at village basis

(iii) Central banks at district level and state co-operative banks at Apex level

18. Autonomous body

(i) Organization and management is in the hands of members

(ii) No dominance of anyone

(iii) No interference.

19. Socio-economic Movements
    (i) It is an indication of social and economic development
    (ii) It brings honesty, independence, self-help feelings
    (iii) It helps in economic upgradation
20. Cultural and moral development
    (i) It is a cultural movement
    (ii) Its ethical part is more powerful
    (iii) It gives moral support to weak as unity

Benefits of Cooperation

Economic Benefits

Cooperatives helps to rationalize distribution patterns increase purchasing power and promote consumer protections, narrow the housing gap. They contribute to the modernization of small-scale production in agriculture, fisheries, handicrafts and industry. They ensure improved quality and greater volume of production and more efficient marketing of increased output. They stimulate productive capital formation among large number of individuals. In a wider sense, cooperative growth is an effective stimulant for economic growth.

Cooperatives are engaged in securing for their members services of various kinds at low costs. These may include services of various socio-economic activities in the consolidation of holdings, the establishment of irrigation schemes, the contouring of land, the procurement of technical knowledge, the administration of credit, the buying of fertilizers, pesticides, seeds, electricity, and machine services, of consumers, goods and services, the processing and marketing of produce, the provision of insurance, health and medical care or education.

Cooperation is also playing a vital role in checking the monopolistic tendencies.

The following is the list of economic advantages of cooperative organizations:

- The substitution of the profit incentive in business by that of service to humanity or production for consumption. (In other words, priority is given to the satisfaction of human needs instead of greed of profits).
- A more equitable distribution of wealth.
- The breaking up of monopolies and trusts, which operate at expenses of consumer.
- The increase of workman's purchasing power an real wages by giving him more and better goods for his money.
- The reduction in cost of distributive system by:
  - Elimination of unnecessary middlemen
  - Removal of useless duplication of services
  - Eradication of such practices as misleading advertisement and high pressure salesmanship
  - The elimination of fraudulent practices like adulteration, short weight, etc.
- The rejection of accounting inaccuracies by encouraging frankness in business.
- The more accurate correlation of demand and supply as a result of the greater certainty and regularity of consumer market.
- Stabilization of employment, which will result from the regularity of demand and the absence of speculation.
- The fair treatment of all labour and general improvement in employer-employee relations.
- The training of people to spend wisely.

Social and Moral Benefits

Cooperation offers not only economic benefits to members but also confers a number of benefits to the society. This is so because the object of cooperation is to transform the member's condition in such a way that he makes his social life richer and happier.

The ultimate aim of cooperation is to develop men-men imbued with the spirit of self-help and mutual help in order that individually they may rise to a full personal life and collectively to full social life (Dr. Fauquet).

Modern life is full of social tensions: Urban *vs.* rural, consumer *vs.* producers, labour *vs.* capital, there are tensions with regard to religion, caste, language, state, race and occupation. Cooperatives tend to lessen these tensions and show all people how they can work together on common group.

The cooperative movement frees its members not only from usurers and profiteers, but also from themselves and their bad habits. It teaches them the virtues that are not always natural to them, such as, orderliness, foresight punctuality and a strict respect for engagements entered into. A cooperative order returns ownership of the means of production, in an indirect form, to the workers, and the class struggle is resolved.

It is the claims of the cooperators that it can be the principal means of bringing about in a peaceful manner social change of a fundamental nature, ushering in a social order non-exploitative, egalitarian, tolerant that harmonizes the dignity of the individual with the well-being of the community.

The social purposes of cooperation are more diverse than economic purposes. They may be to provide unique education in democracy, responsibility and toleration, to train for political power, to evolve an industrial relationship in which the element of authority is much more evenly distributed than in private business, to preserve a strong friendly or family spirit and a sense of pride and power which is impersonal, to encourage a general advance rather than the advance of particular individuals, to secure rations, constructive and unifying approaches to social and economic problems.

Cooperation teaches that man is his brother's keeper and that he can best lighten his own burden by lightening the burden of others, that he can achieve his own happiness only by including within the happiness of others. The cooperative movement is an exercise in fellowship, which seeks to end the exploitation of man by man. The movement teaches man and woman to rise above their own interests and to think in terms of general good.

ICA Statement on Cooperative Definition and Values

Definition

"A cooperative is an autonomous association of persons united voluntarily to meet their common economic, social and cultural needs and aspirations through a jointly-owned and democratically controlled enterprise".

Explanation

The definition emphasizes the following characteristics of a cooperative:

(*a*) The cooperative is autonomous: that is, it is as independent of government and private firms as possible.

(*b*) It is 'an association of persons'. This means that cooperatives are free to define 'persons' in any legal way they choose. Many primary cooperatives around the world choose only to admit individual human beings. Many other primary cooperatives admit 'legal persons', which in many jurisdictions includes companies, extending to them the same rights as any other member. Cooperatives at other than primary level are usually cooperatives whose members are other cooperative. In all case, the membership should decide how it wishes the cooperative to deal with this issue.

(*c*) 'The persons are united voluntary'. Membership in a cooperative should not be compulsory. Members should be free, within the purpose and resources of the cooperatives, to join or to leave.

(*d*) 'Members of a cooperative meet their common economic, social and cultural needs'. This part of the definition emphasizes that cooperatives are organized by their members, for their members. Member needs may be singular and limited, they may be diverse, they may be social and cultural as well as purely economic, but whatever the needs, they are the central purpose for which the cooperative exists. The term 'aspirations' here denotes strong desire or ambition for advancement.

(*e*) 'The cooperative is a jointly owned and democratically controlled enterprise'. This phrase emphasizes that ownership is distributed among members on a democratic basis. These two characteristics of ownership are particularly important in differentiating cooperatives from other kinds of organizations, such as capital-controlled firms. Each cooperative is also an 'enterprise' in the sense that it is an organized entity, normally functioning in the market place; it must strive to serve its members efficiently and effectively.

Statement on Cooperative Values

Cooperatives are based on the values of self-help, self-responsibility, democracy, equality, equity, and solidarity. In the tradition of their founders, cooperative members believe in the ethical values of honesty, openness, social responsibility, and caring for others.

Explanation

- ***Self-help:*** It means one should try to solve his problems with his own effort, means and resources available. But self-help succeeds only up to a point. Therefore it needs joint-efforts with those who have the same problem. They can pool small resources and means, so that they become more potential. In-group individual becomes more powerful, he learns, with experience of other fellow men, this becomes mutual-self-help. Self-help and mutual-help promote cooperatives spirit and key to success of cooperatives.

- ***Self-responsibility:*** coupled with self-help and mutual self-help is the value of self-responsibility. Every office-bearer, member of Board of Directors or management must take responsibility for his personal actions, for the activity as whole and for its impact on society. Similarly each member of cooperative should realize and accept his responsibility towards cooperative and commit himself to it. A cooperative can achieve its object and progress only when every ones involved in its functioning, including employees, feel his accountability and discharge his responsibility with commitment, dedication and sincerity of purpose. This is what the Rochdale Pioneers demonstrated and they succeeded.
- ***Democracy:*** Democracy is a basic value of cooperatives. In the context of cooperative, the essence of democracy is 'conscious decision' based on 'freewill'. Conscious decision means understanding the logic or rationale of taking decisions and be aware of the possible consequences of the decisions and their impact on individual an institution. 'Freewill' means no forcing of the decision from outside. 'Participation' is an integral aspect of democracy. Participation includes attending general body/board meetings, actively giving ones opinion on various matters and issues affecting the society. It also encompasses participation in strengthening internal finance and business.
- ***Equality:*** Equality means equal right and opportunities, right of participation, a right to be informed, a right to be heard, a right to be involved in the decision making. Members are to be associated as equal as possible, without any kind of discrimination of gender, religion, caste, creed, race, amount of share capital contribution, deposits, political affiliation etc. That is why one member one vote is the principle, which establishes equality.
- ***Equity:*** It refers to how members are treated within a cooperative. It means that members should be treated

equal in how they are rewarded for their participation in the cooperative normally through patronage dividends, allocations to capital reserve in their name or reductions in charges. Equity ensures social justice.

- ***Solidarity:*** It is an important base of cooperatives. Solidarity is collectivity. Management have the responsibility to ensure that all members are treated as fairly as possible, that the general interest is always kept in mind, that there is consistent effort to deal with employees (members or non-members), as well as the non-members. It also means that a cooperative has a responsibility for the collective interest of its members. It indicates that society's financial and social assets belong to the group, being the result of joint efforts and participation. Solidarity also means that cooperatives and cooperators stand together. They work together to resent a common entity before the public and government.
- ***Honesty:*** This is most important for survival of cooperatives. Rochdale Pioneers had a special commitment to honesty. Rochdale Pioneers had a special commitment to honesty. Indeed, their identity in the market was distinguished partly because they insisted upon honest business—honest measurement, high quality and fair prices. Cooperatives ideal is honest dealing with members and non-members. Therefore, cooperatives have a bias towards openness. They regularly reveal to their members and others information relating to their performance. Scope of honesty is much wider in cooperatives than what generally is understood. For individual honesty is not monetary honesty only, but also honesty of thoughts, commitments, behaviour and conduct, ho hypocrisy or falsehood, no underhand dealings or false promises, no dishonesty in elections. In cooperatives honesty also encompasses correct maintenance of accounts and balance sheet, correct information to members, objectivity and fairness in personal matters. It prohibits

undue favours of any kind to any one. Individual cooperators honesty, business honesty and managerial honesty brighten the image of cooperatives and their identity. Without honesty cooperatives have no cause to exist, non-future to sustain themselves. Cooperatives will be in peril and danger of self-liquation without honesty.

- ***Openness:*** It means that cooperatives are open to members of community they serve. They have a commitment to serve and assist individuals in helping themselves.
- ***Social Responsibility:*** In fact Social Responsibility and caring for others are overlapping concepts. It means that cooperatives should move beyond caring for members only. They should financially assist or organize activities beneficial to the entire community. However, such activities can be taken up when cooperatives have surplus.
- ***Caring for others:*** It means take interest in and care about other people. This concept stems from humanism. Cooperatives are humane by nature though their main concern is to achieve economic object.

These value concepts can be only in an individual who is an altruist, pluralist, self-denials, large-hearted, broad minded and above all a humanist, whose eyes become wet seeing others' sufferings; whose conscience revolts seeing others being exploited; whose heart throbs seeing the destitute and the oppressed; who gets happiness and satisfaction in helping others. To such people cooperation becomes a mission and means to solve problems and enable the weak to become collectively strong.

Principles of Cooperation

Meaning

Principles are needed in any institution for its discipline and proper functioning. They help in proper structural set up and organization and management of institutions. Co-operative principles are established with the same objectives. co-operative principles are not imaginary they are based on facts. These principles ensure proper functioning and encourage maximum utilization by their use.

Every organization has its own principles (fundamental truth, law, doctrine, or motivating force, upon which others are based), which are to be observed for its smooth working. The principles are formulated keeping in view the object, pattern of governance, power and authority structure, accountability, organizational framework, financial structure, etc. Organization is recognized, inter alia, with the laid down principles. Any distortion, deviation and non-observance caused aberrations and create various problems. This is a general principle. Cooperatives have their own set of principles, which are universal in their nature, recognition and acceptance. Since the beginning of their origin, cooperatives lay great emphasis on them. They manifest the nature of cooperatives; underline management principle inter-organizational relationship, etc. The operation of these principles, indeed, makes a cooperative a cooperative.

According to different authorities Co-operation has been defined as follows:

> "Co-operative principles are those principles of social science which are utilized in explaining the salient features of co-operation undertaking as well as their administration".
>
> — *P.R. Dubhashi*
>
> "Co-operative principles are such by laws which administers the activities of co-operative organization."
>
> — *George Davidovic*

The basis of co-operation is co-operative principle. Without principles co-operation is baseless can not stable and efficient in management and efficient in its activities and its basic aim of mutual help cannot be fulfilled.

Principles of co-operation are changed with change in concept of co-operation. The principles of co-operation can be studied as follows:

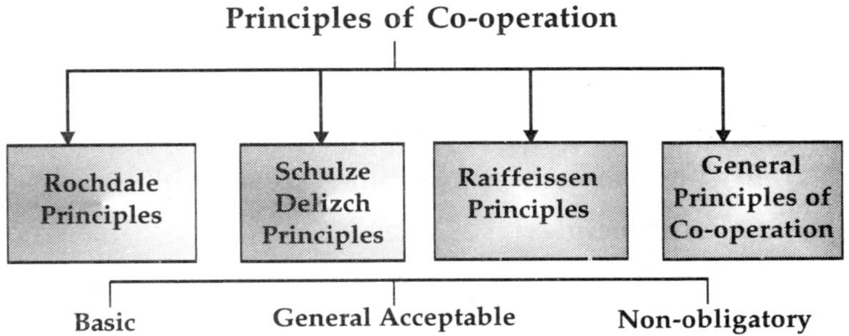

Rochdale Principles

1. These principles were propounded by Rochdale pioneers as it was started with consumer store at village Rochadale (England) on 21 December 1844.
2. The basic aim was to check exploitation by industrialist and mutual help was the objective.
3. To continue the India successfully some principles were laid down known as Rochadale principles of co-operation as:
   (*a*) Democratic control
   (*b*) Open membership
   (*c*) Fixed interest on capital
   (*d*) Dividend on purchases
   (*e*) Cash transaction
   (*f*) Pure and unadulterated products
   (*g*) Provision of education
   (*h*) Political and religious neutrality
   (*i*) Self-help

Schulze Delizsch Principles

1. It was started by Mr. Schulze in Germany in 1849 based on the following principles:
   (*a*) Self-help without outside help
   (*b*) Wider area
   (*c*) Division of profit according to work
   (*d*) High rate of interest on capital
   (*e*) Limited liability of members
   (*f*) Specialisation in trade
   (*g*) Ten per cent of profit in reserve fund.

Raiffeissen Principles

1. These principles were implemented in rural agriculture credits by Mr. Raffesion in 1862
2. Some principles laid down are as follows:
   (*a*) Self-help through state help
   (*b*) Limited area of operation
   (*c*) Distribution of profit not compulsory
   (*d*) Balance of profit to reserve fund
   (*e*) Member liability unlimited
   (*f*) Investment of capital not necessary for membership
   (*g*) Work by a board of directors with service control.
3. These principles were accepted by international co-operative alliance in 1921.
4. These principles were divided into two parts in 1973 by committee of international co-operative alliance as:
   (*a*) Obligatory principles
   (*b*) Non essential principles

Obligatory principles includes open membership, democratic control, dividend on purchases and limited interest on capital while nonessential principles included religious and political neutrality, cash transaction, promotion of education.

5. From 1963 international Co-operative Association followed these principles without division as a whole.

General Principles of Co-operation

These can be studied by dividing into three parts:

A. Basic Principles
B. General Accepted
C. Non-obligatory

A. Basic Principles

1. *Membership*

(i) Open and voluntary membership
(ii) All can be member who can bear responsibility
(iii) Membership is irrespective of social, political and religious discrimination
(iv) Any member can be member of any society.
(v) Member should be in need of benefit and society.
(vi) Whenever a member desire can leave the society
(vii) One cannot be compelled to remain a member
(viii) A person may be induced to be a member by introduction of benefits of co-operation

2. *Democratic Administration*

(i) The basis of co-operation is democratic pattern
(ii) Member performs the function of administration
(iii) They can appoint or nominate representative
(iv) One man one vote is the basis although a person may purchase more items
(v) General council is the Apex authority
(vi) Everyone has to follow the decision of Apex authority

3. *Distribution of surplus*

(i) Surplus will be distributed among members after making provisions for development of trade of co-operative society, arrangement for collective services

(ii) Profit will be distributed on basis of exchange by members with society

(iii) The main objective of society is not profit earning but surplus is an incentive to its members

4. *Limited Interest on capital*

(i) Interest paid on capital shared be with low rate

(ii) Capital is not master but servant in co-operative society

(iii) Fixed rate of interest on capital is essential to make the movement popular

5. *Political and Religious Neutrality*

(i) Co-operation movement is really an economic movement

(ii) Its objective is service along with economic up gradation of members

(iii) Every one irrespective of caste, creed, religion can be member of society

(iv) By political neutrality here mean to express himself with any fare and his ideas with freedom

6. *Principles of Honest Trading*

(i) Profit is the motive of co-operation

(ii) By removing the services of middle man its aim is to serve consumers more better

(iii) Consumer protection is now the prime objective of co-operation

B. Generally Accepted principles

1. *Self-help through mutual help*

(i) It is based on fact that each for all and all for each

(ii) It is union of weak and poor persons

(iii) It is for interest of have-nots

(iv) Self-help through mutual help is the basis

2. *Service Spirit*
   (i) Service is main aim of Co-operation
   (ii) It is not possible without feeling of sacrifice
   (iii) If is not only commodity trading
   (iv) Man is important that commodity and profit

3. *Justice and equality*
   (i) It is a weapon against injustice
   (ii) Its aim is equality
   (iii) All are equal and surplus should be distributed without any discrimination
   (iv) It is based on democratic decentralization

4. *Principles of joint ownership*
   (i) Co-operative society is not owned by a person
   (ii) It is joint property and an asset of all the members
   (iii) It works for common interest
   (iv) It avoids concentration of powers and wealth

5. *Cash transactions*
   (i) It believes in cash transaction
   (ii) Credit transaction needs more capital
   (iii) It avoids bad debts
   (iv) It encourages economy by cash transactions

6. *Principles of unity and fraternity*
   (i) First society than the principles
   (ii) Each for all is the basis
   (iii) One inspires to work above the personal interest.
   (iv) It encourages unity and brotherhood

7. *Principle of economy and efficiency*
   (i) Sources co-operative societies are limited
   (ii) Maximum satisfaction from limited resources is tried
   (iii) It is possible by economy and efficiency both

8. *Federal structure*
   - *(i)* Federalism is the basis of organisation of co-operative structure
   - *(ii)* These institutions at national level, then state level and district level and village level
   - *(iii)* It creates a systematize administration
9. *Principle of Training*
   - *(i)* Every member is trained for efficient management
   - *(ii)* Co-operative principles and their implementation is taught by training
   - *(iii)* Officer and members both are given training

C. **Non-obligatory Principles**

1. *Principle of Honorary Service*
   - *(i)* Honorary service was expected at initial stage
   - *(ii)* Then society as less number were helpless to hear the financial burden
   - *(iii)* After 1949 this practice of honorary service is not there not its has outlied its utility
2. *Principle of Consumer Protection*
   - *(i)* The are of co-operative is now very wide
   - *(ii)* New it has covered many areas as fishery, co-operation housing society, co-operative consumer stores, poultry farm etc.
   - *(iii)* Even public distribution system is now based on co-operation
   - *(iv)* Co-operative can protect consumer by giving wide protection
3. *Principle of publicity or complete disclosure of information*
   - *(i)* The principles, objectiveness and benefits of co-operation should reach to public

(ii) Publicity with respect to its operation make the society known by its deeds, and therefore it may be a surest

(iii) Every person should known the accounts

4. *Principle of state patronage*

(i) Co-operative is free organisation

(ii) It is not government organisation but people's organisation

(iii) It should depend less on government

5. *Principle of Unity*

(i) Common interest can be only be of people of common status

(ii) It creates unity

(iii) organised prople can check any exploitation can solve any problem

6. *Principle of stability*

(i) Co-operative organisation can be maintained are the basis of stability

(ii) A table organisation can plan proper and can implement plan properly

(iii) Out should assist in maintaining stability of co-operative sector

Application of Co-operative Principles

(i) The principles of democratic control and limited interest on capital have been incorporated in laws and by laws of Co-operative societies

(ii) Self-help and economy principles are also followed by credit societies co-operative societies

(iii) Every society is recommended to reserve of education based on spread of education principle

(iv) Distribution of profit has been adopted in Co-operative act

(v) Open membership principle is being followed

Evolution of Cooperative Principles (In the context of ICA)

Historically Cooperative Principles have their origin in the working practices and rules, which the Rochdale Pioneers had evolved, adopted for heir working. The Pioneers had laid down certain rules and objects in what they called as 'Law First' and were also found in the 'Minuets of Proceedings', their practice and decisions of the general body.

Not all the practices of the Pioneers were contained in their rules. There is no mention of sale at current market prices, of dealing only in pure, non-adulterated commodities, of giving true weight and measure, of political and religious neutrality. They adopted and evolved, however, what they found to be sound methods of conducting cooperative business, which they communicated to many societies seeking their advice, so that Rochdale practice became regarded as sound practice and generally adopted by most societies not only in Briton but also all over the world.

Evolution of cooperative principles over 100 years of International Cooperative Alliance (ICA) life has been through three exercises:

1. 1933-1937; crystallization of Rochdale Principles;
2. 1966 ICA Cooperative Principles; and
3. 1995 ICA revised Cooperative Principles.

The succeeding paragraphs deal with the background and evolution of cooperative principles in detail. The following table gives glimpses of Cooperative Principles at various stages.

1934-37 ICA Principles

At the 13th ICA Cooperative Congress held at Vienna in 1930, the French Cooperative Federation submitted a memorandum suggesting that special Committee be set up and defines as to what constituted the Rochdale Pioneers practices, rules or principles and their application.

1934	1937	1967	1995
1. Open Membership	**Main Principles**	1. Voluntary and Open Membership	1. Voluntary and Open Membership
2. Democratic Control	1. Open Membership	2. Democratic control	2. Democratic Member Control
3. Dividend on Purchase	2. Democratic Membership	3. Dividend on Purchase	3. Member Economic Participation
4. Limited Interest on Capital, if any	3. Dividend on Purchase	4. Limited Interest on Capital	4. Autonomy and independence
5. Political and Religious Neutrality	4. Limited Interest on Capital, if any	5. Cooperative Education	5. Education, Training and Information
6. Cash Trading	**Optional Principles**	6. Cooperation among Cooperatives	6. Cooperation among Cooperative
7. Promotion of Education	5. Political and Religious Neutrality		7. Concern for Community
	6. Cash Trading		
	7. Promotion of Education		

Accordingly, accepting the French proposal, the ICA had setup a Special Committee. The Special Committee, after in-depth study of available records of the Equitable Pioneers Society and through a questionnaire identified the following as Rochdale Principles:

- Open Membership
- Democratic Control
- Dividend on Purchase
- Limited Interest on Capital, if any
- Political and Religious Neutrality
- Cash Trading
- Promotion of Education

Reverting to the study and recommendations of the Special Committee, it reported and recommended to the ICA 14th and 15th Cooperative Congress held at London in 1934 and at Paris in 1937 respectively. The Committee examined each Rochdale Principles and how they were being adopted by various cooperative in European countries and the USA. The committee accepted their validity. However, it recommended that the first four Principles, viz. (1) Open Membership; (2) Democratic Control; (3) Dividend on Purchase; and (4) Limited Interest on Capital, should be treated as essential, while the other three, viz. Political and Religious Neutrality, Cash Trading, and Promotion of Education should be treated as optional, because in several countries cooperatives could not be neutral, in the former communist bloc countries. Even in England cooperatives formed Cooperative Party affiliated to Labour Party of England. In some countries Political Neutrality was acceptable, but not Religious Neutrality. Cash trading was considered ideal and desirable, but to make that a permanent condition for recognition or identity of a cooperative was practically difficult. Likewise, education was considered a socially—oriented concept. Moreover, it was also a problem to find enough finance for educational activities. The congress accepted the recommendation of the Special Committee and declared as such.

Background of 1966 Principles

The above mentioned Cooperative Principles remain in vogue for nearly 30 long years. During this period the world witnessed swift changes; the horrors of the Second World War, emergence of several new independent nations in Asia an Africa with problems of economic and social liberation. These nations faced serious economic, social and administrative problems. The most difficult problems were mass poverty, low agricultural productivity and production, food shortage, unemployment, lack of infrastructure, population explosion, and lack of resources for development. Economic planning was adopted in several countries. There emerged cartels and monopolies.

Cooperation was envisaged as important method and instrument to accelerate economic development, to enlist people's voluntary participation in economic planning and implementation of various developmental programmes. Along with national government, ·international organisations like the ILO showed keen interest in cooperative development.

The UN General Assembly adopted Resolution emphasizing importance of cooperative in socio-economic development. During this period, there has been fast progress of cooperatives in various countries.

In the above background the international cooperative leaders considered init necessary to review whether there was any need to modify the Cooperative Principles. The ICA Congress held at Bournemouth in 1963 recommended to the ICA Central Committee to constitute a commission to examine the application and validity of existing Cooperative Principles and suggest modifications if necessary. Accordingly a Commission was set up under the Chairmanship of Prof. D.G. Karve, an Indian. The commission suggested a new modified set of Cooperative Principles, which was adopted by the 23rd ICA Cooperative Congress in 1966 at Vienna. The new Cooperative Principles dropped the optional principles of Political and Religious Neutrality and that of Cash Trading and made Promotion of Education as necessary principle. What is more significant was that a new Principle what is shortly known as 'Cooperation among Cooperatives' was added for global integration of cooperative efforts. Such a principle was much needed to formalize horizontal and vertical integration of cooperative from village to national and international levels for efficient working of the federal structure, which has been developed in all the countries. For cooperatives to become an economic system, it is necessary to provide functional support to each other at various levels. Unity is the philosophy of cooperation—unity among individual cooperators as well as cooperatives. Isolation is cause of weakness, whereas integration is a vital source of strength.

1995 Cooperative Principles

The 1966 Cooperative Principles guided the cooperatives all over the world for merely 30 years up to September 1995. This period from 1966 to 1995 also marked a number of political and economic changes. There were significant political developments in Central and Eastern Europe and USSR. Communism and communist bloc have been disintegrated. The system of centrally controlled and directed has been done away with; there is revival of institution of private property and ownership in the erstwhile communist countries. There is economic transition towards globalization of economy by encouraging marketization or competition-oriented, privatization and liberalization of national economies. There has been continuation of population explosion and fast urbanization, environmental pollution of every king, managerial revolution, technological and scientific development, industrialization, agricultural development and diversification, emergence and dominance of multi-national corporations, and a kind of economic war, greater awareness about individual's liberty and rights, etc. Another significant development in the cooperative world in the intervening period (1966-1995) has been that early dominance of the European cooperative movements has been weakened or overshadowed by the cooperatives of developing Afro-Asian and Pan American cooperative movements. Of the total individual membership of ICA, two-third belongs to Asian continent itself. There has been fast diversification of cooperatives.

In the above background, ICA again thought to review the 1966 Cooperative Principles and to amend them according to global economic situation and requirements. This time initiative was taken by the former President of the ICA, Lars Marcus himself, when he raised the question of 'Basic Cooperative Values' at eth ICA Congress held in 1989 at Stockholm. Finally the ICA Congress held at Manchester in September 1995 considered a 'Statement on Cooperative Identity' and revised Cooperative Principles, as suggested by Prof. Ian Mac Pherson on the basis of his study and opinions received from various individuals and institutions. The Congress adopted the following revised Principles, which were also endorsed by the ICA General Assembly.

First Principle: Voluntary and Open Membership

Cooperatives are voluntary organization, open to all persons able to use their services and willing to accept the responsibilities of membership, without gender, social, racial, political or religious discrimination.

Second Principle: Democratic Member Control

Cooperatives are democratic organizations controlled by their members, who actively participate in setting their policies and making decisions. Men and women serving as elected representatives are accountable to the membership. In primary cooperatives members have equal voting rights (one-member-one-vote) and cooperatives at other levels are also organized in a democratic manner.

Third Principle: Member Economic Participation

Members contribute equitably to, and democratically control, the capital of their cooperatives. At least part of that capital is usually the common property of the cooperative. Members usually receive limited compensation, if any on capital subscribed as a condition of membership. Members allocate surpluses for any or all of the following purposes: developing their cooperative, possibly by setting up reserves, part of which at least would be indivisible; benefiting members in proportion to their transactions with the cooperative; and supporting other activities approved by the membership.

Fourth Principle: Autonomy and Independence

Cooperatives are autonomous self-help organizations controlled by their members. If they enter into agreements with other organizations, including governments, or raise capital from external sources, they do so on terms that ensure democratic control by their members and maintain their cooperative autonomy.

Fifth Principle: Education, Training, and Information

Cooperatives provide education and training for their members, elected representatives, managers and employees so they can contribute effectively to the development of their cooperatives. They inform the general public, particularly young people and opinion leaders about the nature and benefits of cooperation.

Sixth Principle: Cooperation among Cooperatives

Cooperatives serve their members most effectively and strengthen the cooperative movement by working together through local, national, regional, and international structures.

Seventh Principle: Concern for Community

Cooperatives work for the sustainable development of their communities through policies approved by their members.

Expansion

Cooperative Principles are more than commandments; they are also guidelines for judging behaviour and for making decisions. It is not enough to ask if a cooperative is following the letter of the principles; it is important to know if it is following their spirit, if the vision each principle affords, individually and collectively, ingrained in the daily activities of the cooperative.

The principles that form the heart of cooperatives are not independent of each other. They are subtly linked; when one is ignored, all are diminished. Cooperatives should not be judged exclusively on the basis of any one principle; rather, they should be evaluated on how well they adhere to the principles in their entirety.

1. The 'Voluntary' and Open Membership Principle

Voluntary principle implies that people cannot be made to be cooperators, they must be given the opportunity to study and understand the valued for which cooperatives stand. They must be allowed to participate freely. If membership forced, such members should be involved so that they develop voluntary attitude.

Open membership means that cooperative is open to all persons who need and are able to use the services of cooperatives and willing to accept the responsibilities of membership without any artificial discrimination. But where cooperatives are for specific purpose, e.g. housing, there may be understandable and acceptable reasons why cooperatives may impose a limit on membership. "Willing to accept responsibilities of membership", reminds members that they have obligations to their cooperatives.

2. Democratic Member Control Principle

Within cooperatives 'democracy' includes considerations of rights and responsibilities. It means fostering the spirit of democracy within cooperatives. 'Controlled by the members' mean members participating in setting the policies and making decisions. It means members ultimately control their cooperatives and they do so in democratic manner. 'Accountable to membership' phrase reminds elected representatives that they hold office in trust of the immediate and long-term benefits of members. Cooperatives 'belong to members' and not to elected officials. Elected officials are accountable to members. They are Trustees on behalf of members. Member control also prohibits a non-member becoming office bearer through nomination to the Board by the Government or through process of cooption.

3. Member Economic Participation Principle

In cooperative, capital is servant and not master or organization. Cooperatives exist to serve the needs of members, this principle describes how members both invest in their cooperatives and decide how to allocate surpluses. Members can contribute capital in three ways, viz.: (1) Share capital; (2) Reserves, which is owned collectively; (3) Depositing their part of their dividend and on special requests for specific activity.

4. Autonomy and Independence Principle

Cooperatives in all parts of the world are very much affected by their relationship with the state. Government determines the legislative framework within which cooperatives may function. In their taxation, economics and social policies, governments may be helpful or harmful in how they relate to cooperatives. For that reason all cooperatives must be vigilant in developing open, clear relationship with governments. When cooperatives enter into agreement with organizations, they must retain their freedom ultimately to control their future.

5. Education, Training, and Information Principle

The principle emphasizes the vital importance played by education and training within cooperatives. Education means more than just distributing information or encouraging patronage, it means engaging the minds of members, elected leader, managers and employees to comprehend fully the complexities and richness of cooperative thought and action. Training means making sure that all those who are associated with cooperatives have the skills they require in order to carry out their responsibilities effectively. Education and Training are also important, because they provide excellent opportunities where by cooperative leaders can understand the needs of their membership. They should be conducted in such a way that they continuously access the activities of the cooperatives and suggest ways to improve or to provide new services. A cooperative that encourages effective two-way communication between its members and leaders and leaders, while operative in an effective manner, can rarely fail.

The principle ends by recognizing that cooperatives have a particular responsibility to inform young people and opinion leaders—politicians, public servants, media representatives and educators about the nature and benefits of cooperation.

6. Cooperation among Cooperatives Principle

Cooperatives must also recognize the necessity of strengthening their support organizations and activities. It is crucially important for different kinds of cooperatives to join together when speaking to government or promoting the cooperative way to the public. In order to build an integrated cooperative system it is necessary that cooperative should cooperative among themselves. They should not compete with their own constituent members.

7. Concern for Community Principle

Cooperatives are organizations that generally exist for the benefit of their members. Cooperatives have special responsibility to ensure that the development of their community economically, socially and culturally is sustained. They have the responsibility to work steadily, for the environmental protection of these communities. It is up to the members, though, to decide how deep and in what specific ways a cooperative should make its contributions to their community.

Classification of Cooperatives

There was lesser number of societies in the earlier stages of formation. They were organised here and there for a particular purpose only. So there was no need for classifying the societies. Now, there are a number of societies. Their purpose, area of operation, place of operation, business undertaken and the services done are different. Hence, classifications of societies are necessary for proper planning and development.

Prof. C.R. Fay's Classification

The societies may be classified in various ways. According to professor C.R.Fay, the societies may be classified as follows:

1. Cooperative Banks or Credit Societies
2. Agricultural Cooperative Societies
3. Cooperative Labour Societies.
4. Cooperative Stores.

The above classifications are not complete. They were classified before 1960. The cooperative societies are found everywhere. All classes of people enjoy the benefits. Hence, they should be classified covering all societies as follows:

1. Agricultural Producers Marketing Society.
2. Agro-Engineering Society.
3. Consumer society.
   (*a*) Urban stores
   (*b*) Rural Stores
   (*c*) Staff and students stores
   (*d*) Employees Stores
   (*e*) Canteen and Restaurant

4. Cooperative Union.
5. Credit Society
   (*a*) Agricultural Service Society
   (*b*) Land Development Bank
   (*c*) Financing Bank
   (*d*) Urban Bank
   (*e*) Urban Credit Society
   (*f*) Employees Credit Society
6. Dairy society
   (*a*) Milk producers Society
   (*b*) Milk Consumers Society
   (*c*) Dairy Farm
7. Farming society
   (*a*) Joint Farming Society
   (*b*) Collective Farming Society
   (*c*) Tenant Farming Society
   (*d*) Land Colonisation Society
   (*e*) Gramdhan Sarvodays Society
   (*f*) Bhoodan Service Society
8. Fisheries Society
   (*a*) Fisheries Society
   (*b*) Fisherman Production-cum-Marketing Society
9. Housing Society
   (*a*) Building (Housing) Society
   (*b*) House Building Society
   (*c*) House Construction Society
   (*d*) Township
   (*e*) Tenancy Housing Society
   (*f*) Rural Housing Society
   (*g*) House Sites Society
   (*h*) House Service Society

10. Industrial Society
    (*a*) Artisan industrial Society
    (*b*) Technicians Industrial Society
    (*c*) Producers Industrial Society
    (*d*) Industrial Service Society
11. Labour Contract Society
12. Lift Irrigation Society
13. Miscellaneous Society
    (*a*) Barber's Society
    (*b*) Cattle or Duck or Goat or Pig or Poultry or Sheep Breeding Society
    (*c*) Indian Medical Practitioners Pharmacy
    (*d*) Printers Society
    (*e*) Rural Electric Society
    (*f*) Salt Workers Society
    (*g*) Washermen Society
    (*h*) Writer's Society
    (*i*) Other Miscellaneous Society
14. Oil Seeds Growers Society
15. Processing Society
    (*a*) Sugar Mills
    (*b*) Spinning Mills
    (*c*) Textile Processing Mills
    (*d*) Industrial Tea Factory
16. Training Institutes
17. Weavers Society

The structure of a society is classified as follows:

(*a*) Primary Society
(*b*) Central Society
(*c*) State Society
(*d*) National Federation

Cooperatives could be classified in many different ways because their characteristics differ so much. If you were to classify people, you could use many different bases—height, weight, colour of hair, pigmentation, income, occupation, religious affiliation, and many others. So it is with cooperatives. The purpose in mind, on doubt, becomes the criterion as to which basis to use. An outline of the principal types of cooperatives follows:

I. **By Size**

1. Volume of business done-sales, amount of loans made, etc.
2. Number of members or patrons served.

II. **Area Served By (where members reside – not where sales are made)**

1. Local—market area about a single community.
2. Regional—large area of one state or of several states.
3. National—members residing in many states.
4. International—members of two or more countries.

III. **By Type of Membership**

1. Locals—persons or firms of a single locality are members.
2. Contra lines associations—persons residing in an area much larger than a small locality such as a state or region.
3. Federated:
   (*a*) Local associations are members of central associations.
   (*b*) Central associations are affiliated with national cooperatives.
4. Hybrid type—individuals and locals are members of the central company.

IV. By Legal Status

1. Unincorporated—a multiple partnership arrangement.
2. Incorporated—a legal entity created by law or sanctioned by it.

V. By Financial Arrangement

1. Capital Stock—shares of common stock and sometimes also preferred stock are issued.
2. Non-stock or Membership Type—no stock issued; membership is non-assignable and not transferable to others.

VI. By 'Who' Constitutes the Membership

1. Producers—such as farmers, fishermen, foresters who have products to sell or supplies to purchase.
2. Consumers—purchasers of consumption goods or services.
3. Workmen—self-employed; operators of their own plants.
4. Businessmen – to purchase merchandise for sale and/or buy supplies for use in their private businesses.

VII. By Principal Functions or Business Activities

1. Production associations.
2. Processing associations.
3. Marketing associations.
4. Service associations.

Self-Learning Activity

Try to answer the following questions on your own.

1. Define Cooperation (ICA 1995 definition)?
2. What are the benefits of cooperation?
3. Give an account of the value 'social responsibility'?

4. List out Raiffeisen Principles?
5. State the ICA 1995 Cooperative Principles?

Summary

- The concept and meaning of co-operation has been given by utopian socialists, religious thinkers, sociologists, economists and reformists in their own way in the context of the circumstances prevalent in their respective countries. ICA 1995 definition on cooperatives is universally accepted.
- There are economic, social, moral and educational benefits of cooperation.
- The principles of cooperation have been restated many times according to the changes and advancement in the business environment. Now we have universally accepted seven principles (ICA 1995).
- Cooperatives can be classified by means of size, area, membership, legal status, and so on.

Chapter 4 Issues in Cooperation

The leaders of the cooperative movement have faced a number of problems in respect of the organization of cooperative activities. These problems have been more the concern of the theoreticians than of the practical minded cooperators. In this chapter, we shall discuss those problems and controversies with which the cooperative movements have been confronted within the various stages of their development throughout the world.

Unlimited *vs.* Limited Liability

The foremost problem faced by the cooperators has been, whether a cooperative organization should be established on the basis of unlimited liability or limited liability. In almost every country of the world, the cooperative societies, in their earliest stages, especially in the field of agricultural credit were set up on the basis of unlimited liability. With the extension of the application of the principle of cooperation to economic activities in urban areas, the controversy between unlimited liability and limited liability assumed serious proportion. However, this controversy was set at rest by evolving a pattern suiting local conditions. Liability means the responsibility of obligation of the members of a trading concern for making good the losses, debts, or deficits in the assets of the concern. In losses in the assets of the society it mean members' obligation to make up the losses in the assets of the society at the time of its winding up or liquidation. The liability of the members may be of two types: limited and unlimited. Limited liability is of three types, viz., *(i)* liability limited to the value of the shares; *(ii)* liability limited to multiple of shares; and *(iii)* liability limited by guarantee. In the first case the liability of a members is making up the losses sustained by the society is limited to the amount, unpaid on the shares held by him. In the second case the guarantee is fixed as a multiple of the share value and in the third case the liability of each member is liable to make contribution to any deficiency in the assets of the society on its winding up. The chief features of unlimited liability, in particular reference to a cooperative society may be: *(i)* unlimited liability cannot be enforced so long as the society is alive; *(ii)* the individual members cannot be sued by the creditors. The claims are to be submitted to the liquidator, who would levy contribution on the members in such proportions, as he may deem proper; *(iii)* the losses will first be recovered from the defaulter, and then from their sureties. In case the losses are not recovered from these persons the liability for making up the losses will first fall on the reserve and other funds, then on the share capital, then on the limited liability of the members and lastly on the creditors.

In a cooperative form of business whether the liability of the members should be limited or unlimited is a debatable issue. Each kind of liability is good in its own place. The success of cooperation does not depend on the liability of its members, but on the good organization, sound business methods, healthy objectives and the loyalty of the members. The nature of the loyalty need not change according to rural or urban surroundings or according toe he nature of activity undertaken by a cooperative society. It depends upon the area of operation, size of membership, element of risk involved in business and the status of the members. Broadly speaking, if the area operation of a society is wide, the size of membership is large, the element of risk in business is great and the members are of large means, the liability may be kept limited while in other cases, it may be unlimited. Theoretically, each type of liability has its merits and demerits, and the merits of the one are the demerits of the other and vice versa.

Points in Favour of Unlimited Liability

1. Unlimited liability creates confidence in the creditors, and the society is able to attract sufficient deposits and loans from non-members at reasonable terms.
2. It creates a sense of collective responsibility and mutual vigilance among the members.
3. It leads to efficient management because of the fear of enforcement of liability in case of loss to the society. Loans are granted for productive purposes and prompt action is taken towards the recovery of loans.

Points against Unlimited Liability

1. It has been pointed out that well-to-do people are scared away from the membership of the society because they fear that in the event of losses occurring in the society they may lose all their property without any fault of theirs. The Maclagan Committee (India) had in unequivocal terms stated that, "We have not found that the adoption of this form of liability (unlimited), where the safeguards against loss are properly understood has any appreciable effect in keeping out the rich peasants, nor have we met with any demand for the substitution of limited responsibility". The Committee further states: "The unlimited liability, as it now stands, has contrary to the anticipations of many, been unreservedly accepted by the people and we have evidence before us to show that it constitutes an important factor in the confidence

reposed in societies both by central institutions, inside the movement, and by the Joint Stock Banks outside it. We see every reason, therefore, for adhering to the principle that Agricultural Credit Societies should be societies of unlimited liability, whether they are without shares".

2. Unlimited liability is ineffective so long as there is no bar on the alienation of property.
3. Large business organizations cannot be run on the basis of unlimited liability because mutual vigilance and knowledge is not possible due to a wide area of operation and large membership.

Single *vs.* Multi–purpose Societies

A society engaged in one activity or function, is known as a single purpose society, while a society, which is engaged in more than one activity, is known as a multi-purpose society. Almost in every country of the world, the cooperative movement was started with the establishment of a single purpose society but later, more particularly after the Great Depression of the multi-purpose cooperative is greater to farmers than to urban dwellers. When the working of the primary agriculturists' credit societies was found unsatisfactory, the cooperative leaders gave thought to their revitalization. It was also realized that unless a sincere effort was made for an all-sided improvement, lasting economic benefits to the agriculturalists were not possible. A rural credit society, it was through, should not only supply credit on easy terms, but should also assist its members in achieving the idea of "better farming, better business, and better living". The society should be able to cover the entire life of the agriculturists. Multi-purpose societies form a considerable part of agricultural cooperative in countries like Japan, Germany, India, Yugoslavia, Czechoslovakia, etc, while single purpose societies have exclusively been organized in countries like Denmark and Holland. In theory, the question of single *vs.* multi-purpose society has been a subject of frequent discussion.

The organization of a multi-purpose society can be supported on the following bases:

- It strengthens the bond among the members and results in a higher degree of integration;
- It requires the members to contribute less share capital;
- It helps ensuring that all the members in a village are concentrated in one society;
- Administrative costs being low, the cost per unit of production is also low;
- The viability of the society is assured;
- It facilitates the appointment of trained and technically skilled persons;
- The stability of the society is increased because the risk of operation is spread more evenly over the whole area;
- There is usually a mutual stimulation between activities;
- The combination of credit, marketing and supply gives the society a key position in the life of eth agriculturists. Supervision of loans and their recovery become considerably easier;
- Integrated farming programmes can be undertaken;
- The combination of marketing, supply and credit usually decreases cash transactions and hence the cash requirements of the society.

The following are the disadvantages of a multi-purpose society:

- The burden put on the management is considerably heavier;
- A manager expert in all the lines of business is difficult to find;
- The dispersal of efforts in a number of activities leads to the neglect of some of them;
- The bookkeeping system becomes more complicated since separate records are required to be kept for various activities;

- The exact costs for certain operations are difficult to assess owing to the difficulties of credit allocation of overhead expenses;
- Mixing of trading and banking entails a considerable risk, which may not be properly controlled;
- Conflicting interest might arise within the membership.

The decision, whether a multi-purpose society should be organized or a single purpose society, will depend on the size of the society, activities to be undertaken, the structure of membership, stage of development, the type of management, federative structure and tradition of the country. So far as the size of the society is concerned it seems that above a certain size, single purpose societies are better situated. A great deal depends on the kind of activities, which are to be undertaken. Services requiring a high degree of technical knowledge and highly qualified staff should be organized in a single purpose society. In developing countries where degree of specialization is fairly less marked, the scope for multipurpose societies is very wide. The size of the members' economic units or farms is an important influence in the formation of multipurpose societies. Densely populated areas with small farms are more suitable than the areas with commercialized medium and large-scale farms. Where members undertake different types of farming or where they belong to different occupations, they may not have equal interest in all activities. In this situation, a conflict can easily arise among the membership from the fear of being neglected. It is also important that any new activity is undertaken at the right moment. It would be killing if a new activity is undertaken at a time when the society is struggling with the task in hand. Only when the society is firmly established in its current line of business, additional business may be taken up. Again, for the successful working of a multipurpose society it is essential that the management should comprise trained and dedicated people; otherwise a multipurpose society is likely to face great obstacles. One good secondary organization with a well-functioning extension service can do much to make up the deficiencies of the management.

Which type of society should be organized, will also depend on the tradition of the country. In a country where the multipurpose societies have played a considerable part in agricultural cooperative movement, a similar society will face less difficulty than in a country where the tradition is for the establishment of a single purpose society.

Centralized *vs.* Federation

The difference between a federated type of association and a centralized association is largely a mater of degree. While the former starts from the bottom and grows upwards and it decentralizes authority among its constituent units, the latter starts from the top. The other points of difference between the two are as follows:

- In the federated type the farmers are members of local associations, which in turn, are members of district associations, which are federated into central exchange. In the centralized type the farmers are directly members of the central exchange, and there is no intermediary between the two;
- The federation works with the object of reducing the cost of marketing and obtaining the best prices by providing efficient marketing services and supplying quality products. The main object of a centralized type, on the other hand, is to control price by controlling the market supplies;
- A federation works through rendering efficient marketing services, whereas a centralized association attempts to gain control over the bulk of crops for the purpose of increasing the bargaining power;
- In a federated type of association, the farmers are owners of local associations, which are the owners of the district exchanges and the central exchange is

owned by the district exchanges. In a centralized type farmers are the direct owners of the central exchange;

- In a federated type of association farmers elect directors of the associations, which in their turn, elect directors of the district associations and the directors of the central exchange or federation are elected by the district exchanges. In a centralized type of association the farmers elect delegates at district meetings, which elect the directors of the central exchange;
- Members' contracts are not considered essential in a federative system, whereas in a centralized system such contracts form a vital part of the business;
- The federative type of association does not insist on a definite percentage of crops to be sold through it, whereas, the centralized association insists that at least 75 per cent of the crops should be sold through it;
- In a federative system the functions of packing, sorting, grading, etc, are the concern of the local association, while the federation is concerned only with supervision and advice and finding trade outlets. Under the centralized system, marketing functions are performed by the central organizations;
- In a federative type of association more emphasis is given in efficient marketing services and quality products in order to get the best possible prices. In a centralized type of system the monopoly of control over a large volume of crops is favoured, in order to control the prices.

Small-sized Societies *vs.* Large sized Societies

The idea of small-sized societies has convinced many cooperators and they opt for small societies in order to maintain the proximity, loyalty and patronage of the limited membership. Small-sized societies are based on the concept of one-village-one-society.

Advantages of small-sized societies

- Small-sized societies are suited to the developing countries. As majority of the farmers are illiterates, it is easier to get credit and other services from a small society situated in their own village.
- A small society is easier to manage and may be within the reach of the managerial capacity of farmers. As the membership is small, they can know each other and can have contact, which will be useful to judge the credit worthiness and repaying capacity of various farmers.
- The cost of running small society will be less and farmers can run it honourably.
- As the members are few, the entire credit needs of the farmers could be met by a small society. During times of recovery also difficulties would be little to recover loans. Due to their personal touch the board members can contact the defaulters and ask them to repay the loans.

Limitations of small-sized societies

- Small-sized societies have become outmoded. They cannot undertake multifarious activities to meet the credit, as well as non-credit needs of the farmers.
- Small-sized societies are not suitable to raise rural resources by way of deposits. To raise deposits a society must provide minimum banking facilities, which cannot be provided by a small society.
- At present viability is the accepted concept of a village society. By having small societies viability cannot be attained.

Advantages of large-sized societies

- A large-sized society could be able to cover a wider area of operation covering a few villages. The membership of such societies could also be increased.

- A large-sized society command better operational efficiency. This is possible by means of raising adequate resources and increasing the business.
- Deposit mobilization would be easier task for large-sized societies. As the society is in a position to have its own building, it can create a confidence in the minds of depositors by having a sound owned funds structure.
- The large-sized society can appoint adequate number of paid staff and run the society efficiently.
- Credit, service and supply activities can be effectively discharged by a large-sized society.
- After a particular stage it can cover the non-agricultural population and it can also become a 'growth center' by encouraging small-scale and cottage industries and encouraging ancillary occupations like diary and poultry farming.

Issue on Merger, Consolidation and Liquidation

Cooperative Merger

All the world over, there is a clear trend noticed, in the direction of increasing the size of the individual organization, through mergers and amalgamation with other willing and eligible organizations, either belonging to the same trade or working as complementary to the main activity of the central organization. This is happening irrespective of the form of organization. The need for merger or amalgamation is felt because of the fast pace of technological developments in almost every field of economic activity; whether in production, distribution to other service sectors. The competition is becoming fierce as a result of increasing scale of production and operation. At the same time the costs of management are also showing tendency towards increase. All these forces working in different directors have been compelling the business organizations to grow in size either on their own, or through securing combination with similar other organization.

The process of merger and amalgamation is comparatively easy in case of private sector units, or for that matter, in case of public sector units as well. However, in case of cooperatives the process is fraught with main problems and obstacles. They are human, sociological, economic, financial and legal. In spite of these, as stated earlier, the pace of mergers in the cooperative sector of the highly developed countries has been increasing. In these countries, cooperatives have come to be treated as a part of the private sector. They do not have any special supports of the governments in these countries. The decision to reorganize the structure through mergers or amalgamations is entirely taken by the representative bodies of the specific cooperatives. The process there also is not that smooth and the cooperatives have to overcome the obstacles mentioned earlier. All the same, under the pressures of time and need for survival, it is catching-up as the time is passing. For instance, in Great Britain, the Independent Commission on Consumer Cooperative Movement, has recommended a broad plan for reducing through amalgamation, the number of primary consumer cooperatives over a decade (by 1954-64), in order to be able to face the increasing competition from the private distributive trade on the basis of efficiency of service. In the sector of agricultural associations (cooperatives) in UK, the same problem is experienced and endeavours are being made by the movement to secure as expeditious a progress as is possible through mergers and amalgamations. The efforts and experience of the cooperative movements in countries like U.S.A., Canada and other continental countries has not been much different. The trend also has encouraged the amalgamation and merger of units in the agricultural sector.

Developing Countries

Cooperative movements in some of the developing countries cannot escape pressures of time, technology and other advancements. The networthy feature of the cooperative movement in developing countries has been the dominant role of the State in regard to promotion, direction and development of the cooperative movement. As for merger and amalgamation there is resistance in developing countries to do so. There are many cases being made to avoid mergers by requiring the government authorities to entrust additional business to the rural primary cooperatives which can make them viable (which they are not today). Similarly, in the cooperative processing sector the need for merger or amalgamation may be felt in the near future. The consumer sector is not an exception to this trend.

Merging two or more cooperatives is a difficult task. There have been a few honourable exceptions but their achievements have been successful more because of enlightened leadership that was in command of the affairs of the concerned cooperatives. This is trend in developing countries as far as merger is concerned.

Consolidation

Consolidation of cooperatives is way to have a strong and vibrant cooperative for the benefit of members and employees, and others related to the development of those cooperatives. The mis-coception and lack of understanding of the complex problems involved on the part of the human elements, both members and employees have been responsible for resistance to consolidation or mergers, however desirable it might be. These barriers to consolidation have to be removed through a carefully planned programme of education. Both, the management including the board of directors and membership at large, would have to be educated and guided through studies and analysis of the facts affecting the growth and development of the concerned cooperatives so that objective decision-making in favour of consolidation may become feasible. This may help to establish credibility as to intentions and the benefits that are to follow consolidation for both the members and the employees of the consolidated cooperatives.

The stages of consolidation may include the followings:

1. An outline of a programme to guide the cooperatives in favour of consolidation has to be indicated;
2. It may be necessary for the management to analyse the cooperative's economic growth potential assuming that it may operate independently with no change in technology or production capacity;
3. The comparison of the projections flowing out of the alternative plans may help in establishing the need for consolidation with other cooperatives;
4. The leaders of cooperatives, on the basis this exercise, may be able to take proper decision on consolidation;
5. The financial statements of the cooperatives should be analysed;
6. Steps have to be taken, as a part of the planned development, to secure the uniformity in operations, accounting system, etc, which may help to assess the economic situation of cooperatives;
7. After all assessment with the whole-hearted cooperation of the members and employees the consolidation process may be done.

The need for consolidation of the cooperatives in the changing economic conditions cannot be avoided and ignored. However, it is desirable that the decisions on consolidation through merger or amalgamation of cooperatives are taken with open heart. In any case, even in developing countries, it would be undesirable for the State or any other party to secure merger or amalgamation or consolidation with the help of ordinances or administrative fiats. The need for consolidation may be real but the exercise of units involved may have to be handled skillfully in a climate of whole-hearted cooperation of the people involved namely, the members and the employees.

Liquidation

Recognition and honour generally extended to those who had the foresight and skills necessary to create a cooperative. But it also takes foresight to recognize when a cooperative should liquidate—and it takes much courage to act on that realization. Typically, cooperatives are created when other businesses are not providing necessary services or when competition is not functioning. Sometimes competition provides new or superior services or prices and returns from cooperative activity evaporate. In such cases cooperatives should liquidate to stop erosion of equity. Even if equity is not eroding but returns are zero, farmers can find a better use for their funds.

Recognising the need: It is critical that cooperative directors and mangers frequently evaluate their competitive and financial position and determine the need to merge or consolidate while they still have sufficient financial strength. Feasibility studies should indicate when an activity should be dropped.

The difficulty is in determining the stage of a recent reversal. Ia it a sign that the worst is yet to come, or is it the darkness before the dawn? In other words, management must decide whether the change is temporary or fundamental. In some cases the problem can be corrected and the cooperative will return to profitability. In other cases there may be no hope because the damage is so severe or the negative factors are beyond control of the cooperative. Or members can vote to liquidate, having determined that the cooperative has performed its task and is no longer needed. Poor performance can be linked to poor management or the evaporation of the cooperative's economic justification. Management may be incompetent, having become involved in moral turpitude or perhaps having speculated unwisely in the future market. In other cases the cooperative may have inherited a high-cost structure that it cannot easily change. A competing business with a lower-cost structure may be capturing substantial patronage. A fundamental decline in demand may also result in losses.

Alternatives: Feasibility studies should indicate when an activity should be dropped. Methods of cooperative reorganisation through liquidation include the following:

- Sell assets of weaker cooperatives to a neighbouring cooperative and thus retain essential services for members.
- Sell just the non-productive assets of the cooperative.
- Sell all the assets of the local cooperative to the regional cooperative and have the regional provide member service, or convert the operation from a federated to centralized cooperative.
- Liquidate the assets, dissolve the cooperative, and recognize the cooperative under a new financial structure.
- Sell the assets to the regional and lease back the facilities in order to retain local member service.
- Liquidate assets and dissolve the cooperative to protect the remaining member equity.

Disposing of a vertical stage does not necessary eliminate service to members. Diversing of horizontal facilities could leave some members without services if the facility is operating at the first level from members.

Legal Procedures: Dissolution or liquidation is the process by which a cooperative ceases to do business, liquidates its property, and distributes equity to shareholders and others. Liquidation may be voluntary or involuntary. Voluntary dissolution is initiated either by the board or the members as a body, and member approval is required. Typically, members appoint trustees to carry out the dissolution process. They wing up the cooperative's business and liquidate the assets.

One of the more important tasks is to distribute assets. According to most laws, property remaining should first be applied toward debts and obligations of the cooperative. Any remaining surplus should then be apportioned among members. Although a few statutes give detailed directions for distribution, most place considerable emphasis on what the articles, bylaws or agreements say about distribution on dissolution.

A sample legal document gives an example of a bylaw provision on dissolution distribution. It says:

Upon dissolution, after: (1) all debts and liabilities of the association shall have been paid; (2) the par value of stockholders' shares returned; and (3) all capital furnished through patronage shall have been retired without priority on a pro rata basis, the remaining property and assets of the association shall be distributed among the members and former members in the proportion which the aggregate patronage of each member bears to the total patronage of all such members, unless otherwise provided by law.

Cooperatives may establish other priorities, depending on the intended plan of operation and limitations in statutes and other laws. Each of the plans takes careful study to protect member assets and to retain essential services. Most cooperative laws are carefully written to protect members in the liquidation process. These laws require that members be given adequate information for decision making and that a substantial majority of the members approve the liquidation plan.

Existing cooperatives can be restricted in several ways. They can combine with other cooperatives, make alliances with other firms, liquidate, and reorganize internally. The appropriate scope and organizational structure is dictated by the environment, by the job to be done, and by the resources available. Within these constraints, what evolves depends on the management and leadership skills of those involved. They will succeed only if they have the ability to recognize and overcome problems.

Self-learning Activity

Try to answer the following questions on your own.

1. What do you mean by limited liability?

2. Single or multi-purpose cooperatives—debate?
3. Small is beautiful—critically comment regarding cooperatives?
4. Why might a cooperative look for a merger partner rather than construct a new processing plant? Which factors are unique to cooperative? Contrast these issues.
5. Why might another cooperative decide to grow internally rather externally?
6. Distinguish mergers from consolidations and acquisitions, and discuss why a cooperative may select one over the others?

Summary

- The issues related to cooperatives are: Limited vs. Unlimited, Single vs. Multipurpose, Centralized vs. Federation, Small vs. Large Scale Cooperatives. Cooperatives may be organized by considering these issues based on the requirements and significance.
- Cooperatives may design strategies to merge or consolidate or liquidate. In the competitive market economy the cooperatives through these strategies they try to survive and sustain.

Legal Status of Cooperatives

Incorporation

To conduct its business effectively, a cooperative must exist as a legal entity separate from its members. Incorporation is necessary to achieve such status.

Like other corporations, cooperatives obtain significant advantages from incorporation. The primary one is limited liability. Under incorporation, the personal liability of the individual owner/members for the co-op's losses is limited to the amount of equity each member has invested in the co-operatives.

The documents necessary to incorporate a co-op are the articles of incorporation and the bylaws (see below for instructions on preparing these documents). Filing the articles of incorporation creates the co-op as a legal entity; while the bylaws provide the co-op with guidelines for conducting business. It is advisable to obtain legal counsel to review the articles of incorporation and bylaws.

Legal Documents Pertaining to Cooperatives

In order to exist legally and function effectively, a new cooperative must develop the following legal documents:

1. Articles of incorporation

2. Bylaws
3. Membership application
4. Marketing agreement

These documents form the legal and operational basis for the co-op. They should provide a solid foundation on which to build a new business, and should be developed with care and legal counsel. Each document is discussed separately below.

1. Articles of Incorporation

The articles of incorporation are filed with the state when the co-op incorporates. They should be the first document the co-op develops.

A cooperative exists as a legal entity when articles are filed and accepted by the state. The Department of Financial Institutions (Secretary of State) has copies of the proper articles to file. The Articles of Incorporation set out the basic characteristics of the cooperative, including its name, address, and type of business. The specific information required by law is described in the state statute. Note that articles of incorporation are legally binding; all subsequent documents adopted by the co-op must be consistent with the articles. Articles can be amended by procedures established in most cases by state statute.

A copy of the cooperative articles of incorporation form appears in the Appendix. Although these may be used as a model to draft articles for your co-operatives, we strongly suggest that a qualified co-operatives lawyer review your draft articles before adopting them.

Articles of Incorporation for Cooperatives*

Incorporation is usually the best method of organizing. Each State has special enabling laws under which cooperatives may incorporate. It may be preferable to incorporate under the state's general corporation enabling act, but structure bylaws to operate as a cooperative.

Incorporation gives the cooperative a distinct legal standing. Members generally are not personally liable for the debts of an incorporated organization beyond the amount of their investment. The articles indicate the nature of the cooperative business. The articles should specify rather broad operating authority when incorporating even though services may be limited at the beginning.

These articles usually contain the name of the cooperative, principal place of business, purposes and powers of the association, proposed duration of the association, names of the incorporators (in most States), and information about the capital structure. In some States, the names of the first officers of the association must be included.

Filing the articles of incorporation (usually with the Secretary of State) activates the cooperative corporation. After the organizing committee approves the articles, the attorney files for the corporation charter and includes the recording fees. Once chartered by the State, the cooperative should promptly adopt bylaws.

*From Galen Rapp and Gerald Ely, "How to Start a Cooperative," Cooperative Information Report 7. Washington DC: United States Department of Agriculture, Rural Business—Cooperative Service. Revised September 1996.

2. Bylaws

The co-op's bylaws provide a more detailed description of the cooperative's internal structure and operations. They are a set of written rules for how the co-op will function and govern itself. Bylaws are not usually filed with the state in which the co-op will operate, but they are considered legally binding on the cooperative and its members.

If you draft the bylaws yourself, we strongly recommend that you have a lawyer who is knowledgeable about cooperatives review your bylaws before presenting them to the membership for approval. This will ensure that no aspect of your draft is in conflict with the articles of incorporation or your state's statutes.

An outline of the major topic areas that the bylaws should cover appears below:

Membership

Identifies the qualifications for eligibility and procedures for joining the cooperative, including requirements for purchase of stock, if any. Describes the procedure by which membership may be ended, either voluntarily or involuntarily.

Meetings of Cooperative Members

Identifies the date for the annual meeting; how and when any special meetings may be held; requirements for notice of upcoming meetings; procedures for voting and requirements for a quorum; order of business at the annual meeting.

Directors and Officers

Specifies the number and qualifications of directors; procedures for electing directors and length of terms; election of officers by the board; frequency of board meetings and requirements for notice of board meetings; any special meetings; compensation of board members and requirements for a quorum.

Duties of Directors

States the director's specific powers and responsibilities, including: guiding the cooperative and articulating its mission, goals, and policies and periodically reviewing those goals. Authorizes directors to employ a manager, define the manager's duties, determine his or her compensation and evaluate his or her job performance. Specifies the director's responsibility to maintain an appropriate accounting system and have the co-op's books audited or reviewed annually. This section also specifies the board's responsibility to indemnify directors, officers and management against liability.

Duties of Officers

Specifies the duties of the president, vice president, secretary, and treasurer. Also describes the terms of officers and excused absences from board meetings.

Membership Capital Contributions

Specifies the required equity contribution by members and the method by which the co-op will collect the contribution; what type of stock the cooperative has the authority to issue; and any requirements regarding the co-op's stock certificates.

Profits and Losses

Specifies how the co-op's profits, if any, will be distributed based on each member's patronage with the co-op. In addition, any losses experienced by the co-op must be allocated across the membership.

Equity Redemption

Gives the board authority to determine at what time and in what manner the cooperative will redeem members' equity in the cooperative.

Non-member Business

Specifies how the cooperative will distribute the benefits, if any, resulting from business with non-members.

Dissolution

Identifies a procedure for dissolving the cooperative, and specifies the distribution of any remaining assets.

Amending the Bylaws

Specifies a straightforward method by which the bylaws may be amended.

3. Membership Application

This document is used to apply for membership in the cooperative, and should include the prospective members name, address, telephone, and signature, as well as a statement that the individual agrees to abide by the co-op's bylaws and meets all membership qualifications.

It also specifies the equity contribution required (the number of shares of stock being purchased or the amount of the membership fee if it is a non-stock co-op), which is often submitted at the same time as the application.

This application, approved by the board of directors and signed by the co-op president, is the primary legal proof that the individual is a member of the co-op. However, a stock certificate can also serve to recognize that the person has been accepted as a member of the cooperative. Careful records should be kept of membership agreements, stock sales and other transactions between the member and the cooperative for tax purposes.

4. Marketing Agreement

The marketing agreement, used primarily by agricultural marketing co-ops, is a contract between each individual member and the co-op's membership as a whole. It is intended to benefit both the member and the co-op by setting out the respective obligations of both parties in terms of product delivery, sale, and payment.

As a contract, the membership agreement should carefully specify the production commitment of the producer (measured in either volume or acres), and the specific products to be marketed; describe how the value of the producer's goods will be determined and when s/he will be paid for them; specify any actions that are considered in breach of the contract; and include an Act of God statement that releases both parties from their commitments to the contract in the event of a natural disaster which substantially harms the producer's crop.

It is highly recommended that the co-op seek a knowledgeable lawyer to review the marketing agreement draft before putting it to use. A couple hours of a lawyer's time up front could save the co-op a great deal of time and money down the road.

Combined Membership/Marketing Agreement

Membership Application for Cooperatives, including a Sample Outline*

This form has five main parts: applicant's statement asking to become a member of the cooperative, signature of the applicant, statement of cooperative acceptance of applicant, signatures of the president and secretary, and a statement of the duty and intent of the member.

The application, signed by the member and approved by the board of directors, is the legal proof that a patron is a member. A cooperative should have a completed membership application on file from every member. Membership and the amount of business done with members and non-members are important factors for certain anti-trust and taxation provisions.

Membership Application and Marketing Contract

This agreement between the ________, Inc., hereinafter referred to as the Association, and the undersigned Producer, witnesseth:

The Producer

1. Applies for membership in the Association, and if accepted as a member, agrees to be bound by its articles of incorporation, bylaws, rules, and regulations as now or hereafter adopted.
2. Appoints the Association as agent to sell all the ________ of marketable quality produced an any farm in control of or operated by the Producer, except that required for consumption on the farm.
3. Will deliver such products at such times and to such places in unadulterated form under such conditions as may be prescribed by proper authorities.
4. Will notify the Association of any lien on the products delivered hereunder, and authorizes the Association to pay the holder of said lien from the net proceeds derived from the sale of such products before any payment is made to the Producer hereunder.

5. Will provide capital in such amounts and in such a manner as may be provided in the bylaws.

The Association:

1. Accepts the application of Producer for membership in the Association.
2. Agrees to act as agent for the marketing of products of Producer as herein provided.
3. Will dispose of Producer's products in a manner deemed to be most advantageous for its members.
4. Will account to the Producer in accordance with this contract for all amounts received from the sale of products as herein provided.
5. Will reflect in an appropriate capital account the capital received from each patron.

*From Galen Rapp and Gerald Ely, "How to Start a Cooperative," Cooperative Information Report 7. Washington DC: United States Department of Agriculture, Rural Business—Cooperative Service. Revised September 1996.

The Producer and the Association mutually agree that the Association shall have the power:

1. To establish various plans for making returns to the Producer.
2. To blend or pool proceeds from sales of products of the Producer with the proceeds of the sales of products of other Producers, and to account to or settle with Producer therefore in accordance with established plans.
3. To process or cause to be processed products of the Producer and dispose of the same in the manner deemed most advantageous to its members.
4. To collect from buyers of products the purchase price therefore and to remit the same to Producer under a plan authorized by this contract after making uniform deductions deemed adequate for all necessary expenses and for capital purposes.

In case of a breach of this contract by the Producer, the actual damage to the Association and other producers cannot be determined. Therefore, Producer agrees to pay to the Association as liquidated damages for such breach, the sum of _______ dollars (   ) per _______ on all products that would have been delivered had the Producer not breached the said contract.

And the Association shall further be entitled to equitable relief by injunction or otherwise to prevent any such breach or threatened breach thereof and the payment of all costs of litigation in connection with the exercise of any or all of the remedies available to the Association.

This contract shall remain in effect for an initial term of (   ) years from the date hereof. Following the initial term, the contract may be cancelled by notice given in writing by either party to the other within ten (10) days after any yearly anniversary date, and such cancellation shall become effective on the last day of the second calendar month following the month during which such notice is given.

Date _______

Producer's signature _______ (_______)

Address____________

Social Security No. _______ County_______

Accepted this day of _______. 20___. _______, Inc. By _______, President By _______, Secretary

(Some State laws provide for filling or recording cooperative marketing contracts in a county recorder's office to give notice to third parties that the contract exists. And acknowledgment if the contract is to be filed or recorded.)

Membership Certificate

This certifies that _______ of _______ is a member of _______ Association and is entitled to all of the rights, benefits, and privileges of the Association.

Date _______ _________

(President)

Cooperative Board of Directors

(Adapted from 'Liability of Directors' by Robert Guenzel, Nebraska Cooperative Council)

A director of a cooperative has a special fiduciary relationship with that co-op and with its members. Cooperative directors have a duty to conduct the co-op's affairs in the members' interests; they are trustees of the members' property.

It is the duty of the board to hire and evaluate the performance of the cooperative's manager. If the manager fails to perform adequately, the board has a responsibility to the members to respond effectively.

Directors should always use their best business judgment in conducting the co-op's affairs, making decisions as reasonably prudent people would. Directors should use reasonable care and skill to obtain knowledge useful to them in making such decisions. They must be willing to ask questions, even if such questions are inconvenient for co-op management. They must be willing to take steps to obtain sufficient appropriate information to make good decisions.

This does not mean, however, that the directors can ensure that the cooperative will be financially successful. Directors are required to use their best judgment; if the members feel that a director has not done so and one consequence is that the co-op has not made money, they can exercise their right to elect a different director.

A person nominated for a director's position should carefully consider the responsibilities inherent in that position. Directors may be liable for damages if they are found to have exercised less than their best judgment.

Criteria for Separating Cooperative Board and Executive Decision Areas

There is no fine line of distinction between the executive's and the board's authority for specific action. The following ten criteria may be helpful in distinguishing board and executive decision areas.

Criterion 1

Ultimate accountability to stockholders or members is vested in the board of directors, who may subsequently grant certain authority to officers, agents, and employees as permitted under the corporate charter, bylaws, and applicable laws. The executive or general manager, in turn, is accountable to the board and initiates action within the boundaries of authority granted by the board.

Criterion 2

The board of directors is primarily concerned with idea decisions; executives are primarily concerned with action decisions.

Criterion 3

Decisions on overall objectives, policies, and goals of the company are the responsibility of the board.

Criterion 4

Decisions related to attaining objectives and goals are the responsibility of executives.

Criterion 5

Decisions involving long range and consequential commitment of resources, which include facilities, finances, or manpower, are the board's responsibility.

Criterion 6

Decisions involving long range and consequential commitment of resources, which include facilities, finances, or manpower, are the board's responsibility.

Criterion 7

Decisions related to the assurance of capable executive succession by providing for executive depth and training are the board's responsibility.

Criterion 8

Decisions specifying the ideal pattern or model of board behaviour and performance, and the review of and perpetuation of this ideal through indoctrination and training of directors, are the board's responsibility.

Criterion 9

Control over the executive and of board performance, decisions involving long range and substantial financial commitments and financial structure, objectives and policies, and public and member relations are the board's responsibility.

Criterion 10

Control over operations and over subordinate managers and employees, decisions involving budgets, procurement, production, and marketing plans, and industrial and employee relations programs are the responsibility of executives.

The following are some decision areas that are often performed by the board, management or shared.

Board Decisions Solely

1. Defining corporate objectives, policies, and goals (but with opportunity for management participation and recommendations for setting goals).
2. Long range financial commitments, including sources and type of financing.
3. Selection of chief executive (manager) and his salary.
4. Defining duties of chief executive.
5. Filling board vacancies.
6. Employing corporate auditing firm (unless bylaws provide for membership approval).
7. Retaining board legal counsel.
8. Basic changes in financial structure.
9. Approval of major plans and commitments.
10. Matters where stockholder or member decisions are due.
11. Selection of banking, insurance, and related entities.
12. Approval of employee retirement and benefit programmes.
13. Basic affiliations with suppliers.

Management Decisions Primarily

1. Defining operating or management level objectives, goals, and policies within constraints of corporation-wide decisions.
2. Short run commitments of resources.
3. Preparation of budgets, production plans, and market plans for approval by board.
4. Defining duties of division and department heads.
5. Administration of employee benefits programme and salary determination (consistent with salary scales approved by board for key management people).
6. Selection of employees.
7. Short run decisions on sources of supply that do not modify basic board decisions.
8. Selection of management's legal counsel.
9. Employee working conditions.
10. Measurements of employee performance.

Shared Decision Areas

The following were identified by respondents in a survey by the Agricultural Cooperative Service. There is some difference from the above list:

1. Relations with government, industry, and general public.
2. Insurance requirements (but not the source selection).
3. Amounts and sources of working capital.
4. Engaging professional services.
5. Employee benefits plans.
6. Selections of depositories
7. Appraisal of cooperative's performance.
8. Distribution of earnings.
9. Financial relationships with affiliates.
10. Employee bonding.
11. Changes in basic organizational structure.
12. Issuing capital instruments.
13. Authorizing facility construction, expansion, etc.

	Board	Management
Accountability	To Members	To Board
Areas of Concern	Idea Decision, Judge Ends/Purpose	Action Decisions, Manage Means/Activities
Commitment of Resources	Determine Values Long-range, Consequestial Set limits, Monitor	Intermediate and Short-Range Organize and Control Resources
Goals, Policies	Determine Set Policies Regarding Results to be Achieved and Limitations on Activities	Implement
Management Evaluation	Monitor Progress Toward Results Monitor Compliance with Limits	Provide Information for Monitoring
Operations	Determine Values and Goals Set Limits Monitor	Conduct
Perpetuation	Assurance of Capable Management and Board Succession	Support, Participate
Board Process	Determine Structure, Behaviour Performance Evaluation Calender and Agenda	None

Adapted from Leon Garoyan and Paul O. Mohn, "The Board of Directors of Cooperatives." Davis, CA: University of California (1976)

Self-learning Activity

Try to answer the following questions on your own.

1. What do you understand about the legal status of cooperatives?
2. Discuss about the bylaws and other legal documents of cooperatives.
3. Describe the duties and functions of board of directors.

Summary

- The legal status of cooperatives is discussed in this chapter. The legal documents such as articles of incorporation, byelaws, membership application and marketing agreement are also discussed.
- The various duties and functions of board of directors are described.

Framework for Integration of Cooperatives

Dear learners! In this chapter you are going to learn about the cooperative integration concept. The features, methods, and advantages of vertical and horizontal integration are discussed.

Cooperative Integration

Integration is a process of strengthening the cooperative structure. Structural relation is considered to be the foundation of the cooperative system. The growth of the cooperatives and the unity of the structure depend on the principle of cooperation among cooperatives. In the opinion of E.V. Mendoza,

> "The need for cooperatives to expand becomes more imperative in this era of competitive business which is being increasingly dominated by large enterprises. Cooperatives must perforce grow and expand to strengthen their bargaining power and attain greater economies of scale thereby place them in the effective competitive position".

Integration has to be understood as a process of knitting together and not a form of organization. It is primarily concerned with expansion with particular reference to services and not organizational matters.

Therefore it implies a fusion of functions and activities rather than structural configurations. Yet, structural changes cannot be ruled out as a consequence of integration. Basically integration is of two types, namely horizontal and vertical. Integration of cooperatives refers to the combination of cooperatives, which could be horizontally or vertically. This combination is undertaken to benefit from it though it has its own disadvantages.

Horizontal Integration

Horizontal integration implies the general grouping of like business units under one administrative control. It involves grouping together of associations or units with similar business activities. This is usually accomplished through merger of several similar associations or formation of a federation. Horizontal integration in cooperative movement takes place usually through the process of federation rather than by outright merger. In some cases horizontal integration is strengthened by management or membership contracts which stipulate that all member units will perform certain functions in a similar way.

The purpose of horizontal integration is to derive economies of large-scale operation. These economies may be derived due to bulk purchase, cheaper credit, specialization, transport economies, collective publicity, research, professionalisation of functions, etc. The following methods are used to achieve horizontal integration:

1. ***Federation:*** This means formation of a central organization by similar primary organization, eg., central cooperative bank organized by primary cooperative societies in a district/woreda.
2. ***Amalgamation:*** The amalgamation is merger of small cooperative organizations performing the same function with the aim of increasing their viability by forming large scale economic units. It is generally resorted to for reorganizing weak societies into a strong viable cooperative:

(i) *Diversification:* Integration is also achieved by cooperatives through diversification of business. This involves the broadening of the range of services. For example, a supply association dealing exclusively on such farm inputs as fertilizers, seeds and farm chemicals may diversify its operations by engaging in such other lines as farm machinery and equipment, production of manure mixures, etc.

(ii) *Link-up system:* Under this system, two cooperative organizations work closely without losing their individual legal identity. There are different possibilities of the link-up arrangement: between credit cooperatives and marketing cooperatives, between consumers' cooperatives and producers' cooperatives, between labour cooperatives and housing cooperatives, between consumer cooperatives and marketing cooperatives, and between labour cooperatives and producers' cooperatives.

The advantages of horizontal integration are:

1. By means of this integration, cooperatives can increase their power by adding to their range of service. Such diversification expands the opportunities for growth and expansion.
2. The similar cooperatives can derive the economies of large scale operations and improve their operational efficiency.
3. Only by horizontal integration cooperatives can offer effective competition to powerful non-cooperative organizations.
4. This type of integration enables integrating units to get the services of talented functional specialists.

Vertical Integration

Vertical integration is the combination of different business units engaged in successive stages of operation beginning from production of raw materials, through distribution of finished product. The business units combined stands end to end, the product of one serving as input to the next one. That is the combining business units come one after another in the successive stages or levels in the operations through which a commodity moves from the producer to the consumer. The vertical integration implies general dovetailing or 'fusion' of successive stages in the industrial process, within one business organization.

Vertical integration can be one of the most important factors influencing the success of the cooperative movement in the developing countries, as many primary societies would be unable to succeed or would be greatly restricted in their rate of development without the support of federative organizations.

Vertical integration is achieved by the following methods:

Federation: Normally vertical integration is achieved through federations. Processing, wholesaling, manufacturing, value addition, etc., can be achieved by means of federations. Cooperative federations can be organized at different levels, secondary, tertiary or apex; and the level chosen will depend on the objective, stage of cooperative development, nature of service, etc.

Confederation: This is a federation of federations, performing such functions/services common to combining federal organizations eg., the Cooperation Union of Canada, Danish Central Federation of Cooperative Societies, and the Indian Cooperative Union.

Cooperative Association: Another form of vertical integration is cooperative association. A cooperative association is an association of cooperative enterprises for business purposes, ie., an economic institution through which an economic activity is conducted in the pursuit of common economic objective, eg., joint plant set-up by individual cooperative enterprises. It has no purpose apart from that of participating firm.

Forward and backward integration: Vertical integration can be forward integration or backward integration. When a manufacturing unit absorbs channels of distribution or a producer of raw material absorbs a manufacturing unit forward integration emerges. On the other hand when the integration is initiated at or near the consumer level and is extended towards raw material level, it is known as backward integration.

Vertical integration is said to be pure when a firm handles a single product or very similar product over successive levels in the market chain. When the integration affects a number of different or complementary products it becomes complementary integration.

The advantages of vertical integration are:

1. A number of successive selling costs, buying costs and other handling charges normally incurred in transferring commodities may be eliminated and some of the duplications and competitive wastes of marketing may be avoided.
2. Vertical integration facilitates optimal utilization of productive resources and thus reduce costs.
3. Because it is in a position to buy more units of given productive factors at a time, the large integrated firm's bargaining power is enhanced and as a result, unit factor prices may be reduced.
4. Another advantage is the opportunity to absorb middlemen's profits.
5. An important advantage is that production or distribution at one stage can be adjusted more closely to the needs of other stages.
6. More complete vertical integration of many agricultural markets may facilitate the flow of farm commodities from producers to consumers. In such a market system the price adjustments needed to move products through market channels may be made more promptly without delay.

7. Elimination of competition, enhancement of monopoly powers, assurance of input supplies are among the other obvious advantages of vertical integration.

Now we can discuss elaborately on vertical integration through central organizations and vertical integration through federal organizations.

Vertical Integration through Central Cooperatives

Vertical integration of cooperatives is the accumulation of more business processes under closer central control. Vertical integration includes every effort made by primary cooperatives with in the cooperative movement to form central business organizations, promotion and provision services. The intention behind this affiliation is that the performance of the affiliated primary cooperatives can be improved through the carrying out of functions and the provision of services by the central organization which do not lie within the scope of the primary cooperatives.

Vertical integration has contributed to the development of cooperative movement, especially in a competitive economy through giving support and services. The extent (degree) to which the primary cooperatives are integrated within the central organization vary between two extremes.

(i) The primary societies are wholly dependent agencies of the secondary organization. The primary societies are merely collecting or distributing agents and are with little responsibility. Therefore, they are completely devoid of economic decisions and are regarded or recognized as economic branches of the secondary organization i.e., subordination.

(ii) The primary and secondary organizations are recognized as business partners.

There exist many intermediate type of integration between the two extremes mentioned above. However, the actual extent of integration is dependent on a number of factors influencing the relationship between the primary society and the central organization. These factors comprise:

(*a*) Economic viability, competitiveness and operational efficiency of primary societies.

(*b*) Financial dependence on the central organization.

(*c*) Management strength of the secondary organization in relation to the primary ones.

(*d*) Existence of transport and communication facilities between the primary and the secondary organizations.

(*e*) Cooperative and marketing ordinances and other provisions determining the extent of relation.

Even though there are various degrees of relationships, the recommended extent is the one where there is neither subordination nor exaggerated local autonomy but collaboration and integration on the basis of equal partnership.

Vertical Integration Through Federation

This refers to the complete apex-system of vertical integration. The open-system arises from and is principally comprised of federated structure of primary cooperatives brought together in associations which in turn are amalgamated in one single cooperation at the top 'apex'. In the case of affiliation, integration is conceivable only for those cooperatives concerned with the same economic activity as no such coming together takes place between the cooperatives which are involved in different economic functions, i.e. action is undertaken by the central organization on behalf of individual members' businesses interest.

Contrary to the above case, in federation at apex-system, no consideration and distinction is made for various types of activities or the functions of the affiliated cooperatives. These activities can be similar or different unlike affiliated ones. This apex-system is advantageous in removing competition between different cooperative associations since they develop a spirit of mutual cooperation through the apex-system.

After all, what is the importance of vertical integration?

This is basically to assist the affiliated societies to be efficient and stable through:

(*a*) Audit and supervision-service of audit to cooperatives is helpful to sort any irregularity and to take action of remedy. This could be done by accountants, audit institutions, etc.

(*b*) Extension services—these services of extension to cooperatives include:

- Services of information like price quotations.
- Services of business consulting and advise on business operations, investments, plans, feasibility studies, etc.
- Services of property advise regarding location or any aspect of office buildings, shops, plants, etc.

(*c*) Research activities—on various aspects of the society.

(*d*) Settlement of disputes—if any among the members of the affiliated societies, to preserve solidarity and unity.

(*e*) Representation and delegation—in legal matters, labour relations by taking over the function of the manager, in negotiations, policy concerning legislation, etc.

(*f*) Education and training—of members and staff members, especially managerial training to improve the success of the society.

(*g*) Provision of stabilizing fund—if there is sudden lose and need for immediate assistance.

Self-learning Activity

Try to answer the following questions on your own.

1. What is meant by cooperative integration?
2. Dovetail the vertical integration and its forms.
3. What is horizontal integration of cooperatives and spell out its advantages?

Summary

- The framework of integration is discussed in this chapter. The cooperatives, to strengthen their business, can go for both vertical and horizontal integration.

Chapter 7 World Cooperative Movement — At a Glance

On a worldwide basis, modern cooperatives have developed for over 200 years. Cooperative institutions exist all over the world providing essential services, which would otherwise be unattainable. In many Third World countries, cooperatives such as credit unions and agricultural organizations have been very successful in helping people to provide for themselves where private and other corporate capitals do not see high profitability. In 90 countries of the world, over 700 million individuals are members of cooperative institutions. Globally, cooperatives have been able to elevate its position as a powerful economic model. In some countries they are a sizeable force within the national economy.

Origin

Cooperative philosophy though originated with revolutionary characters in the writings and activities of Robert *Owen*, Louis Blanc, Charles *Fourier*, and others. but under the impact of such movements as Christian Socialism this aspect diminished. After some early 19th-century experiments, consumers' cooperation took permanent form with the establishment of the *Rochdale Society of Equitable Pioneers* in England in 1844.

The cooperative movement has had considerable growth throughout Great Britain and countries under its domain and through phases local cooperatives transformed into national wholesale and retail distributive enterprises with involvement of a large section of the population as members. of Cooperative organizations are also formed in the Scandinavian countries, Israel, China, Russia, and France. In the United States the cooperative movement began in the 19th century, first among workers and then among farmers. In 1867 the 'National Grange', a farmers' cooperative, was formed and later this institution exercised considerable political influence.

An international alliance for the dissemination of cooperative information was set up in 1895. Today the major types of cooperatives include those of farmers, wholesalers, and consumers, as well as insurance, banking and credit, and rural electrification. There has been increasing international collaboration among the various kinds of cooperatives and a growing trend toward the establishment of international cooperative distribution.

DEVELOPMENTS IN EUROPE FEW EXAMPLES

Denmark

The first co-operative store was established in 1866, but in fact in 1882 the first co-operative dairy was established. This ushered in the start of the agricultural co-operative movement which by the time of the First World War had expanded to its fullest extent in the shape of co-operative dairies and bacon factories, with production facilities, marketing undertakings in the shape of co-operative egg and butter exports and purchasing organisations like co-operative heavy goods undertakings. An important precondition for this development was the fact that Danish farmers and marginal holders owned their own land, for which reason the co-operative undertakings could be financed by joint liability on the part of the members.

Within the co-operative movement the fundamental principle has been one man-one vote (vote entitlement was not decided by the number of cattle owned, which was prevalent in some other countries). There is no special legislation in Denmark governing the co-operative movement, but from its early days in the 1880s and right up to the present, the movement has developed on the basis of members' needs and the constant practical adaptation of the movement's fundamental principles to the demands of the day. Apart from the principle of one man one vote, which applies in primary production activities, i.e. where there is a question of personal membership, other characteristics of the movement are the open membership and the distribution of profit in relation to the individual member's volume of business with the undertaking. The co-operative movement in Denmark is felt to be an integral part of the community and business, which many of them encounter either as consumers (co-operative stores) or as producers (agriculture, market gardening and fishing). The co-operative undertakings have for generations been seen as practical instruments for protecting of financial interests.

Finland

During its century-long history, the Finnish cooperative movement has played an important role in the development of society and national economy.

The cooperative enterprise, controlled by its members, has been particularly strong in agricultural production , dairies and marketing, since most of the producers have been and still are small-scale farmers. It has been vital for them to join hands in their efforts to procure farm inputs and to market their produce. More recently, the movement has also gained momentum in services such as children's day care and care of the elderly. Further evidence of the viability of the cooperative movement are the hundreds of new cooperatives being started every year in country.

Palestine

The roots of the cooperative movement in Palestine goes back to the year 1933, when the first Palestinian Cooperative Law was published. Tobacco growers and Citrus producers established the first cooperatives., Savings and credit cooperatives in the Palestinian countryside also existed then.

The Palestinian Cooperative Movement encountered different political conditions. As a grassroot socio-economic movement, the Palestinian Cooperative Movement remained voluntary and non-governmental owned and managed by its members based on cooperative values of democracy, social justice, equitable distribution of resources and opportunities. Cooperative activity differs from one cooperative to another depending on members activity and dedication. New studies show that the number of active cooperatives in Palestine is around 400 cooperatives with more than fifty thousands members representing 300,000 families. This number indicates the importance of cooperatives as forming a vital economic sector in the Palestinian society.

Generally, at the end of the Second World War, consumer cooperatives were a major presence in most European countries. They could be found in almost every town and city. Most were still locally owned and controlled democratic institutions responsive to their local community Cooperatives in the modern sense have been around since the people of Rochdale, England founded their co-op in 1844. The consumer cooperatives of Europe were the first to organize group purchasing, wholesales, transportation networks, and a host of allied services, such as banking and insurance. While they were the only retailers doing it, the independent local co-ops were economically successful and they were growing. Fortunately for the cooperatives, it was not until after the Second World War that competition among retailers began to heat up. Chains were forming, wholesales being organized, supermarkets being built. For about 25 years, the co-ops stood and watched the competition take away their market share. The local cooperative societies, with their small corner shops on High Street, were no match for the big supermarkets sitting on cheap land on the outskirts of town.

Movement in United States of America and Canada

In Canada and the US, the roots of the cooperative movement are stuck to the businesses to figure prominently in their national economies. Rural electric co-ops, credit unions, and agricultural co-ops were formed to meet the needs of rural populations, which did not attract investment or where goods and services were provided at unfair prices. In the early 20th century, cooperatives in these two countries began to see a need for national organizations. In the US, cooperatives organized the Cooperative League of the USA, which later became the National Cooperative Business Association (NCBA) which provides networking, technical assistance, and development assistance. It contributed for effective lobbying at the national level for cooperatives. It helped pass legislation which formed the National Cooperative Bank in 1978. Today, NCBA remains the premier cross-sectoral link among co-ops in the United States. Canada enjoys an even stronger network of cooperative support organizations. The Canadian Co-operative Association (CCA), provides educational services to its member cooperatives and sponsors cooperative development in lesser-developed nations. The Co-operative Housing Federation of Canada provides technical assistance to developing and established co-ops throughout English-speaking Canada. Canadian cooperatives have also benefited from the support of the Canadian Mortgage and Housing Corporation. The contemporary cooperative movement is strong and diverse there. Cooperatives exist all over both the countries. Some of the larger cooperatives have an annual income of several billion dollars. In addition to rural electric co-ops, credit unions, and agricultural co-ops, there are cooperatives to serve almost every need namely food co-ops, automotive co-ops, insurance co-ops, housing co-ops, book co-ops... and so on.

COOPERATIVE DEVELOPMENTS IN ASIA

Japan

The Japanese cooperative movement today has 13 million members cooperative societies, which with over 50,000 employees. Over 5 million households participate regularly in nearly 1 million *han* groups. The number of *han* groups has doubled in the past five years.

The reasons for success of the *han* approach

1. They reduce the need for high investment by not having to build or own stores. At least in the early stages, their capital investment went only into distribution centers and small delivery trucks.
2. They take advantage of computer technology to give people at home tremendous ease in ordering and communication.
3. Centralized management and distribution centers are separated. The business side focuses on aggregating and using economic power, allowing participants at the *han* level to concentrate on member activity and democratic participation. Thus the cooperatives offer economic advantages to their members as consumers, while at the same time providing the organizing advantages of decentralization to their members as citizen activists. The combination of the two elements is without doubt the most important example of a successful consumer cooperative to emerge in the 20th Century.

India

During the British rule, Nicholson a British Officer in India suggested to introduce Raiffersen model of German agricultural credit Cooperatives in India. As a follow-up of that recommendation, the first Cooperative Society Act of 1904 was enacted to enable formation of 'agricultural credit cooperatives' in villages in India under Government sponsorship. With the enactment of 1904 Act, Cooperatives were to get a direct legal identity as every agricultural Cooperative was to be registered under that Act only. The 1904 Cooperative Societies Act, was repealed by 1912 Cooperative Societies Act which provided formation of Cooperative societies other than credit. Under 1919 Administrative Reforms act , Cooperatives was made a provincial subject making each province responsible for Cooperative development.

In 1942, the British Government enacted the Multi-Unit Cooperative Societies Act, 1942 with an object to cover societies whose operations are extended to more than one state. The impulses of the Indian freedom movement gave birth to many intiatives and institutions in the post independence era in India and armed with an experience of 42 years in the working of Multi Unit Cooperative Societies and the Multi-Unit Cooperative Societies Act, 1942, the Central Government enacted a comprehensive Act known as Multi State Cooperative Societies Act, 1984, repealing the Act of 1942.

An Expert Group constituted by the Govt of India in 1990, recommended *(i)* to facilitate building up of integrated co-operative structure; *(ii)* to make the co-operative federation organisations responsive towards their members; *(iii)* to minimise government interference and control in the functioning of co-operatives; and *(iv)* to eliminate politicisation.

India has basically an agrarian economy, 71 per cent of its total population reside in rural areas and 29 per cent in urban areas. The rural people need lot of services in daily life which are met by village co-operative societies. The village co-operative societies provide strategic inputs for the agricultural sector, consumer societies meet their consumption requirements at concessional rates; marketing societies help the farmer to get remunerative prices and co-operative processing units help in value additions to the raw products etc. In addition, co-operative societies are helping in building up of storage go-downs including cold storages, rural roads and in providing facilities like irrigation, electricity, transport and health. Thus the co-operative societies in India in fact are playing multi-functional roles both in rural and urban areas.

Based on the recommendations, the Central Government enacted the Multi State Cooperative Societies Act, 2002 which provided for democratic and autonomous working of the Cooperatives, which came into force with effect from August 19, 2002. At present, the Government of India is in the process of formulation of National Policy on Co-operatives which is likely to uphold the values and principles of co-operation recognizing its autonomous characters and attaching priority to professionalism , human resource development and to act as preferred instrument for execution of public policy in rural areas and in sectors where they provide the most effective delivery system. To strengthen their competitive edge in the market total quality control initiatives, management initiatives and cost reduction initiatives will also be taken up. It is now increasingly recognised that the co-operative system in India has the capacity and potentiality to neutralise the adverse effects emerging from the process of globalisation and liberalization, and continue to play an important role in employment promotion and poverty alleviation, both as production enterprises—mainly of the self-employed—and as providers of services to members Although cooperatives are not instruments of employment promotion, they do effectively create and maintain employment in both urban and rural areas and thus provide income to both members and employees in the form of shares of surplus, wages and salaries or profits depending of the type of cooperative.

Thailand

Cooperatives in Thailand, like in all developing countries, have been initiated by the government since 1915 with the prime aim of using as a means to improve the livelihood of small farmers. This is due to the increasing indebtedness problem resulting from farmers who were suffering from the shifting of self-sufficient economy to trade economy. The natural disaster such as drought and flood even added further to create more chronic and severe indebtedness to the farmers. Consequently, they lost their farmland and becoming labourers and thus leaving their debts unpaid. The first cooperative in Thailand named Wat Chan Cooperative was established by the government on February 26, 1916, following the Raiffeisen credit cooperative type with a single purpose of providing farm credit and being organized as a small village credit cooperative to help the severely indebted farmers. The success of this cooperative type in preventing many farmers' land from being grabbed by the moneylenders led to the increasing number of small village credit cooperatives all over the country. The small credit cooperatives had prevailed in the country until 1983 other cooperative types then established in responding to the people's need First 'Cooperative Bank' was set up in 1947 with government funds. Village credit cooperatives were urged to increasingly hold share capital in the Bank with the hope that they would, in future, be owners of the Bank which was their own financing centre. In 1952 and 1953, two provincial cooperative banks were also established. The two provincial cooperative banks were serving their affiliates so well both in their credit needs and depositing surplus funds. These were reorganized as credit cooperative federations, and further reorganized as the "Bank for Agriculture and Agricultural Cooperatives", a state enterprise, functioning as a financial center of agricultural cooperatives including lending directly to individual farmers. In 1968 establishment of the Cooperative League of Thailand, functioning as the apex organization of the cooperative movement.

At present, the cooperatives in Thailand are officially categorized to six types, namely:

1. Agricultural Cooperative;
2. Land Settlement Cooperative;
3. Fisheries Cooperative;
4. Consumer Cooperative;
5. Thrift and Credit Cooperative; and
6. Service Cooperative.

SOUTH AMERICA

Latin America

The Brazilian Landless Workers Movement is the largest social movement in Latin America and one of the most successful grassroots movements in the world. Hundreds of thousands of landless peasants have taken onto themselves the task of carrying out a long-overdue land reform in a country mired by an overly skewed land distribution pattern. Less than 3 per cent of the population owns two-thirds of Brazil's arable land.

While 60 per cent of Brazil's farmland lies idle, 25 million peasants struggle to survive by working in temporary agricultural jobs. The Landless Workers' Movement is a response to these inequalities. In 1985, with the support of the Catholic Church, hundreds of landless rural Brazilians took over an unused plantation in the south of the country and successfully established a cooperative there. They gained title to the land in 1987. Today more than 250,000 families have won land titles to over 15 million acres.

In the following sections some of the country's movement is discussed in detail for more understanding about the world cooperative movement.

Cooperatives in England

England's toad lane is a place where the origin of model cooperative is traced back. It was during the industrial revolution that the birth of cooperatives took place. The industrial revolution had completely overhauled the entire social and economic life of Englishmen. Domestic industries were replaced by factory industries. The rural population started shifting its habitation from villages to towns and cities, industrial revolution and mining districts in the expectation of bettering their lot. Improved means of transport and communication broke down the isolation of many places. People started depending more and more on the outside world for employment and the supply of goods and commodities. To some this change was a boon while to others it was a source of great insecurity and poverty. Much of the distress was due to the effects of the Napoleonic wars. The factory system created new problems for the government and the people, namely *low wages, payment in truck, unemployment, and labour disputes, exploitation of child labour and slums.* Factories were ill-lit, ill ventilated, overcrowded and in sanitary. Safety precautions and device were neglected.

Such were the effects of the industrial revolution and there seemed to be no way out. The economists, political thinkers and social reformers, all started applying their mind towards finding out a solution to these problems. Adam Smith and his followers expounded the theory of competition on the one hand and on the other hand Robert Owen pointed out the way of escape from the evils of competition through the organization of equitable associations, which are quasi cooperatives. Beer (1985), in his history of British socialism, has rightly said that ' the working of classes learned socialism from Owen.' Owen's socialism was cooperative in nature and not militant. His struggle was not against usurpation and wickedness but against error and ignorance.

Robert Owen(1771-1858)

Robert Owen was born on 14th May, 1771. He achieved great fame as a captain of industry. In his early days he worked as a laborer in the factories and ships and acquired intimate knowledge of the difficulties faced by the workers. By and by, he went on making progress and invented small machines. Later on, he married the daughter of the owner of the new Lanark mills, Glasgow. After the death of his father in law he becomes the proprietor of the mills. Robert Owen was very humane and kind. He didn't believe in the accumulation of wealth. His chief concern was human happiness, which he believed was determined by human character, which was chiefly the product of circumstances in which human beings lived.

The cooperative movement in a real sense began with Robert Owen—a factory manager, a Utopian Socialist, a pioneer of industrial cooperation and trade unionism, and an advocate of communal living. Owen (1771-1858) envisaged villages including farmlands and small-scale industry, all operated cooperatively by the citizens of the villages who would live communally.

Owen's communities were originally conceived as a cure for unemployment but later as a way to replace private capitalism and competition with self-employment and with conditions that should provide universal happiness. He planned that such communities would consist of about 1000 people, 1500 acres of land, with common buildings and apartments for individual families; and would cost between $200,000 and 250,000. Wealthy sympathizers of Owen's schemes were to finance such projects rather than the inhabitants of the communal villages. Such villages were attempted at New Harmony, Indiana (1825-27); and at Orbiston, Scotland; Ralahine, Ireland; and Queenswood, England. All failed.

This failure, however, did not keep Owen from preaching cooperation as the best solution to mankind's problems. Because of the stimulus of his teachings cooperative societies, labour exchanges (where handicrafts were exchanged presumably on the basis of the amount of labour involved in their making), trade unions, and magazines for workingmen started about 1820 and afterwards. Most lasted only a short time, but the seeds were sown for a later harvest of cooperatives.

Owen was an idealist more than a realist, visionary rather practical and an advocate of industrial cooperation, not of consumer distributive cooperation. Owen declared, "Profit-making was necessarily the exploitation of man by man. Profit upon price for individual gain and the accumulation of useless and unnecessary individual wealth brought in to action the lower passions of human nature; and a false estimate of all things ensued and everything became valued by its cost instead of its intrinsic worth. Cunningness and deception usurped the place of wisdom and sincerity."

As already stated, the schemes of Owen undoubtedly ended in failure, his principles and ideals have continued to inspire the cooperative movement. These principles are:

1. abolition of private profit;
2. voluntary association;
3. common ownership of the means of production; and
4. The utilization of the wealth of the community for increasing the happiness of mankind.

Owen had more grandiose ideas, encompassing agricultural and industrial production, education, housing, and commercial distribution—the whole gamut economic activity on a cooperative basis. No doubt, Owen (called by some the *Father of Cooperation*) believed it far more important for persons to increase their incomes, to improve their living conditions, and to free children from debilitating factory employment than to save a few pennies on retail buying.

Dr William King—Father of Distributive Cooperation

Dr. William King (1786-1865) of Brighton, England was a social reformer and a realistic advocate of consumer cooperation. He learned about Robert Owen and accepted much of Owen's social philosophy although he differed with him as to how to achieve its ends. King was a physician and soon became interested in improving the welfare of the working people of Brighton. To this end he became involved in organizing an Infants' School (1823), the Brighton Provident and District Society (1824), the Brighton Mechanics' Institute (1825), a Subscription Library (1826), the cooperative Benevolent Fund Association, and the Brighton Cooperative Trading Association (1827). Some of this lasted only a short time.

Beginning in May 1828 and continuing for two years, Dr. King published at his own expense a small magazine called 'The Cooperator'. Its 28 issues contained King's important contribution to cooperative thought and were a source of inspiration, information, and instructions on cooperation in general and cooperative shop keeping in particular.

King was much more realistic and far more understandable about cooperation than Owen. His plan was relatively simple. He urged the workers to: Save their money, invest their money in their cooperative retail store, pay cash for merchandise, and operate democratically. Publicize the cooperative movement so it might grow and become effective. Reinvest the 'profit' or net earnings in the store to enable the store to employ its own members who would make things to be sold in the store or to other buyers.

King taught that cooperatives should start small with members supplying the original capital (Owen relied on wealthy outside investors to supply the funds for large-scale operations). He also believed that cooperatives should not pay a patronage refund but the net earnings should be put in a reserve fund and used for the good of all the members so as to enlarge the cooperative's activities in production, crafts, and provide employment. He did not object to Owenite self –sustaining cooperative communities provided they were set up with the members' own capital and restricted to Christians. (King was a deeply religious man who believed that the spirit and ethics of the Gospel were those of cooperation also.)

In many respects Dr. King was more responsible for the extension of the cooperative idea and for the organization of many cooperatives than Robert Owen ever was. King was truly the "Father of Distributive Cooperation," the inspirer of consumer' cooperative stores in England where as Owen encouraged self-employment and communal living and started no stores. King's little periodicals were distributed throughout England. It advocated the kind of cooperation within reach of the common man in its realistic, albeit optimistic, proposals. His was a grassroots, bottom-up, simple scheme of organization contrasted with the far more expensive top-down plan of Robert Owen. As a result, the movement grows from a few societies in 1826 to around 300 shops in 1830—many patterned after King's Brighton Cooperative Trading Association. (Kings ideas may also have influenced American cooperation—a Mr. William Bryan, treasurer of a cooperative at Brighton, England came to New York in 1829 and helped organized a consumers'. cooperative store in that city in 1830).

The Rochdale Pioneers

During the early period of cooperative development, one of the societies, which had sprung up in 1830s, was at Rochdale (Rochdale Friendly cooperative Society), England. Dr. King's writings might have influenced this early Rochdalian cooperative because James Smithies, one of the leaders among the 28 Rochdalians, was inspired by King's 'The Cooperator' and showed it to the Rochdalians. A nucleus of this determined group continued to work actively for social reform. From the work of this nucleus, the cooperative movement in Great Britain was able to achieve outstanding success. The foundation of this success was not new. It was based upon the intelligent combination of various ideas, which had been tried by previous cooperatives. The failures of the past became the warning signals of later years so that firmer foundations could be laid.

A Consumers' Cooperative Store, started in Toad Lane, Rochdale, England on 21-12-1844, and continuing to this very day, provided the organizational and operating pattern that became the prototype for other consumers' cooperatives, both at the retail and wholesale levels, the world over.

These 28 Rochdalians had high hopes and aspirations. They hoped not only to establish a store for the sale of provisions but also to acquire homes in which their members might live; to manufacture articles that the society's members might need as well as to provide employment; to acquire land on which to produce products needed by members; and to employ those members out of work or those whose wages were very low. They wanted to "establish a self-supporting home colony of united interests" and to "arrange the powers of production, distribution, education and government" in the interest of its members. And finally, "for the promotion of sobriety a temperance hotel (was) to be opened in one of the Society's houses as soon as convenient." This was, indeed, an ambitious programme, and how different it was from the purposes which cooperatives today state as their reasons for organizing.

The business practices (later called as Rochdalian Principles), which these pioneers laid down for operating their store on Toad Lane were not individually novel but the combination of all them are essentially new. These practices were:

- Capital should be of members own providing and bear a fixed rate of interest. (Limited interest on equity capital).
- Only the purest provisions procurable should be supplied to members (to do away abominable adulteration of food).

- Full weight and measures should be given. (Provide honesty in weighing).
- Market prices should be charged, and no credit neither given nor asked. (Cash trading; no charge accounts; charge prevailing prices).
- Profits should be divided in proportion to the amount of purchases made by each member (Patronage refunds).
- The principles of 'One Member One Vote' should prevail in government, and the equality of the sexes in membership (democratic control).
- Management should be in the hands of officers and a committee elected periodically by the members. (Representative government and control of the cooperative).
- A definite percentage of profit should be allotted to education. (Provision for education in cooperation).
- Frequent statements and balance sheets should be presented to the members (member information).
- No inquiry should be made in to the political and religious opinions of those who apply for membership. (Political and religious neutrality).

Note that these Rochdalian rules were devised to run a small grocery store and although they have wide application, they are not necessarily appropriate for all types of cooperatives. Such principles as democratic control by member users, limited dividends on equity capital, and operations at cost (with its corollary that if gross margins or incomes exceed costs, refunds will be made on a patronage basis) are almost universally followed. But cash trading, charging prices that other dealers charge, sending out frequent statements and balance sheets, or even setting aside a part of the new savings in an educational fund are not adhered to by all associations. The success—one might add, the phenomenal success—of the Rochdalians was by all means the shot in the arm that the cooperative movement needed in its doldrums days of the mid forties (Hungry Forties). Rochdale became the beacon for others to follow.

Cooperatives in Germany

Germany was the first country in the world to apply the principles of cooperation in the field of credit. The cooperative credit movement was started in Germany in the middle of the 19th century. At that time the economic condition of Germany was extremely deplorable and the peasantry and artisans felt crushed under the heavy weight of indebtedness. Famines were common phenomena. Usury was the order of the day. The Jews ruled over the market and the poor labourers and farmers had no way out to buy articles of their requirements from them and sell their products to them. The Jews were not only buyers and sellers but moneylenders as well. German peasantry and labourers were thus passing bad times and were almost broken. Henry W. Wolf has beautifully narrated the conditions of the farmers and the labourers. He says "Among the poor peasantry the distress was great. Every little wattle cottage and tumbled down house was mortgaged; most of the peasants' cattle belonged to the Jews. There was little employment on the roads or in the forests; the sole available means for netting a few additional shillings; the poor land yielded but a bare pittance; and famine and ruin stared the poor inhabitants in the face. There was no one to turn to help but the 'Jews'. Immediately steps were required to take them out of these miserable conditions. During those periods, only two cooperators only Raiffeisen and Schulze took keen interest to alter the situations.

Herr F.W. Raiffeisen (1818-1888)

Herr F.W. Raiffeisen (1818-1888) and Herr Franz Schulze (1809-1883) the two pioneers in this field took initiative and started introducing various measures of relief. They started their schemes at about the same time but their field of operation was entirely different. Raiffeisen tried to reduce the sufferings of the people living in the rural areas while Schulze adopted the new measures for giving relief to the people living in the urban areas. Both were convinced that the lot of people could be improved only if they were taken out of the clutches of the 'Jews'. They had realized that providing monetary help was not a permanent solution, and any time, in adverse circumstances, the people could fall a prey to the Jews. Hence, they thought that people should be made to take part effectively in any step aimed at ameliorating their condition. Self-help was considered to be the only way out.

It was Raiffeisen who contributed the maximum to the spread of the cooperative movement in Germany. He was the Mayor of Weyerbusch. He had witnessed how dishonest moneylenders created poverty-stricken farmers. His commune was in the grip of famine. He sought the support of the Government and got some grain. He appealed to the people for help. He employed bakers on wage basis for preparing breads. He also organized a 'Poor people's committee' which provided food to the poor and recovered the loan after the expiry of the specific period. In 1849, he was transferred to Flammers field where he organized 'Union in Aid of Impoverished Farmers'. The funds for this union were raised on the security of the rich persons of the locality. This union achieved great success and rescued a number of farmers from the jaws of greedy Jews. Raiffeisen was then transferred to Heddesdorf where he set up the 'Heddesdorf Beneficent Society' whose members were also well-to-do people. These people deposited money with the society on interest. Loans were given to deserving farmers and artisans for productive purposes. Although the society was a grand success, Raiffeisen did not like the idea that the poor people should be at the mercy of the rich. He therefore, 'enrolled as members of the society. Accordingly, a new society was constituted under the name of 'Heddesdorf Credit Union'. The memorable phrase, 'each for all and all for each' was coined there. The movement gained momentum and in a short time many credit unions were organized. The Grand Union of Rural Cooperatives also known as 'Raiffeisen Union' was set up in 1877.

Characteristics Features of the Raiffeisen Societies

- Membership was limited to the rural masses, especially farmers and cultivators.
- Unlimited liability of the members.
- Small area of operation.
- Small loans were given to the members, which were recovered over a long period.
- Loans were given on the basis of personal security of the members and only for productive purposes. Emphasis was on the *personal character* of the borrower.
- Nominal share capital.
- Profit earning was not the motive and even under the cooperative law only a small portion of profits was distributed to the members as dividend.
- Losses and profits were transferred to the reserve fund and endowment fund. The endowment fund was indivisible.
- The management was honorary.
- Emphasis was given to moral as well as material well being.

Herr Franz Schulze (1809-1883)

Schulze was a judge in his native town of Delitzsch. He had seen the miserable condition of the people, especially of low means, with his own eyes. In 1849, he organized in association with his friend Dr. Bernhardi, a friendly society for Relief in sickness and later established an association of shoemakers for the purchase of raw material. In 1850, he founded the first credit association with the funds provided those who were well-off and who did not require any financial help. Schulze was conscious of this situation and, therefore, he emphasized that no one could obtain loan from the association unless he was its member. Two years later, in 1852, Schulze founded a society at Delitzsch, which was based on cooperative principles. He obtained the required capital through the sale shares. He was a wonderful propagandist and his efforts bore fruits quickly. He published a book in 1856, which contained the principles of cooperative banking as formulated by him. The number of banks started by him increased rapidly, and in 1859 organized a congress of these banks. The congress decided to set up 'The General Union of German Industrial Societies'. He was its director till his death in 1883. He was also responsible for securing from Prussia the first cooperative law in 1867, which later on was made applicable to the entire country.

Characteristics Features of the Schulze-Delitzsch Societies:

- Membership was limited to artisans, industrial workers and middle class people living in cities and towns.
- Limited liability of the members.
- Large area of operation.
- The amount of loans advanced was bigger and the period of the repayment was short.
- Loans were given on the security of tangible assets. Although loans were advanced for productive purposes, no supervision over the utilization of the loan was made.
- A strong share capital
- Profit earning was the chief motive and rate of dividend was quite high.
- Not much emphasis was given to the reserve fund. Reserve fund was used for making up losses, but it was required to be made good as soon as possible.

- The management was paid.
- The chief concern was with the material well being of the members.

Cooperative Movement in Denmark

Besides developing voluntary movement, the movement is self-made, introduced and nourished by common men who make up the membership of the cooperative societies, without any advice or support from abroad, without state control or state help. Denmark has no cooperative legislation. The different types of cooperative societies have been organized freely, adjusting themselves according to local needs and conditions. Owing to the absence of cooperative legislation the cooperative movement presents varying forms ranging from strict conformity to the classical Rochdale stores to semi-public institutions. The basic principle guiding the movement has been:

- To strive on a no-profit basis for the direct economic benefit of the members who have founded the societies and their sole owners.
- The voluntary cooperative movement organized on democratic lines has been serving the Danish families in the villages and in town's since the last quarter of the last century and will continue to serve for ages.

The Danish movement is the superb example of voluntary effort of common men for alleviating their economic, political and social status. In this respect, Denmark is the torch bearer to other countries of the world. Surprisingly, the cooperative movement in Denmark was started with the establishment of consumers' stores in accordance with the Rochdale principles. The first cooperative store was established in 1886 in Thisted.

Agricultural Cooperative Movement in Denmark

Agricultural cooperative movement in Denmark, like other cooperative movements, is the product of social and economic conditions that prevailed during the last quarter of the 19th century. The system of marketing had undergone considerable changes. The Danish farmer had to face a keen competition at the hands of the cheap American agricultural products. Their export trade was subject to serve restrictions imposed by the governments of importing countries. The immediate need was, was therefore reducing the costs of production to the minimum. This required re-organization of the agricultural industry and the maximization of production. The Danish agriculturalist realized that this could be possible only through cooperation. Again, in the beginning of the last century most of the land was under the possession of feudal landlords. The cultivation was done by peasants and the fruits were reaped by the barons. The cultivator didn't have the freedom to improve agriculture. By 1885, most of the tenancies were converted into free holds as a result of the land reform introduced by the benevolent rulers. The position was undoubtedly improved but to a limited extent. As the holding were small and scattered, the economic position of cultivators.

Cooperative Dairies

The first agricultural society, Viz., the royal agricultural society was organized in 1979 with the chief objective of developing agriculture. By and by, the number of such societies increased. The societies improved the conditions of the farmers. During the last century the Danish farmers were mainly dependent up the production and export of grain. They had to change to dairy farming mainly because they could not compete with America in the supply of cheap corn and because of an increase in the demand for Danish butter in England. In the beginning butter was produced by ordinary churning method. It was in 1880 that the use of separate machine was made and a number of private creameries came into being. In 1882, a creamery was set up in Hjedding. This creamery proved to a great success. Encouraged by it, many other cooperative creameries were set up in the country. Today, the cooperative dairies occupy the front position in the cooperative system of Denmark. The area of operation being small, fresh supplies of milk can be had every day. There are no transport bottlenecks, and no cold storage difficulties are faced. After the butter and cream have been taken out, the skimmed milk is given to the farmers which are used as cattle feed. The butter making process in Denmark is a highly specialized one. The Cooperative dairies employ highly technically skilled staff.

The cooperative dairies have the following special features:

- The product is immediately connected with the raising of raw materials.
- The manufacturing is carried on the land close the place of production. Consequently, there is saving of time. The cost of production is minimum since no transportation cost is involved. The primary cooperative society deal with the various problems of industrial organization.
- On account of specialization, highest standards of efficiency are maintained, and therefore the price of the produce is quite low.
- The marketing system is highly organized. Consequently all the economies of large scale buying and production are enjoyed by the farmers. They employ trained staff who posses day-to-day knowledge of market requirements, and therefore, they are able to cut down the cost to the minimum. Their method of packing is excellent, specially suited to transshipment for export.

In Denmark the entire export trade is controlled by federations. Marketing through federations has a number of advantages:

- Because of the transportation of goods in bulk, cheaper transport facilities can be availed of;

- The dairy products have been standardized in quality, packing, finishing, etc.;
- The cost of packing is very low;
- The prices are stabilized and competition is avoided;
- The local societies are supplied with up to date information.

The Danish cooperative dairies are not only interested in business but are also interested in improving economic condition of the farmers. It has been fully realized by them that the interest of the trader and the producer can come together. They try to get the farmers high price for their products. They impart training to the farmer not only in business methods but also in cattle rearing. The farmer is made to realize that his interest is linked with the reputation of the Danish dairies. The education in the principles and methods of production is therefore automatic and is imparted through practice.

Let us see some of the broad areas where Danish dairy cooperative were found model:

1. *Constitution and working*; Members are required to supply milk according to the terms of contract which continues for 15 to 20 years after which the dairy is wound up and started afresh. The farmers take loan from commercial bank or savings bank for the purchase of machinery and equipment. The milk is collected from the members daily. It is tested and pasteurized. The cream is separated from the milk and butter is prepared. Skimmed milk is given back to the farmers for being used as cattle feed. The farmers are paid according to the fat contents of the milk supplied by them.

The Chief functions performed by dairy cooperatives are:

(*a*) To process the milk supplied by the members;

(*b*) To provide funds for investment;

(c) To give advice on cattle keeping and to provide technical knowledge regarding feeding and breeding of animals.

The Cooperative dairies have set up their creameries in central places in the area of operation. The goods produced by these dairies are sold under the trade mark 'LURBRAND'. It is a mark of quality and goods bearing this seal are easily sold out in Denmark, England and Germany. The principles followed by these dairies are:

- Open membership within the area of operation;
- Members are not required to contribute anything byways of shares;
- Liability of the members is determined in proportion to the milk supplied by them;
- Democratic management;
- Distribution of profits in proportion to the value of milk supplied by the members.

2. *Capital*: The working capital of the dairy raised from the members. The members are paid interest on these deposits. The rate of interest is quite low. The initial capital of the cooperative is raised from a bank and is paid out of the profits
3. *Profits*. In the beginning a fixed rate of profits is allowed on the capital afterwards it is deposited in to the reserve fund and whatever is left, is distributed among the members in proportion to the value of the milk supplied by them.

Factors for the Success of Cooperative Dairies

The success achieved by the cooperative dairies in Denmark can be attributed to the following factors:

- The manufacturing of products close to place of production has been responsible for keeping the cost of production minimum.

- The principle of unlimited liability has made the member to take keen interest in the working of the dairy.
- Owing to the policy of prompt payments made to the members for the milk supplied by them, the members' loyalty is assured.
- The policy of making payment for the milk according to its fat contents ensures the supply of good quality milk.
- The importance attached to proper feeding of the cattle and the system of testing dairy cattle and the breeding of the cattle by the control societies and cattle breading societies respectively has not only led to the improvement of bread of the cattle but has also led to the improvement of the quality of milk.
- The services offered by butter export associations to the local dairies have not brought profits to the members only but to the society as well.
- Production and export of butter under the trade mark 'LURBRAND' has not only led to the standardization of the production of butter but also assured the consumers of supply of good quality butter.
- The use of highly sophisticated machines and specialized techniques for the production of butter has established the reputation of the Danish cooperative dairies on a firm footing.

Difficulties of Adopting Danish Model in India

Cooperative dairies in India have confined their activities only to the collection and sale of milk while those in Denmark have been dealing in the supply of milk and milk products. It does not mean that in India cooperative dairies do not undertake the production and sale of milk products. However, it remains a fact that in India cooperative dairies do not undertake the supply of requirements of the farmers to the extent they do in Denmark. There are a number of reasons for such state of affairs:

- The milk producers are not adventurous and lack initiative;
- Although the number of cattle is many times more in our country as compared to Denmark, the milk yield is comparatively very low. Consequently the question of preparation of milk products like butter, cheese etc.., does not arise;
- The poverty of Indian farmer has also been responsible for the growth of such institutions. The farmers have no staying power. He is illiterate and traditional and therefore any plan formulated for augmenting his prosperity ends in utter failure;
- Since the quality of milk per cattle is very low, the cost of collecting milk from distant places is very high and also untimely; chiefly because the means of transportation are not developed well, and it is highly difficult to contact remote villages especially during rainy seasons;
- It is universally known that the quality of milk cattle in India was very poor and therefore, their milk yield is also very low. Consequently the quality of milk is also poor and the percentage of fat in the milk is so low that standardization of milk or milk products is not possible.

Characteristics Features of the Danish Agricultural Cooperation

The brilliant success achieved by the Danish agricultural cooperative movement has been mainly because the movement is people's movement. It has the support of the entire nation. The rural population in Denmark is homogenous and there is not colour or caste distinction. The cultivators are literate and understand clearly their responsibilities towards the national and village life. The characteristic feature of the movement can be enumerated in brief as under:

- Strong specialization of the societies is one f the most distinctive features of the movement. The farmers do not let the existing societies cope with all the problems and prefer to establish a new society whenever a new problems crops up. He may be a member of many different cooperative societies. This keeps the society in size and leads to functional efficiency.
- Since the farmers are literate they posses a high sense of loyalty.
- A standardization of products and maintenance of high quality have enabled Denmark to retain its export markets. The fear of losing the market has led to prudent management.
- The movement has emanated from the hearts of the people, as an urge for bettering their lot. It is an automatic growth and not the result of the efforts of any external agency. It is entirely independent. The state has neither helped not has ever tried to supervise or control the cooperative societies. This is why the movement has never faced a bad time.
- The technical and scientific advice is always readily available to the farmer from the movement. The faith in the movement is preserved and Zeal for hard work is maintained.
- The unique feature of Denmark's economy is that it is a land of arable farms and hence the production and supply of dairy products is constant and regular. The system of arable farming has provided additional support to the movement.
- Last but not the least important fact about the movement is that the societies have a limited area of operation.

There is no gainsaying the fact that the prosperity of the Danish farmer has been possible only because of the cooperative movement. The movement has covered the entire life of the Danish farmers. The farmer is now not only a cultivator he is also a producer, a manufacturer, a distributor, trader, a banker and an insurer. He does not suffer from inferiority complex. He considers the interest of the community above his own interest. The movement has thus unified the agricultural life of the people in Denmark.

No element of subsidy, regulation, or control from the government or others exists in Denmark. There is no legislation governing the movement, no public registration of the cooperative society, no rules on forms of organization or audit. Surprisingly enough, the self-government of the cooperative has been conducted in such a way as not to give rise to any abuse. This is due to the fact that the individual cooperative societies have been organized with clear cut rule, which are acceptable to the members and are applied reasonably by the boards of the management. Besides an organizational apparatus has been created with joint efforts of all cooperatives, which has helped the society solve problems which cannot be solved individually. This is the reason that the need of state control or supervision was never felt in Denmark.

Main Features of Danish Cooperative Movement

From the foregoing account of the progress of the Danish cooperative movement we can now briefly state the chief characteristics of the movement:

- It is essentially a voluntary movement and has not received any encouragement from the state.
- The members are of strong character; they are devoted and loyal to the movement because they are hard working and sociable, intelligent and educated.
- Specialization and organization of Federations is another secret of its success.
- The management of these institutions is democratic. Democratization has led to an effective quality control; consequently the products have been standardized and export trade has flourished;

- The movement is guided by specialize and technocrats;
- Again, cooperative training has been combined with agriculture as well as general education. Obviously the cooperative movement must flourish under such a favourable movement;
- Another important feature of the Danish cooperative movement is that cooperative organizations have adopted business principles in their true form. They adopt the latest techniques in planning of business and trade, production, marketing, finance, auditing, etc.

Ethiopia can learn a lot from The Danish experience but, under the present circumstances it is impossible to adopt the Danish system of cooperative dairies chiefly because our agriculturist are illiterate, traditional in their outlook and pessimistic in their nature. In Denmark the cooperative movement and the farmers are two inseparables, but in Ethiopia the cooperative organization are considered as stop-gap arrangement or source of temporary relief. The people do not treat cooperatives as their own organization; may be because the movement has been thrust up on them from above.

Cooperative Movement in Japan

The cooperative movement started in Japan in the middle of the 19th century. Cooperative credit organization known as '*koh*' were the first to be established. The basic principle behind the organization of these institutions was that a group of friends would contribute to a savings pool to be used as a loan fund. The members could borrow from this fund in times of need and paycheck gradually by making deposits to the fund. The 'koh' type of credit organization originated during the 14th century. The mutual banks, which are now a powerful and popular type of organization, are based on 'koh' principles.

Agricultural Cooperatives of Japan

The phenomenal rise of Japanese post-war economy can safely be attributed to the hard and systematic work done by these agricultural cooperatives [called JA or JA Group or even JA Movement] in consolidating people, land resources, producing the needed food and providing the needed services to the community.

The JAs are a good example of an integrated framework in the service of the farmers. They deliver multipurpose services and operate as multi-function economic institutions directly responding to the felt-needs of the members. They serve the members at the same time being under the control of the members.

Their services range from the *'Cradle to the Grave'* [This slogan has presently been pushed into the background mainly due to the economic capabilities and capacities already achieved by the agricultural cooperatives. The fact, however, remains alive because the organizational structure and the system still firmly exists and has been integrated in the services provided.

The Japanese agricultural cooperatives stand committed to "3-H Agriculture—Healthy, High Quality and High Technology". The Japanese Agricultural Cooperative Movement had successfully introduced a number of innovations which are of great relevance to the Movements.

Some of the interesting features of the agricultural cooperatives of Japan have been:

- Sustained and progressive amalgamation of cooperatives to make them more economically-viable and service-oriented;
- Farm guidance and better-living services to achieve a high degree of communication with the members and to enrich their economic and social life;
- Protection of interests of farmer-members through mutual insurance, healthcare;
- Carefully planned and well-executed marketing and supply functions through specially-created and cooperative-owned holding companies;

- Production of quality consumer goods and services;
- Implementation of the 'joint-use' concept e.g., joint marketing, joint purchasing, joint-use of capital, joint use of facilities etc.;
- Successfully interacting with the government through a process of policy dialogue and lobbying inside and outside legislature;
- Education and training of farmer-members through a network of cooperative training institutions;
- Ensuring higher economic returns to the farmer members through a process of 'value-addition';
- Encouraging women and youth to form associations to compliment and supplement the work of agricultural cooperatives especially in taking care of and sustaining the interest of the young and the aged in the honoured profession of farming;
- Encouraging the farmer members in controlling pollution to produce and market the healthy, safe, and nourishing agricultural products to safeguard the interests of consumers; and
- Extending technical collaboration and cooperation to the developing Movements.

In the light of the experiences of Japan, potential factors that would influence the operation of cooperatives Ethiopia are:

- Customs of mutual help and assistance in rural areas;
- Introduction of new crops and technology to increase productivity;
- Active participation of women members through women's associations;
- Employment of capable and professional managers;
- Acquisition of operational facilities and linking credit with marketing;
- Guidance and education for improving production technology; and

- The cooperative being a member-centred institution rather than the cooperative being a 'cooperative-centred' institution.

Based on the above factors, some general requisites for an effective operation of an agricultural cooperative could be derived. These include:

- Promoting members' participation—economic and organizational;
- Increasing membership by encouraging non-members, women and young people to join agricultural cooperatives; and
- Promoting the utilization of cooperative services by members.

Success Factors of Agricultural Cooperatives in Japan

Experiences of agricultural cooperatives in Japan and the results of various studies in Japan have identified several factors which are responsible for the success of agricultural cooperatives. Some of them are:

- Cooperatives are member-driven, member-controlled and member-responsive organizations;
- Cooperatives are efficiently managed by experienced, trained and professionally qualified staff under the supervision and control of democratically-elected board of directors;
- Principles of 'accountability' and 'answerability', 'role model', ethical behaviour and good governance are employed;
- Adherence to the 'joint-use' concept e.g., joint marketing, joint purchasing, joint use of capital, joint use of facilities;
- Elected officials [board members including the presidents and auditors] are compensated. [It is assumed that honorary elected officials tend to be more expensive to the organizations. Besides, the era of

honorary elected positions have gone, as not many people have neither the time nor the inclination to serve in such capacities];

- Cooperatives have integrated their operations with the needs of their member households;
- Well-integrated vertical structures of cooperatives exist and these provide support in order to enable the base level cooperatives to effectively and efficiently service their individual members; the federal cooperatives provide advisory services, technical know-how and back-up support services;
- Cooperatives undertake comprehensive programmes for member education in order to facilitate the process of members' participation, members' involvement and empowerment; and for training of staff and members of board of directors;
- Cooperatives undertake value-added operations: choose, assess and employ appropriate but advanced technologies; and forge forward integration in order to gain competitive advantage in the market place;
- Cooperatives establish viable and strong linkages with external research and development/ extension agencies in the field of agriculture and technology;
- Cooperatives strive to become self-reliant, accumulate capital and develop other resources in order to remain free from all external controls and directions; and
- Cooperatives are open, ethical, caring, and socially-aware institutions.

They display social concern in their business operations and in their relations with customers, employees and members, and the community at large.

The Ethics of Mutual Cooperation in Japan

The mutual cooperation among cooperatives is not invented by Japanese cooperatives rather by the needy Rochdale pioneers who coined the term cooperation among cooperatives, which later become the pillar of ICA's principles. The integration of business activities in cooperatives could enhance economy of scale. However, this is only possible if the primary cooperatives are strong. The experiences in the Asian countries show that Cooperative Movements, which have resorted to merger, consolidation and amalgamation at all levels, have become more stable and self-reliant. In some countries, the cooperatives shifted from the three-tier to the two-tier cooperative structure and at the same time they merged and consolidated their primary cooperatives. In other countries, they merged and consolidated at the primary and secondary levels where both receive vertical support from the national level. In this structure, the integrated activities are not overlapping as the primary, secondary and tertiary cooperatives have their own defined role. The problem arises when this discipline is not respected, and when the secondary level cooperatives begin to compete with their own affiliates. Instead of competing with the affiliates, the principle of collaboration and mutual economic benefit should be adopted.

Value-addition Through Agro-processing

It should, however, be noted that value-addition does not take place through undertaking processing activities alone. Marketing plays an important role as well. Marketing of graded, properly packed semi or fully processed products still adds some more value than the marketing of basic material. The JAs have been able to establish 'on-line' contacts with the farmers, farmers' groups, and financing agencies, wholesale markets, major bulk buyers and consumer groups. For that matter, no agricultural cooperative can survive and bring benefits and services to its members if it is unable to market the produce of its members. Members want not only to sell their produce as fast as possible, but also with higher economic returns and take the money home. It thus becomes the responsibility of the cooperative to assist the farmers in not only selling the members' produce but also selling it with advantage.

Cooperatives have, therefore, to be on an alert look out for markets and means of marketing the products of their members. The development of value-added agro-processing. Industry motivates the farmers for improving productivity and further opens up possibilities of industrial development. The basic requirements are: sound marketing, modern technology, quality control and a better flow of information. Based on the integrated agricultural cooperative marketing network, agriculture can work as the biggest safety net in the process of adjustment by softening the rigors of inflation as well as by raising income and employment for weaker sections of the society in the Region.

Cooperatives and Members' Expectations in Japan

The main point is that the members should not run after their cooperatives to provide them with services and facilities—it should be the cooperative which should, on its own, be keen to offer a variety of services and facilities to the members which they need. Member is a radiant factor from which the power of agricultural cooperatives emanates. Member is the key and the main source of economic strength of the cooperative. A member should not feel that he is dependent on the cooperative. He has several other options which may not be as economically attractive for him. It is the cooperative which should be dependent on the member. It is often heard that cooperatives do not do enough for them. For the cooperative, the focus should be on the member and his business potential, rather than on itself.

Farmers need money and that money has to be a reasonably good return for the investments made. To secure returns, two factors are very important: *Value-addition* and *Marketing*. The process of marketing is more difficult than that of production. It requires an intimate knowledge of market trends. It should be scientific and well-organized, otherwise the farmer runs the risk of not getting the full value of his produce and the investment made.

In cases where cooperatives are not able to respond to the marketing needs of the members, middlemen thrive and the farmer-members get sucked into the vicious circle which the cooperatives are supported to break. Provision of post-harvest services, warehousing, and grading, packaging, shipment and market information are the essential links in the chain of marketing.

Cooperatives are often blamed for non-performance mainly due to lack of participation on the part of their members. In agricultural cooperatives the entire business moves around the economic benefits which the members expect from their cooperative.

Farmer members are eager to sell their produce and obtain timely and sufficient funds to increase their produce. Their expectations from the cooperative generally revolve around:

- Guidance, advice and support in matters of farm technology;
- Supply of farm inputs e.g., fertilizers, farm chemicals, farm machines and implements etc.;
- Easy accessibility to the sources of credit for purchase of improved seeds, maintenance of fields, investments in long-term items e.g., tube wells, farm cattle etc.;
- Assistance and advice on environment-related issues e.g., disposal of animal wastes and others;
- Improvement and development of infrastructure e.g., grading centers, packaging facilities, forwarding facilities, plastics and pipes etc. etc.

Farmers on their own individual strengths cannot harness all these services and facilities. They would naturally expect their cooperative to develop such services and provide them to the farmers when needed. Members also expect their cooperative to find suitable marketing avenues, which involve: supply of market information, warehousing, value-addition possibilities by erecting some agro-processing facilities and maintaining some business contacts with wholesale markets and bulk buyers.

These expectations naturally become the responsibilities or tasks to be undertaken by the management leaders of the cooperative, which include the Board and the managers. It then becomes a plan of action for the cooperative. All efforts are then made to implement the plan. If the expectations are not met members get disjointed from the cooperative. Their participation in business and organizational affairs get reduced, which a cooperative can hardly afford. A manager is, thus confronted with several problems e.g., identification of markets, methods and techniques of handling members' produce, ensuring adequate returns to the member-farmers and maintaining their loyalty and relationship with the cooperative. Managers with experience, capacity, capability, tact, clarity of business ethics, and professional competence can overcome such problems.

Lessons from Japan Agricultural Cooperatives

Based on the experiences of agricultural cooperatives at the primary, secondary and national levels in Japan, the following lessons can be derived:

- Government should give more importance and provide greater support to agriculture if agricultural cooperatives are to perform satisfactorily;
- Cooperatives would function well with least government intervention. Discipline and good governance contributes much to the efficient operation of cooperatives;
- Cooperatives should be non-political and self-reliant organizations. Complete trust and confidence is necessary for cooperatives to succeed;
- Cooperatives should be managed in a more business-like manner—these are not social clubs or charity organizations;
- Cooperative's guidance and active participation is valuable in the formulation and execution of farm production plans.

- Knowledge of scientific farming, provision of high quality inputs such as seeds, and mechanization are important factors for enhancing productivity;
- Technological innovations that are pertinent to the changing needs of agriculture and the environment should be promoted;
- Introduction of new technology and methods of production is needed to develop agriculture;
- Cooperatives should provide advice to farmers on crops to plant which earn them higher income. Regular dialogues among farmers, cooperatives and market authorities should be undertaken to resolve problems. For success the farmers' orientation should be on improving productivity and quality;
- Organization should be led and managed by energetic, professional and dynamic persons. Business should be conducted in accordance with modern management principles;
- Elected officials viz., Board members including Presidents and Auditors should be paid. Honorary elected officials tend to be a drain on the resources of the cooperatives; and
- Improved packaging and marketing are important to enhancing the business operations of cooperatives. Agricultural cooperatives could be encouraged to participate as wholesalers in the market and hence, enhance the benefits of their members; and good grading and packaging add to the final price of the product and enable efficient handling and distribution.

These lessons can very well form the basic guidelines for the leadership of agricultural cooperatives elsewhere.

Lessons Relevant to the Developing Agricultural Cooperative Movements

Some of the most recent experiences of the Japanese Agricultural Cooperative Movement would indicate that the agricultural cooperatives have to be run on strong economic lines and direct their total efforts and service at the farmer-members who are the owners of the institutions and users of services. These are discussed briefly below:

1. Creation of a Corporate Identity

With a view to bring unity within the agricultural cooperatives and to highlight the quality of JA products, the Movement adopted a Corporate Identity—JA [representing the Japanese Agricultural Cooperative]. 'JA' is printed on all products which are supplied through the agricultural cooperatives channels. CA 'JA' is recognized as a strong commercial group just like any other CI and the brand is associated with fresh, healthy and good product.

2. The Concept of Cooperative Companies

Since there is a legal limitation on the agricultural cooperatives to carry out business with non-members, the cooperatives have created companies which are wholly owned and controlled by cooperatives. JA-Zen Noh is a case in point. Zen-Noh [the National Federation of Agricultural Cooperatives] is Japan's federation of agricultural cooperatives, one of the largest in the world. Most of the 4.7 million farm households in the country belong to one of Zen-Noh's 1,600 primary level cooperatives. In cooperation with prefecture federations and primary level cooperatives, Zen-Noh serves its member-farmers by purchasing and distributing the materials and equipment for agricultural production and the necessities of daily farm life.

It has created companies and corporations to undertake this business. Another organization, Uni coop Japan is also a company promoted by the agricultural cooperatives to import and distribute a variety of commodities needed by the agricultural cooperatives in the country. With a view to consolidate its presence and power in the market, the JA Zen-Noh is going ahead with the process of amalgamation. The prefectural economic federations are increasingly merging with the national federation.

3. The Concept of 'Joint-Use'

The concept is widely implemented not only in the agricultural cooperative sector but also in other industrial sectors. It overcomes the problems of procurement of funds and harnessing of resources. This concept implies joint purchasing, joint marketing, joint use of capital, and joint use of facilities.

4. Collaboration with Private Enterprises

This concept is based strictly on the principle of pure business. The JAs often use their extra industrial capacities to meet the requirements of other enterprises. Some of the JAs have been filling bottles for juice makers, coffee processors and even for popular brand companies.

5. The Concept of One-Window Service

It is generally observed that the office a primary cooperative is alike a cooperative complex where the members transact their business at one place. The JA usually houses the bank, insurance service, travel agency, farm distribution centre, farm guidance services etc.

6. Amalgamation of Agricultural Cooperatives

The main aim is to strengthen the JA group and to make the cooperatives economically viable. There is an 'amalgamation' trend in the country—banks, telecommunication companies, automobile companies and other business houses are merging together to enhance and consolidate their economic strength.

JAs have been following this programme with the following objectives:

- Making the farming operations viable;
- making the cooperatives strong and viable; and
- Facing the market competitions bravely through a strong collective bargaining power.

The process has been slow and painful. Some of the problems faced by cooperatives in the process of amalgamation have been:

- *Division of assets and liabilities*;
- Placement of personnel;
- Difficulties in arriving at consensus; and
- Egoistic attitudes of local leaders.

The process is based on consensus and with the agreement of all the members. Government directives or instructions have no place in the process. While there are several good merits of the process, several demerits have also been cited.

Some of the drawbacks of the process of amalgamation have been stated as:

- Cooperatives will become too large to manage;
- Cooperatives will lose contacts with the members;
- Members will feel distanced;
- Bureaucratic tendencies will develop;
- Leaders due to their power and wide area of influence and business operations will get involved in local politics or may get involved in party politics;
- Failure of a large cooperative will result into huge economic losses, etc.

Some of the amalgamated cooperatives have, however, shown good results.

7. Farm Guidance Activities

This concept is not only to provide technical information to the farmers on cultivation of various crops but also to assist their farmer to increase their income. The farm guidance activity revolves around the total economic business of the farmer as well as of the cooperative. The farmer is guided on technical and economic aspects of particular crops e.g., higher income can be derived by taking up floriculture instead of rice, or cultivation of a special variety of rice, or a special kind of tomatoes, and by the application of methods of cultivation e.g., hydroponics cultivation etc. The main aim of this service is to enhance the income. Without provision of this service, the JA is not called as a multipurpose cooperative. Farm guidance is the key to the success and strength of the business of the JA. The service is linked with farm planning, provision of farm inputs and other supplies, and marketing of the ultimate product. Farm Guidance advisors are now targeting the commodity groups/producers group in order to increase their production and business.

8. Regional Agricultural Promotion Planning [RAPP]

In the production of food the JAs are the basic units. Each farmer produces a production plan; the JA collates these plans and produces a comprehensive regional plan. The municipal administration and prefectural governments and the national government develop their respective plans, and support the basic farmers with inputs, technical advice, equipment and recognition. The RAPP not only produces a comprehensive agricultural promotion plan, but also summarizes a few other things e.g., the quantity and quality of rice, barley, corn, fruits and vegetables, the approximate requirements of fertilizers, farm chemicals, farm implements etc. This data enables the JAs to prepare the supplies and timing of these supplies.

9. One-Village-One Product Concept

The JAs have supported the members to specialize in their respective products. Members are encouraged to improve upon the product. The cooperatives provide all the needed technical and promotional support. These village products eventually become the specialized products of the respective prefectures. Some of the examples are: Nagano's Fuji oranges, Kyoho Grapes, are the result of the application of this concept.

10. Diversification of Agricultural Practices

JAs are not restricting themselves to produce rice and vegetables alone. They have taken up other activities e.g., herbs garden, green tourism promoted by the JA-Sawada in Gumma prefecture. The members of this cooperative decided to pool their lands to create a very large herbs garden which has assumed importance for green tourism in the country.

11. Farm Management Centres

These technical units are created to provide all services and equipment related to farming to the farmer-members. They provide technical information on the equipment, their use, and maintenance. Farmers find it very convenient to obtain all their supplies and the required technical information and guidance from one single point.

12. Producer-Consumer Contact Markets

These are often called 'Morning Markets'. The JA provides space to farmer-members to sell their products [fruits, vegetables, flowers, potted plants etc.] directly to the consumers without going through the process of middleman or local markets. These are usually located in one corner of the JA or its 'A-Coop' Store. The idea is also to give a chance to the busy citizen/consumer to come in direct contact with the producer—the farmer, thereby creating a kind of goodwill for the farming community and the JA.

13. The Concept of Double-Check in Accounts

Business transactions are double-checked to avoid any error or mishandling.

14. The Concept of Savings with the Cooperative

Members are encouraged to deposit their savings with their cooperatives. This helps capital formation thus overcoming the shortage of funds.

15. Chemical-free Food/Agriculture

In effect, cooperatives stand for the betterment of the community in which the propagation of healthy, safe environment is a base. The concept is to meet the growing demand for "Fresh, Healthy, Safe and Chemical-free Food".

Farmers are advised to gradually increase the use of bio-fertilizer and avoid use of farm chemicals. Farmers who are engaged in dairying, hog-raising and poultry business are often confronted with the problem of disposal of wastes. These are natural bio-fertilizers which could enhance the quality and safety of farm products. Under this concept the farmers are entering into purchase and sale agreements with each other, thereby, increasing the economic transactions and producing the safe and chemical-free products.

16. Women's Associations

These are supporting the JA in many ways. These are informal groups but the structure is parallel to the JA structure—from the basic step to the national level. These associations supplement and compliment the social and economic activities of the JA besides enriching the social aspects at the family level. They also contribute significantly in the operations of JA's 'A-Coops' — large size departmental stores run by the primary cooperatives. In fact, these associations try to promote the business activities of JAs.

17. Ethics and Good Governance in Agricultural Cooperatives

By tradition the Japanese society respects the rule of law. The JA Board is responsible for the business operations, and in the event of economic losses, all the members are obliged to make good such losses. The elected officials e.g., board members and auditors are paid officials and their term of office is fixed. Decision-making and implementation process is based on the principles of 'accountability' and 'answerability'. There is a good and harmonious relationship between the chief executive and the Board. The Chief Executive is the Managing Director of the JA [who sits on the Board and is naturally well-informed of the trend of discussion and the decisions taken]. There are good ethics within JAs and everyone in power in the organization—small or big—takes care of the members. Care for the community is another important factor for the success of JAs. These are: taking care of the aged through welfare homes and supply of their food and household requirements, medical facilities, establishment of child nurseries etc. These services are instituted because these are the needs of the community and the cooperatives have not to seek the permission of the government or any other authority to initiate such facilities and services except for obtaining the approval of their members. The JAs have good working relationship with the local governmental authorities and other non-governmental organizations.

18. Open Membership

The JAs have opened their doors to farmers and non-farmers in the form of Full Members and Associate Members. In the provision of services to both the categories there are no restrictions—the only difference is the right to vote. Associate members are not qualified to vote. Since the cooperatives are community/village based, it is the duty of the cooperative to serve all the members of the community. Also the inclusion of Associate Members helps increase the capital base and business operations of the JAs. In many countries, agricultural cooperatives do not serve the non-members and do not have the practice of formally accepting non-members as associate members.

Problems Faced by the JAs

The present stage of development of the Japanese agricultural cooperatives is the result of 100 years of experimentation, innovations and improvements. These successes are not devoid of impediments. Some of the problems encountered by the JAs have been identified as follows:

These are some of the problems that were barrier to the growth of Japanese Agricultural cooperatives;

- Lack of ability for management and ability of planning and development;

- Lack of leaders' management ability;
- Lack of products development ability;
- Inadequate system of national/regional level research institutions;
- Insufficient study and research of consumers' needs and trends of market;
- Failure to establish brand names;
- Lack of development of distribution channels;
- Lack of understanding between processed foods and perishable foods;
- Inadequate linkages with the public information, events planning;
- Insufficient public relations in rural areas;
- Shortage of raw material faced when enlarging the business scale;
- No linkages with Regional Agriculture Promotion Plan [RAPP];
- Raw materials are expensive;
- Operations are based on season;
- Shortage of assorting commodities;
- JA factories tend to operate independently;
- No establishment of cooperation system with members for management.

Agricultural cooperatives provide all types of economic and social services to their members. They demand effective, enlightened and skilled leaders. They need initiatives and services to sustain the interests of their members through the provision of education, training, guidance, extension and farm inputs, farm credit and marketing opportunities. They have to be run on democratic lines. They operate within the framework of national guidelines, but at the same time fulfill the demands of domestic and international markets. Agricultural cooperatives, to be effective and acceptable, must take the members' views and their felt-needs into consideration. An active communication has to be established and sustained between the management and the members, and between the leadership and the management. Agricultural cooperatives have no reason to be afraid of the open market pressures if their members remain united and respond to the needs of the market. The unity of members is the strength of the cooperative business.

The pillars of strength of the Japanese agricultural cooperatives consist of, among others:

- amalgamation of primary cooperatives; restructuring of JA organization from three-tiers to two-tiers to generate greater efficiency in management and provision of services;
- farm guidance to ensure higher productivity with due consideration for environment;
- better-living activities in association with the women's associations;
- continuous policy dialogue with the government; acceptance and application of farm technology; and
- dissemination of information and technology among farmers in Japan and abroad.

Self-learning Activity

Try to answer the following questions on your own.

1. Write short notes on: Danish milk/dairy cooperatives?
2. What do you understand about consumer cooperation in UK?
3. Give an account of Indian cooperative movement?
4. What are the lessons that can be learnt from Japanese cooperative movement?
5. Write a note on American cooperative movement.

Summary

- This chapter has dovetailed the cooperative movement in various countries. Continent wise analysis has been made to have full idea about cooperative movement in the world.
- Detailed picture has been given for some countries where a certain type of cooperative movement is familiar.

African Cooperative Movement

The development of the productive forces and the relations of production of the new sovereign states in Africa is taking place at a time of socialist and national liberation revolutions, a time characterized mostly as a transition from capitalism to socialism on a world wide scale. The extension and development of the national liberation revolutions in Africa inevitably involves these countries in a search for ways and forms for establishing new social relations that meet the interests of the broad working population and facilitate the revival of their economies.

The objective need to establish a new type of economic and social relations in the young independent states and the search for ways and forms for improving these necessitate a theoretical study of the socio-economic events taking place there and, in particular, revelation and assessment of the role of cooperatives in economic and social affairs, and determination of their future prospects. Many changes have occurred in recent years in the economies, political and social relations of the developing countries. Major qualitative and quantitative ones have taken place in the cooperative movement: its role has increased in connection with the further progress of agrarian reforms and cooperatives have gained markedly in strength in the organisational sense.

Their importance has risen. In many countries cooperatives do not remain passive while the choice is made of either a capitalist or a socialist course of development. Of particular importance is the practice of cooperatives organizing collective methods for carrying out individual type of work in agriculture, as well as in construction and manufacturing industry.

The broad scope of the cooperative movement in the African countries and its contribution to the break-up of old forms of production relations and the establishment of new ones urgently demands scientific investigation of the processes taking place within the cooperative movement in the best ways of exerting a purposeful impact on many economic and social factors. In some state, cooperatives have been used quite successfully to stimulate the development of productive forces and the creation of a national economy independent of foreign capital. As evidenced by many, many examples, government bodies almost everywhere assign cooperatives an important place in the fulfillment of economic, social and political tasks. The cooperative movement in the new sovereign state is a major social force. There were about 20 million in Africa. Cooperatives unite a large number of working people in Algeria, Ghana, Nigeria, Tanzania, Ethiopia and other states. In many countries of Africa, the working people do not yet have their own political parties, with the result that their joining together in cooperatives acquires considerable political significance. Most members of cooperatives in developing countries come from the most numerous part of the population—the toiling peasantry. Consequently, cooperatives functioning among the peasantry also contribute substantially to solving these vitally important economic problems. The cooperative movement is now one of the main factors in the socio-political sphere of the new sovereign states. There is a real opportunity to make use of cooperatives, being the most mass-scale organizations of the peasantry, for establishing a union between industrial workers and agricultural labourers.

And yet the cases when contacts have been established between industrial workers and the members of agricultural cooperatives in Algeria, Tanzania, Ethiopia and some other countries indicate a real opportunity for using the cooperative movement to influence the setting and attainment of common goals and tasks of workers and peasants in their struggle for social progress. The programme documents and resolutions of many communist and workers' parties focus particularly on the importance of and need for using the cooperative movement as one of the chief instruments for uniting the workers and peasants. Only active participation by the working people in the struggle for social progress made possible a solution to the extremely complex economic and social problems that have arisen in the path of the new sovereign states.

The cooperative movement in the countries of Africa has many specific features ensuring from the protracted colonial dependence of these countries, their economic and social backwardness, and also their geographical conditions, which leave an imprint on the nature of production activities and the way of life of the African people. The activities of the first cooperatives, which arose in a number of countries before they had gained independence, were, therefore, totally dependent on the exogenous authorities. The legacy of the colonial past could not but affect the cooperative movement even once the colonies had gained political independence. The retention of outdated forms of cooperative management, inactivity on the part of rank-and-file members in deciding economic and administrative issues, an acute shortage of money, a lack of qualified experts, the continuing influence exerted on cooperatives by caste and other traditions, tribal chiefs, tribal relations, and so on, all have a marked effect on the work of cooperatives in the countries of Africa.

Yet there are general laws of development inherent in the cooperative movement. The formation of the simplest types of cooperative took place initially only in the sphere of exchange. Cooperatives are now beginning to exert an increasing influence on people's production activities, and the goals and nature of the work of cooperatives are changing. In the developing countries particularly in African countries, especially those with a socialist orientation, cooperatives are used by the national-democratic forces as an instrument in the anti-imperialist and anti-feudal struggle for establishing a new type of production relations excluding oppression and exploitation.

The Status of Cooperatives in Africa

In a number of African countries, the cooperative movement began to emerge at the beginning of this century, but the objective conditions for the broad development of cooperation were lacking at that time, since in most of these countries commodity-money relations were only very slightly developed and the economic and social life of society was entirely in the hands of the colonialists. Under colonial dependence, the ideas of the cooperative movement infiltrated only slowly into the countries of Africa. The people were skeptical about them, since they often came from the colonial authorities.

A certain role was played in the creation of the first cooperatives in the colonies by cooperative unions in the metropolitan countries, which tried to establish there the same sort of cooperatives as their own in terms of structural principles. These cooperatives spread the ideas of class cooperation among the rural population. A substantial influence was exerted on the spread of the ideas of the cooperative movement by the activities of the ICA, which was set up in 1895. The ICA widely distributed literature on the cooperative movement and its importance, principles in various countries and invited cooperators from everywhere to their meetings and seminars. At first, the ICA served the interests of the colonial powers; it praised their activities in the colonies, preached the need to maintain and increase the private property of people belonging to cooperative organizations, thereby striving to isolate the cooperative movement from the impact of advanced ideas and views.

In the colonies, the cooperative movement could not develop widely: cooperatives were set up primarily among representatives of the metropolitan countries and served their interests. The colonial authorities kept the cooperatives under constant strict control. Cooperatives could only be set up and function on the basis of laws issued by the colonizers. Cooperatives organized without the knowledge of the colonial administration did not usually last long, owing to material difficulties, a lack of qualified personnel, or instructions issued by the colonial authorities that they be dissolved. Cooperation took place primarily among people connected with the production of export crops and only rarely among producers of agricultural produce for domestic consumption.

The following table depicts the formation of first cooperatives in Africa:

Table 8.1: Formation of first cooperatives in Africa

Africa	Year of formation
1	2
Egypt	1908
Kenya	1908
Botswana	1910
Mauritius	1913
Uganda	1913
Zambia	1914
Libya	1915
Senegal	1916
Burundi	1921

(Contd...)

1	2
Morocco	1922
Algeria	1923
Zaire	1924
Tanzania	1925
Congo	1926
Ghana	1928
Nigeria	1928
Sudan	1930
Togo	1931
Sierra Leone	1936
Madagascar	1939
Guinea	1940
Ethiopia	***1945***
Dahomey (Benin)	1947
Somalia	1950
Chad	1955
Rwanda	1956
Mali	1960

Note: Adopted from The Cooperative Movement in Asia and Africa by V. Maslennikov, 1983.

Cooperative Movement in Africa – After the Liberation

In the late 1940's, as a result of the upsurge of the national liberation struggle waged by the people of the colonies, and the decisive support they received from the countries of the socialist community, the colonial system of imperialism began rapidly to collapse. As the African countries gained their independence, the role of cooperatives increased noticeably in importance. In a number of countries they became an organizational force capable of influencing both economic and social processes.

During this period, State control of the economy in many countries was geared to strengthening commodity-money relations in economic affairs, increasing the production of agricultural and industrial output, creating the infrastructure and organizing the training of skilled local personnel. In a number of states, great hopes were laid on the cooperatives in fulfilling these tasks, particular attention being focussed on the activities of cooperatives among the peasantry. In Algeria, Ethiopia and other countries, government bodies began to provide cooperatives with land on privileged conditions, and to assist them in building facilities essential for their activities. These measures speeded up the rise in the number of cooperative members. Not in all countries, however, was the plans outlined for the development of the cooperative movement and an increase in its role in socio-economic affairs fulfilled successfully there being a number of reasons for this.

There were times when one and the same cooperative came under different departments, which could not manage them effectively owing to their limited influence over the various aspects of the economic and social functions of the cooperative movement. The absence of a single management centre for the cooperative movement constituted a substantial brake on its further development in some countries. The situation was exacerbated by the newly liberated countries' lack of money for giving the cooperatives the necessary economic assistance. The low general education level of the masses of the working people and their lack of managerial experience also left their mark. The outcome was that the necessary control on the part of the rank-and-file members could not be recognized in the cooperatives, and the government supervision over the activities also often failed to yield expected results. In addition, a negative impact was exerted on the development of cooperatives by the foreign market. The number of cooperatives was only increased in these countries but there is no remarkable qualitative growth found in these countries.

The development of the cooperative movement is greatly affected by the social changes taking place in the liberated states, and the specifics of the economy, traditions and customs of each given country. The development of cooperative movement and the increase in its influence on the working masses are convincing evidence of its major political and social role. At the same time, experience has shown that, unless the working masses are drawn into the cooperative movement on a wide scale and there is sound management, no socio-economic changes can be achieved.

Cooperative Development Policies in Africa

Sound cooperative development is directly influenced by the cooperative development policy of the government and of other cooperative promotion institutions. It is one of the most important factors determining the creation of a favourable climate for cooperative development since it lays down the framework within which cooperative development activities take place. It gives cooperative promotion a particular direction which can be favourable or unfavourable for cooperative development. In the following, this aspect of cooperative development policy in African countries is analysed with regard to its present situation, the problems associated with it and measures for improvement in the cooperative development policies.

The Situation of Cooperative Development Policy

One of the most important factors responsible for sound cooperative development is the existence of a consistent, realistic and well-planned, long-term cooperative development policy of the government. A good example of such policy statement is the Sessional Paper No. 8 of 1970 of Kenya. The Gaborone Conference emphasized the need for such a policy in each country and as a result steps have been undertaken in many African countries to formulate policy statements, have them approved in Parliament and to integrate such policies in the national development plans. Progress has been very diverse in various countries, as may be seen from the following examples:

In Bostwana, the government policy on cooperatives has been clear although there was a felt need to include a specific policy statement on cooperative development in the country's national development plan. As a result, a policy statement on cooperative development was drafted and submitted to the government in the late 1986 for its approval and notification.

In Kenya, cooperatives have been accorded an important role in the implementation of the government's development policy as laid down in the Sessional Paper No. 10 of 1965 on "African Socialism and its Application to Planning in Kenya". Further, the specific policy on cooperative development has been laid down in the Sessional Paper No.8 of 1970 and No. 14 of 1975 on Cooperative Development Policy. However, the swift changes within the cooperative movement in the last few years have made this Sessional Paper obsolete and created a need for its reviewal.

In Lesotho, the government's commitment to the promotion of viable socio-economic people's organizations, which include cooperatives, has been emphasized at various occasions. However, there is still a dire need for a clear national policy statement on cooperative development and legislation, which is lacking so far and which could contribute to the development of a viable and autonomous cooperative movement if implemented effectively.

The cooperative development policy of Mauritius follows the national objectives of agricultural diversification, industrialization and employment creation. The government has identified a number of problem areas which have to be tackled in the future such as the improvement of audit and supervision, the diversification of cooperatives into industrial areas, education and training of members and employees, the participation of women and youth in cooperatives, the promotion of cooperative research and cooperative trade and the financial autonomy of the cooperative movement.

In the 1980's the cooperative development policy of Tanzania could be derived from a variety of declarations and guidelines concerning cooperatives, although no single, comprehensive policy statement on cooperative development existed. Among the sources which throw light on the government policy on cooperatives were the African Declaration of 1967, which still forms the basis of the socio-economic development in Tanzania and is geared towards promoting socialism and self-reliance through cooperatives. The party directive on production-oriented cooperatives of 1985 formed a further base for cooperative development in the country. The directive summarizes the various policies, decisions and directives of the party and the government since the Arusha Declaration and strives for the promotion of production-oriented cooperatives.

Zimbabwe has laid great emphasis on having a cooperative development policy for the country. A cooperative policy paper was approved by the government in 1983. A new cooperative development policy paper has been issued together with the enactment of the new cooperative law in 1990. The establishment of a national cooperative training institution and of a cooperative bank has been envisaged in the policy paper as well. Cooperative development plans are an integral part of the national development plan and the ministry's policy on cooperative development is integrated into the national policies of social and economic development. The attitude of the State in Zimbabwe towards cooperative development is hence positive. The State has been the driving force behind the development and expansion of the cooperative movement after independence.

In Guinea, a new cooperative development strategy has been introduced since 1984 which does not differ very much from the policies pursued before 1984. Administrative structures have been decentralized and a cooperative promotion institution of the State has been established, namely the Service National d'Assistance Technique aux Cooperatives (SNATC).

In Tunisia, at the beginning of the decade 1960-70 the political party which took over the government proposed a program for the cooperativisation of the country. In short, it was an utopian and ill-conceived project which ten years later ended in disaster. In Madagascar, the economic development programme conceived and launched in 1964 by the government of the First Republic proclaimed that a cooperative is at the same time one of the means and one of the fundamental objectives of development. The basic law of 1964 laid down in more detail in section 31 that cooperative organizations and in particular the buying and selling stations have to participate in the execution of this plan. This was an unrealistic ambition which could not be implemented in view of the prevailing situation.

In Burundi, the Party Union Pour le Progress National (UPRONA) as well as the government planned a general policy in favour of using cooperatives for achieving development goals. The Central Committee of the party devoted a good deal of its work at its second session in July 1985 to the programme of cooperativisation. The IV Economic and Social Development Plan for the period 1983-1987 devoted several pages to cooperatives.

In Ethiopia, the history of the cooperative movement dovetails the policy of cooperative development during three regimes, viz., Imperial, Derg and present FDRE government. During Imperial period and Derg regime cooperatives were organized as a government policy, say a target approach was followed. During the present FDRE period some policy reforms have been made and cooperatives are organized for the development. Now slowly the cooperative movement with new Cooperative Proclamation No.147/1998 is flourishing in the country.

To sum up, it can be stated that irrespective of which power laid down the national policy on cooperative development, this policy was always basically motivated by political problems and goals and was not devised to create favourable climate for cooperatives. Political parties and governments wanted to take over the existing cooperative structure especially in the rural areas, in order to have a better control of the population and to use them for carrying out tasks planned from above. These policies were utopian, ambitious and neither in consonance with the existing realities and needs nor with the means at their disposal. The people concerned were not given the chance to participate in the elaboration of these national programmes.

Weakness and Problems of Cooperative Development Policy

The role of governments in cooperative development and the relationship between the State and cooperatives are two important factors in the African context. It has been seen that a great majority of African governments have recognized cooperatives as instruments for socio-economic development. They used top-down approach of initiating and promoting cooperatives hence continuing with a readily available model which existed from colonial times. The relationship between State and cooperatives over the decades have changed and vary from country to country in Africa. However, in spite of the differences, the intervention of the State in the cooperative movement has generally increased over the years.

Official attitudes towards cooperatives can be mani-fold. The State might be hostile to cooperatives as was the case in countries like Ghana in 1960 and Tanzania in 1975 where cooperatives were dismantled overnight and restructured. Secondly, the State might be neutral or indifferent to cooperatives and show no interest in them except for providing legal framework. This is now the case in Senegal and Cameroon under their new development policies. Thirdly, the State might have a top-down approach to cooperatives whereby it participates in the organization, management, supervision and control of the cooperatives using them to siphon off their surplus earnings but also taking charge of their losses and, if necessary, keeping them alive artificially. Finally, the State might have a benevolent approach to cooperative development whereby it creates a favourable climate for the development of cooperatives, provides them assistance and incentives without infringing in the affairs of the cooperatives.

The experiences in the African countries have shown that the most common patterns of the relationship between the State and cooperatives seem to be either of massive State paternalism and control or a hostile approach to cooperatives. Cooperatives have lost their self-help character and members see themselves as suppliers to a para-statal organization. This is the result of violation of cooperative values and principles. Since membership was made compulsory, surpluses were extracted through marketing boards and government officers intervened in the day-to-day affairs of cooperatives.

In most countries there seems to be confusion as to what direction cooperative development should take and how to go about achieving this goal. One notices great contradiction in the plans and activities of the State with regard to cooperative development.

A further problem concerning cooperative development policy seems to be the lack of continuity in many countries. Frequent and sudden changes in policy have wide-ranging negative effects on cooperative development as was the case in Tanzania and Ghana. This includes the frequent changes of Ministries responsible for cooperatives and changes of leading officials of the civil service from one post to another. Many cooperative development policies in African countries have turned out to be unrealistic. As a result there are large discrepancies between the officially declared policy and its implementation.

Measures for improving Cooperative Development Policies

One of the basic ingredients for the creation of a conducive climate for cooperative development is to have an effective cooperative development policy and implement it successfully. However, before any development policy for cooperatives is formed, one has to be clear about the concept and objectives of cooperative development. This would mean that the State has to take a clear decision whether it wants to follow the concept of State-sponsored cooperation whereby the cooperative should finally become self-reliant institutions or whether it wants to follow the concept of State-controlled cooperatives, where the cooperatives are used as instruments to fulfill its development goals by implementing development programmes of the State. This discrepancy between proclaimed policy and policy implementation needs to be removed and a well-planned strategy of either State-sponsored or autonomous cooperation needs to be implemented.

A proper concept can only be conceived by the State with the participation of the cooperative movement and the NGOs concerned. The results of such a participatory process should then be coined an official policy for the development of cooperatives and other SHOs. The formulation of such a policy is frequently a process of political bargaining, of coordination and of harmonization of conflicting interests and often ends up in a compromise. However, it is important to find a consensus and lay down the policy in a policy statement. Such a statement has to be:

1. Clear, ie., avoid the ambiguity of combining State-sponsorship of SHOs with State intervention and State-control;
2. Consistent, ie., follow a logical pattern in which all components of the program of State-sponsorship fit together;
3. Realistic, ie., be based on solid research and knowledge of facts, taking full account of present possibilities and constraints and future probable development, especially with regard to the speed of socio-economic change, the scope of self-help activities, the target population and available resources for self-help promotion; and

4. Officially pronounced, ie., be published in form of white paper or a statement of objects and reasons of the cooperative law.

Any constructive policy statement on the development of cooperatives should highlight the government's role and intention to promote cooperatives and how it intends doing so, a clear description of the role which cooperatives and other SHOs are to play in the economic system of the country. Cooperative development policy has to be continuous and long-term and should be laid down in a policy paper. However, the implementation should be subject to periodical reviews so as to be able to accommodate new trends which may occur as a result of the development of the country.

The most important step, however, is to have seriously committed government which has sincere intentions of promoting cooperatives without controlling them. The de-officialisation cannot be achieved simply by making an official statement to this effect. It is necessary to clearly limit the function of the cooperative department officers. Government officers should withdraw totally from interfering in the management affairs of cooperatives at all levels. Further, cooperative development policies need to be integrated at all levels of development planning. This implies that cooperatives must be given a voice in planning national development programs, including measures for the promotion of cooperative development in sectoral programs. Cooperatives should be represented in the policy making and programme reviewing organs of the government.

At the regional and international level there are a number of policy statements and recommendations. Perhaps the most important of these is the ILO Recommendation No. 127 which has assumed a position of being the basis for discussion on cooperative policies in developing countries today. The recommendation outlines in a concise form the basic ingredients of a national cooperative policy, the methods to be adopted and the measures to be taken to implement these policies.

Besides the initiatives of the ILO, the resolution taken at the series of Ministerial Conferences of East, Central and Southern African countries organized by the ICA (in Gaborone 1984, Lusaka 1987, and Nairobi 1990) also mark a progress in formulating cooperative policies in Africa. The conferences are trend setters and encouraging factors in the process of creating a favourable climate and conditions for cooperative development.

Cooperative Legislation

Most of the African countries have experienced decades of colonial rule. One of the results of this period of foreign domination is the existence of parallel systems of original local norms and values and value systems imported from and imposed by the former colonial powers. Such dualism of value system and structures exists in the field of law as well as other fields of life. In most of the African countries there are widely spread informal organizations based on local custom and rules of unwritten customary law working side-by-side with officially recognized, registered cooperative and pre-cooperative societies operating under modern, ie., imported cooperative legislation. The colonial origin of modern cooperative law and the fact that many of the provisions of this modern cooperative legislation—although following internationally recognized cooperative principles —are alien to the majority of the people in developing countries and sometimes run counter the prevailing traditional systems of norms and values, are among the root causes for the problems encountered by promoters of cooperative development in Africa up until today.

The cooperative legislation in the 22 countries covered by a report can be subdivided by their origin into three categories:

1. Countries following the classical British-Indian Pattern of Cooperation: Botswana, Egypt, The Ghana, Lesatho, Mauritius, Nigeria, Tanzania and Zimbabwe;

2. Countries following the French Model of State-controlled Cooperatives: Algeria, Burkina Faso, Cameroon, Chad, Cote d'Ivoire, Guinea, Madagascar, Mali, Niger, Senegal, Togo and Tunisia; and
3. Burundi as a former Belgian dependency.

Out of these countries, six tried to develop their own cooperative development policy and legislation following socialist models for a shorter or longer period of time, replacing one imported model by another, namely Algeria, Guinea, Madagascar, Mali, Tanzania and Tunisia. But except for Algeria and Tunisia, they returned to their original system with some modification. Ten of these have developed special legal provisions for pre-cooperative forms of organizations. Burkina Faso (Village Groups 1983), Cameroon (Common interst Groups 1992), Cote d'Ivoire (Groupements a vocation cooperative 1966), Guinea (Groupements Villageois ou de quartier 1985), Madagascar (fokonolona), Mali (tons villageois), Niger (groupements mutualistes villageois 1978), Senegal (associations d'interet rural 1960-83), Tanzania (Provisionally registered cooperatives 1968 and villages and Ujamaa villages 1975-1982), Zimbabwe (provisionally registered pre-cooperatives 1990).

The two models still strongly influence the legislation governing cooperative societies in most of the African countries. Apart from radical changes, replacing colonial models with socialist structures, the innovative force of law-making in the field of cooperative legislation has been rather limited.

The Classical British-Indian Pattern of Cooperation

Cooperative legislation in the African countries having experienced British colonial rule was almost uniform at the time when these countries reached independence. All these countries used cooperative legislation based on the classical British-Indian pattern of cooperation. In a nutshell, the ideas underlying this model are as follows:

- The objective of government is to encourage the development of self-reliant economically viable cooperatives;
- For an initial period, the government sponsors this development by offering guidelines, advice and supervision, carried out by a specialized government agency;
- The policy of government is to hand over its promotional functions to cooperative support structures as soon as possible, limiting its role to skeleton functions like registration, cancellation of registration and normative control.

During 1930's the Model Cooperative Societies Ordinance was applied without major changes by the British dependencies which had not already introduced this type of cooperative law. In recent years, efforts have been undertaken in some countries to correct the shortcomings of this legislation. The central assumptions on which the entire concept is based, are not respected in the laws and in their application, namely that government influence on cooperatives is strictly temporary, that it only serves to make cooperatives self-reliant as soon as possible and that government shall phase out as soon as the cooperatives are strong enough to look after their own affairs.

The French Model

During colonial times the French colonial government introduced a type of semi-public provident society, the SIP in what was then called Afrique occidental francais (AOF) (French West Africa), established by administrative circulars in 1902 and 1909 with bylaws to be approved by the governer and under the control of the district officer. The Africans saw SIPs/socialist africaine de prevoyance—SAPs as extensions of the colonial government.

After the Second World War, SIPs/SAPs continued to operate, but parallel to them the liberal French cooperative legislation of 1947 was declared applicable in the overseas territories. In 1955, the direct application of the French cooperative law in the French dependencies was repealed and a decree governing the legal status of cooperatives in French overseas territories came into force. During the years 1977-83 a new legislation for village groups and cooperative societies was developed in a process of participative law-making. This was revised again in 1990. Still some countries opted for models of cooperative legislation following socialist patterns.

New Trends in Cooperative Law of the African Countries

When analyzing the recent development of cooperative law in the African countries, several new trends emerge in policy statements and revisions of cooperative legislation, namely the recognition of cooperatives as private SHOs of their members, a pluralism of forms of SHOs, a rethinking of the role of government in cooperative development, improvement of the external conditions for cooperative development in the economic sphere, and participative law-making.

Recognition of cooperatives as private SHOs of their members: For decades cooperatives in Africa were treated by policy-makers, development planners and foreign donors as if they were development tools which governments could use to implement their programs and to exercise control mainly over the production of agricultural cash crops for export markets. It has become inevitable to allow citizens to form genuine SHOs financed and controlled by their members and operating in their members' interest. This has, for instance, been declared at the First African Ministerial Cooperative Conference in Gaborone, Botswana in 1984, where it was stated that governments should be prepared to release those income-generating activities presently being run by parastatal bodies to be undertaken by cooperatives so as to help them in attaining self-reliance and that governments were willing to help cooperatives attain increased strength and capability.

Pluralism of forms: During colonial regimes and in many African countries up until very recently, State controlled registered cooperative societies were the only officially recognized form of organizations. In due course people wanted to have their self-help organizations based on the cooperative principles and values. Apart from the legal forms of simple SHOs in the Feench speaking countries, various kinds of associations, groups, societies and clubs are formed as alternatives or preliminary stages of registered cooperative societies and these alternatives developed as a means to bypass rigid cooperative structures will lose some of their attractions.

Rethinking of the role of government in cooperative development: Structural adjustment programmes are forcing governments to reduce their involvement in economic affairs, to deregulate and liberalize the markets and to give more room and responsibility to private initiative. This means the role of government in cooperative development should be reconsidered with a trend to limit government's control over the cooperatives. Government's role in promoting cooperatives will concentrate on creating favourable conditions for private business organizations including cooperatives and offering education, training and consultancy services to those who seek these services.

Improving the external conditions for cooperative development in the economic sphere: Instead of promoting cooperatives directly by grants, soft loans, subsidies and tax exemptions which tend to make them dependent on donors and serve as justification for government control, cooperatives have to be allowed access to income-generating activities so as to enable them to build up their own capital base and to become truly independent. The proceedings of the First African Ministerial Cooperative Conference in Gaborone contain the recommendations on these lines for improving the external conditions for cooperative development.

Participative law-making: In some of the African countries, a new method of participative law-making has been applied which gives cooperatives and their elected representatives a chance to express their views already at an early stage of the process of law making and which emphasizes the free flow of information at all stages of the process of law making relevant reports and drafts available to all interested parties and by having them discussed in workshops, seminars and conferences at all levels.

Causes for Failure of Cooperatives in African Countries

According to Manzi Bakaramutsa of Zaire (1982), causes for failure of cooperatives in African countries are as follows:

Their origins under colonial rule as agencies of cash crop production for export, their continuation under bureaucratic control after independence, the incorporation and actual exploitation of cooperatives by state and parastatal enterprises. But to these he adds some secondary causes of failure, which will need to be noted if independent cooperative associations are to be successfully revived. These include misappropriation of funds, where clan pressure no longer operates, inadequate accounting systems, lack of training and even illiteracy among cooperative members, which leads them to hand over responsibility to managers without democratic accountability.

According to World Bank Report (World Bank Discussion Paper Number 121, 1994) the causes for failure of cooperatives in Sub-Saharan Africa were as follows:

High operative costs, low margins, low turnovers, narrow inventory stocks, fluctuating seasonal demand and trading patterns, and weak infrastructure. In many instances, private entrepreneurs have not found it profitable to break into these markets, yet cooperatives have been expected to succeed.

Professor Hans Munkner, the famous cooperator, has pointed out the causes for failure of cooperatives as follows:

1. Cooperatives were created on a large scale without much preparation, by offering short-term incentives, e.g. access to loans in cash or in kind which otherwise would not be available.
2. In some countries administrative and political pressure was used to impose a model of cooperation on peasants, by creating monopolies for the supply of inputs and the marketing of produce or by making membership compulsory. In all these cases, the intention of the promoters of cooperatives focused on priorities of national development rather than on the interests of the individual members.
3. Cooperatives were conceived primarily as instruments of government for carrying out plans made by Government officials, financed with government funds and accordingly government controlled. The citizens called upon to cooperative (mainly peasant farmers) were seen as persons who were unable to organize themselves without guidance, outside assistance, supervision and control.
4. The models of organization were (and still are) predetermined in almost every detail (e.g. model by-laws are prescribed from which people are not supposed to deviate), government intervention and government control left (and still leaves) no room and no incentive for active participation by cooperative members. But there is also little reason why members should actively participate in such cooperatives:
   (*a*) Their share contribution and liability (if any) are usually purely nominal, so that members do not have to commit themselves and thus have no stake in the cooperative.
   (*b*) Often the rules according to which 'their' cooperatives are operating are not known to them

(e.g. by-laws available only in the official language, which they cannot read and understand; by-laws containing complicated procedures which are different from their rules and values). As a result, there is no member control over office-bearers and employees of cooperatives, many of whom are elected, appointed or seconded from government staff in undemocratic ways.

(*c*) Control exercised by government officers is usually ineffective either because it does not reach the societies due to lack of qualified staff or due to lack of transport, or it does not curb malpractices because of powerful vested interests, and government officers teaming up with influential leaders for their own benefit.

(*d*) Income that could be earned by cooperatives is either siphoned off by high prices for inputs and low prices for produce, by embezzlement and corrupt practices, which go undetected or unpunished, or remain low because of losses due to lack of storage facilities, transport or capacity for processing. Under such conditions it is not surprising that persons refuse to join cooperatives or if compelled to join, show little interest in actively participating in their affairs. Such 'Cooperatives' deserve the bad reputation that they have earned themselves.

In all countries of Africa self-help activities have found other venues for organization such as traditional rotating savings and credit associations (ROSCAs) adapting themselves to the conditions of a money economy, mutual aid working groups of young people (e.g. Nnoboa in Ghana, Nam in Burkina Faso), young farmers' clubs, saving clubs, informal village groups, women's groups, for production and processing of food crops and handicrafts.

Self-learning Activity

Try to answer the following questions on your own.

1. Can you offer measures to improve cooperative development policy in Africa?
2. What are the cooperative models in Africa?
3. List out the causes for failure of cooperative movement in Africa?

Summary

- This chapter is devoted for African cooperative Movement. The details on conditions under colonial dependence, measures for improving cooperative development policy, different cooperative models like British Indian pattern, French models are discussed.
- Causes for failure of cooperative movement are also explained.

Chapter 9 Cooperatives in Ethiopia

These traditional cooperatives are established to provide help or assistance in regard to scarce resources supply such as labour, which are very difficult for an individual to obtain them within a short period of time without external cooperation. On top of this, such types of cooperation are a means for sufficient resource use, namely timely ploughing, weeding, harvesting or building of houses, fence, streets and bridges.

Equib

Equib is a self-help traditional form of saving (credit) cooperative of individuals practiced in both the urban and the rural areas of the country. It is a voluntarily organized money saving cooperation, where each week or month, members get together; collect a fixed amount of money (agreed upon) from each member and hand over the money to a member waiting for his turn. The collected money goes to each member in rotation to serve a defined purpose—such as for the construction of a house, the purchase of a household furniture, clothing, investment on income generating ventures—trade or to meet any other financial obligations.

Eddir

Eddir is properly applied to local associations whose primary, and usually only function is to provide assistance in time of death, but now a days it also includes participation in wedding ceremonies of the member.

Eddir associations in larger towns are organized in neighbourhood basis, while in smaller towns and villages this need not be a factor. Within a given area people will join a particular eddir for a variety of reasons. As noted by Markakis (1974), although eddirs in towns are not ethically segregated, most people prefer to join one that includes a fair number of people from their own ethnic group. Given the religious aspect of the ceremonial functions of this kind of associations, Christians and Muslims have separate eddir associations.

In a few years, the neighbourhood-oriented eddirs have begun to broaden their scope to include matters of general interest to the locality. The status of the new eddir includes general community welfare among their objectives.

Mahiber and Senbete

Mahiber and senbete are found both in urban and rural areas. The membership of the mahiber meets in periodic feast held at each member's house successively. Whereas in the case of senbete members prepare food and local drinks and fetch to the church where members get together every Sundays. The feast takes place in the church compound. As stated by Markakis (1974), while normally membership tends to ethnically homogeneous, it is not unusual to include friends and co-workers who belong to different ethic groups, provided of course they are Christians. This traditional form of organization is established not only for feast purposes but for mutual assistance in time of death and happiness.

Meredaja Mahiber

It is a self-help development association that bears the name of a particular area, region or ethnic group whose development they seek to foster. Their membership is drawn from among the residents who belong to that particular ethnic group or originally came from that particular region.

We can see that there are many different types of traditional social cooperation among the Ethiopian people for various economic and social reasons. Thus the Ethiopian population has got a long standing and experience in pooling resources ad working together for mutual benefit.

Modern Cooperative Movement in Ethiopia

Modern cooperative movement has started at the beginning of 1960s. During this period emphasis has been placed on the need to establish multi-purpose agricultural cooperatives as a major means of:

- providing rural credit;
- storing and marketing farmers' crops;
- providing goods and services for production; and consumption; and
- promoting savings.

The Ministry of National Community Development and Social Affairs was responsible for the organization and development of cooperatives through its Cooperative Department. In 1960, the cooperative movement was started by the enactment of the 'Farm Workers Cooperative Decree' to promote the establishment of modern cooperative institution for farm workers.

However, this decree was limited in scope only to farm workers. Thus, later it was considered desirable to broaden the scope for cooperative development beyond farm workers; and a new legislation was issued in 1966. This legislation was called the 'Cooperative Societies Proclamation'. While the new law and regulations may help to expand the cooperative movement, the establishment of agricultural cooperative has been slow and restricted to cash crops growing areas such as Sidamo, Kaffa (including Jimma and

Agaro) and Wolloga. This was mainly geared towards earning cash and foreign currency.

In general the history of cooperative movement in Ethiopia goes back to the history of 1960 when the first indication of the movement was carried in the 2nd five years development plan (1960/64-1967/68).

Lots of efforts were made to establish and develop cooperatives of various types in the 2nd and 3rd five years development plans. The plans visualize a comprehensive use of different forms of cooperatives with the objectives of:

(*a*) increase in productivity of different resources;

(*b*) raising the saving potential from part of individuals income for the purpose of expanding investment and consequently production and income of the members;

(*c*) improvement of the living conditions of the members through realized income from members production;

(*d*) expand and provide social services such as health, education, and pure water supply to the members;

(*e*) protect the right of all citizens and have equal opportunity of contributing to the economic and social progress.

In the establishment, development and expansion of cooperatives was given due emphasis to both urban and rural (agricultural) areas. In the urban areas, more emphasis was given to the saving, credit, handcrafts and consumers cooperatives.

In the plan, it was also stressed that successful implementation of the cooperative programme was to be assisted by the government. The assistance was also to include the set up of a legal framework to provide fund for training of cooperative supervisors, field workers, or organizers and members. Arrangements were made to provide productive credit facilities and other supportive measures.

The target of the effort was to establish and make a self-reliant of at least twenty cooperatives of different types and carry out all the preparatory works on the basis of the experience gained from the next five-year plan period.

The third Five-year Development Plan (1968 - 1973) tried to continue emphasis on the role of cooperative as the best way of mobilizing the latent organizations and use the under utilized resources such as land and labor. The attention given to agricultural cooperatives was much higher than the other sectors with an overall aim of increasing the capacity of the farmers and the artisan people in cottage and small scale industries.

By the, an ambitious and exaggerated target of no practical ground was laid down to establish about 300 different types of cooperatives in the country. To achieve the target laid down, various arrangements were made including the following:

(*a*) Establishment of national cooperative board consisting of concerned organizations in the expansion of cooperative advice on future course of cooperative development in different parts of the country;

(*b*) Establishment and development of cooperative training centers where organizers, managers, members, supervisors, etc are trained on how to deal with cooperative establishment or organization and further development.

After the arrangement of the above prerequisites, hopes were placed to mobilize and pool quite good sum of money from the contribution of the members.

After the implementation of the 1979 National Policy of Cooperative Organization, Agricultural Cooperatives have increased in size and membership, particularly in the period between 1980/82-1984/85.

According to reports from the Ministry of Agriculture, the Agricultural Producers Cooperatives (APCs) by the end of June 1985 numbered 1856, of which 1255 are the *Melba*, primary stage, 601 are in the *Welba*, secondary stage, and none in the *Weland*, advanced stage. The number of agricultural producers' cooperatives has increased by 71 per cent compared with five years ago. Membership in the cooperatives has also reached 132,872 households. This is 3.4 times the 1980/81 producers' cooperative membership figure. Taking the Central Statistical Office data 4.4 as the average household size in rural Ethiopia, the producers' cooperatives contain 1.5 per cent of the 1984 rural Ethiopia population and 2.4 per cent of the rural population who were organized under peasant associations.

In June 1985 the Agricultural Producers' Cooperatives owned 491,324 hectares of arable land, of which 44 per cent was cultivated. The total acreage owned increased by 57 per cent and the cultivated land by 30 per cent over that of 1984. Each producer cooperative owned, on average, 264 hectares of land, of which 115 hectares was cultivated land. Each household, on average, owned 3.7 hectares of the total land and 1.6 hectares of the cultivated land.

Causes for Failure of Cooperatives

Causes for the Failure of Cooperatives during Imperial Period (1960-1974) and during Derg Period (1974-1991)

Causes for the failure of Cooperatives during the Imperial Period

The first cooperative society in Ethiopia was started during the Imperial Period in 1960. Efforts were taken to introduce and strengthen cooperatives during the planning period. The stipulated target to establish three hundred and twenty cooperatives during the second (1963/64 – 1967/68) and the third five-year development plan (1968-73) were not achieved. Only 112 different types of cooperatives were organized and registered up to the end of the third-five year development plan. Among the total number of cooperatives organized, 76 were farmers' cooperatives; while the rest consist of different sectors mainly handcrafts and marketing cooperatives.

Even though, various efforts were made the goals were not that much realized as anticipated. Several factors are accounted for the failure, including:

1. Oppressive land tenure system and domination in the agricultural sector. To be successful in farming, a cooperative should be established by farmers who own resources of which land is the major factor of production in agriculture. By then majority of farmers were tenants or share croppers. This enabled the rich and affluent farmers and land-lords to play a leading role in the establishment of cooperatives to adjust the conditions to their own benefit. The have-nots were thus, pushed away to the corner of poverty line and were demoralized to participate in cooperative development.
2. Inadequate trained manpower to propagate the idea on how to organized and manage cooperatives.
3. Inadequate budgetary allocation for the purpose of promoting of cooperatives which reflects poor interest of the government to the expansion of cooperatives. On top of this, the bank credit and collateral policy was not convenient for the poor farmers to get credit for cooperative and farm development. Actually, the farmers as such did not have access to bank credit. Subsistence and traditional forms of production with no surplus production for the formation of reserve capital was thus, among the farmers' problems of the time to limit the expansion of cooperation throughout the country.
4. Lack of efficient marketing system:
   - Low price of farm products;
   - High price of inputs;
   - Inadequate transport services.

Main problems of Cooperative Organization in post-Revolution Ethiopia (post-1974)

Though, there were many convenient situation for organization, development and further expansion of cooperatives in Ethiopia (such as land reform and establishment of Peasant Association—as training school for collective work), there were various problems that contributed for the failure of cooperative movement, including:

1. Distorted training system of man-power

   Cooperative organizers were trained in socialist political ideology than in cooperative discipline who were known as 'production and political cadres'.

2. Lack of coordination between cooperative principles and state policy

   Cooperative principles clearly show ways and of means of organization cooperatives, the place and time of organizing cooperatives, the pre-requisites of organizing cooperatives.

   Whereas,

   (*a*) ambitious cooperative organizers (government agents), neglected pre-requisites and jump to higher forms of cooperatives (e.g. from Malba to a complete collective form of Wolba), step-by-step and gradual development of cooperatives (elementary and simple forms of cooperatives could have been used to introduce and show advantages of cooperative work and train collective work);

   (*b*) neglecting of cooperative principles especially voluntariness (free will), conviction of membership, rather used forced cooperativization method, especially following a quota system in different peasant associations and woredas.

   (*c*) Interference of the government in production and marketing of agricultural outputs of the cooperative members.

Instead of following a competitive marketing system, the government used a complete centrally controlled marketing.

For example, the government used to fix prices of agricultural outputs of cooperative members.

The observed consequences were:

- Low supply of goods and services by suppliers;
- High demand of goods and services;
- Black markets (and skyrocketing prices);
- Quota system of supply; and
- Food/goods rationing.

This action has demoralized the farmers and they considered that a cooperative to be the most hated agency serving the government.

However, prices are not of stimulating factors of production, but in the case of Ethiopian cooperatives, prices were highly demoralizing and frustrating. Because the government fixes prices of farm products without considering cost of production and imposes quota system of supply.

For example:

- The Agricultural Marketing Corporation (AMC) used to buy food crops at low prices and farmers were obliged to give their quota and this also was in initiation of black markets.
- The Ethiopian Coffee Marketing Corporation (ECMC) used to buy coffee from the farmers on quota basis at low prices. Thus, farmers in some regions (such as Hararghe) replaced their coffee farms by chat an food crops.

3. Credit availability

Credit was not available at the desired time and place for all cooperatives. Only very few favoured cooperatives with legal status could get credit.

4. Poor record-keeping

   Even if there were some formats prepared by the Ministry of Agriculture, they were too complex and inappropriate to the farmers. For others credit was not accessible and the interest rate was incompatible with their level of income generation.

5. Premature start of cooperatives

   Cooperatives usually started before studying their feasibility in the community (see the methods of organizing a cooperative)

6. Inadequate member support

   This problem stems from:

   - Poor communications on a cooperative as a whole;
   - Poor business performance;
   - Lack of members' appreciation of what they can and cannot expected the cooperative to accomplish.

7. Cooperatives were frequently imposed from above

   Even where and when the rural population has no idea as to what a cooperative is and has no interest in cooperatives, the government used to force farmers and other producers to establish cooperatives.

8. Cooperatives were misused by the government

   The government used cooperatives:

   - As a means of imposing or pushing forward specific policy objectives;
   - To perpetuate government control or even to extend political control to the village level.

   For example: farmers' producers' cooperatives were used as an instrument for the expansion and consolidation of socialist ideology in the farming community.

9. Cooperative were charged with inappropriate tasks, which conflict with interests of the members.

For example cooperatives were used as a means of:

- Ideological work;
- Forcing individuals for membership;
- Tax collection – as an agent of the government.

10. Cooperatives take more of the character of bureaucratic governmental institutions than of organizations of/for their own members.

Thus, from this one can conclude that, cooperatives in Ethiopian were no longer pretend to be politically neutral because:

- Cooperative leaders were supporters (members) of the workers party of Ethiopia of the Derg regime and most are members of parliament;
- All important decision and actions were ordered and directed by the party and its instrument—the state;
- Cooperatives had lost their internal autonomy as well as their freedom of action;
- Cooperatives had become the obedient servants of the state.

Suggestions for the Speedy Growth of Cooperatives in Ethiopia

The cooperative movement in Ethiopia was organized in the year 1960 with the passing of The Decree No. 44/1960 with the following objectives, to form the Farm Workers' Cooperatives.

(*a*) Arrange for production, processing, transportation and marketing of agricultural products;

(*b*) Operate and administer livestock and agricultural and other machinery owned by the cooperative for the benefit of its members;

(*c*) Promote good farming and agricultural practices;

(*d*) Promote cooperation among cooperatives; and

(*e*) Promote cooperation among cooperatives generally by the pooling of common resources and the taking of other action to this end.

In 1966 the decree of 1960 was replaced by cooperative society proclamation No. 241/1966. The main objective of this proclamation was improving the standard of living of the farmers, better business performance and improved methods of production by:

(*a*) reducing cost of credit;

(*b*) reducing the cost of goods and services for production and consumption;

(*c*) minimizing and reducing the impacts of risks and uncertainties;

(*d*) spreading knowledge of practical technical improvements; and

(*e*) may otherwise contribute to achieve the above-mentioned objectives.

In actual sense the formulation of this proclamation has benefited wealthy commercial farmers. This proclamation has led to the organization of different types of cooperatives such as:

- multipurpose and farm cooperatives;
- thrift and credit cooperatives;
- handicrafts and small scale industry cooperatives;
- consumer cooperatives; and
- other forms of cooperatives.

But during the Imperial Period the progress of the cooperatives was very slow and vast majority of the cooperative became failure due to mismanagement, corruption, poor accounting system, lack of leadership, etc.

With the political change during 1974, cooperatives were given a new shape in the form of Proclamation No. 138/1978, which replaced the proclamation of 1966. This proclamation was enacted on the ground of socialist ideology and centralized economic planning system. This has led to the complete collapse of the previous cooperatives.

Again a political change took place in the year 1991, which had its effect on cooperatives also. A new cooperative proclamation 147/1998 came into existence and all previous cooperatives legislations became null and void. Again Proclamation No. 274/2002 made provisions for the establishment of cooperative commission and to manage it a commissioner for cooperatives was created. But under the new democratic setup the cooperatives could not achieve the things expected from them. Compared to other neighbuoring countries like Kenya, Tanzania, and Nigeria, the cooperatives in Ethiopia were moving very slow and stagnation exists at present. To revitalize the cooperatives and the cooperative movement, the following suggestions are offered.

1. ***Organization of cooperative banking structure:*** Ethiopia lacks a prominent cooperative banking structure with tier systems, which is very popular in other countries. Only with a strong cooperative banking structure, the cooperative movement can raise resources of its own and be self-reliant in resources in order to protect the cooperative democracy intact. Cooperative banking should be organized from primary level (kebele level), zonal level, regional level, and at national level. At present in regions of Oromiya and Amhara, Regional Cooperative Banks have been established with branches since 2004. But these banks are not pure cooperatives but they are registered as share companies. Without the permission of the cooperative bureau or the cooperative commission the word '*Cooperatives*' should not be allowed to be used. Further, there is an immediate need in Ethiopia to institute a *National Cooperative Bank of Ethiopia*. Such bank can be floated directly by the cooperative commission or by the existing cooperatives around Ethiopia. This national cooperative

bank can mobilize resources and inculcate banking habits in rural areas by means of opening branches throughout the country. It can also play a balancing function role to other cooperative banks and can guide the activities of all other existing and future cooperative banks in Ethiopia. Moreover, the national cooperative bank can act as a spokesman for the cooperatives in Ethiopia and can create link with international organizations like ICA (International Cooperative Alliance), ILO, FAO, etc.

2. ***Creation of separate Ministry of Cooperation:*** Ethiopia is one of the few countries where there is no separate department for cooperatives. At present the subject cooperation comes under the jurisdiction of the Ministry of Agricultural and Rural Development. In order to give special attention to the growth of the cooperatives (which can provide employment opportunity to vast number of educated youth) a separate ministry for cooperation must be created and a senior and experienced politician must be appointed as the Minister for Cooperation. With the creation of separate ministry of cooperation, lot of funds available with foreign cooperatives and international cooperative agencies can be brought to Ethiopia. Like the federal government the regional governments must also create separate Regional Bureaus.

3. ***Arrangement for cooperative education and training:*** In the cooperative proclamation of 1998, provisions have been made to organize separate structure for cooperative education and training. Again only in Ethiopia at the national level or at regional levels a separate agency is lacking for the provision of cooperative education and training. Only by means of creating a strong cooperative education and training structure, the employees can be given continuous training and the cooperative members can be given training in leadership, management, etc. At present, four educational centers of Ambo College, Ambo;

Debub University, Alemaya University, and Mekele University offer degree programmes in cooperation by means of creating a separate department for cooperatives. As a transitional arrangement the existing four departments can undertake the training of cooperative employees also by means of creating separate wing for cooperative training. At the national level a separate training institute must be organized immediately. In this respect, the help of the International Cooperative Alliance's, Regional Office for East and South Africa located at Nairobi can be resorted.

4. ***Increase in Agricultural Prosperity:*** As Ethiopia is a major agricultural country; the prosperity of the country depends on the prosperity of agriculture. It is a country, which grows specialized crops like coffee and has enormous potential for the future growth of agriculture. But due to lack of irrigation facilities, land ownership rights, marketing problems, etc the country is yet to move towards self-reliance in foodgrains. Food security and agricultural prosperity can give a guarantee for the organized growth of cooperatives. On the other hand, cooperatives can make agriculture prosperous, as has been shown in other developing countries.

5. ***Participation of Women in Cooperatives:*** For the future growth of cooperatives in Ethiopia, the participation of women is very much needed. Women forming part of half of the population, has been very much neglected in the membership of cooperatives, leadership and management of cooperatives in Ethiopia. There is an immediate need to promote the women membership in cooperatives and to encourage and motivate their participation in the cooperatives. Special types of cooperatives like cooperative banks, consumer cooperatives, dairy cooperatives, etc can be exclusively organized for women to improve their role and employment opportunity.

6. ***Revising the Cooperative Proclamation:*** In all countries where cooperatives are fast developing, the respective cooperative legislations have been revised from time to time in order to incorporate the latest trends that are taking place in the cooperative movement. The Cooperative Proclamation of Ethiopia must also be revised from time to time in order to suit the changing needs of the cooperative movement. This also warrants a need to have a separate Ministry of Cooperation at the federal government level.

7. ***Coordination with International Cooperative Agencies***: International cooperative agencies like International Cooperative Alliance (Headquarters Geneva, Regional Office Nairobi), ILO, FAO, other countries national level cooperatives are offering unlimited funds and exchange programmes for employees. Unfortunately, these facilities from international cooperative agencies have not been used by Ethiopian cooperatives at present. This was due to a lack of spokesman for the cooperatives at the national level and lack of a separate ministry of cooperation. So the time has come in Ethiopia to organize national level cooperatives like National Cooperative Bank, National Cooperative Training Institute, National Federation of Consumer Cooperatives, National Federation of Dairy Cooperatives, etc.

8. ***Organization of New Cooperatives:*** At present in Ethiopia only producers' cooperatives and service cooperatives are functioning. Other types of cooperatives like marketing cooperatives, consumer cooperatives, cooperative banks, dairy cooperatives, labor cooperatives, etc are completely absent. There is an immediate need by the thinkers of cooperatives and government to start about such cooperatives to avail locally available resources, to increase the employment opportunities, to increase agricultural and dairy

production, to empower the women-folk and to ameliorate the living conditions of the farmers.

9. ***Using the Words Cooperation and Cooperatives:*** The words cooperation and cooperatives denote a corporate sector called cooperative movement. In other countries strong legal measures have been taken to use above words. Without the permission of the concerned cooperative authorities like cooperative commissioner nobody should use the words cooperation and cooperatives. But in Ethiopia cooperation and cooperatives are used by all people who do not form cooperatives or come under the purview of the cooperative commission. *So, the time has come in Ethiopia to use the words cooperation and cooperatives on a restrictive manner only with the permission of the commissioner for cooperatives.* Suitable amendments to the cooperative proclamation, and even the federal constitution must be made towards this objective.

Self-learning Activity

Try to answer the following questions on your own.

1. Write short notes on: Equib and Meredeja Mahiber?
2. What are the causes for failure of cooperatives in Ethiopia?
3. Can you offer suggestions to improve the cooperatives in Ethiopia?

Summary

- Traditional (earlier) cooperatives like equib, eddir, senbete, meredeja mahiber are discussed.
- A picture about modern cooperative movement is also given.
- Causes for failure of cooperative in Ethiopia are listed down and suggestions to improve cooperatives are also offered.

Chapter 10

Scope for Organizing Various Cooperatives in Ethiopia

Agricultural Cooperatives in Ethiopia

Agricultural cooperatives are the earliest and the oldest cooperatives in Ethiopia. Since the beginning of the development of the cooperatives (1960s) only agricultural cooperatives were given prominence. During Imperial period, Derg period, and the present democratic setup only agricultural cooperatives were organized.

Primary Agricultural Cooperatives

Primary agricultural cooperatives in Ethiopia are called in different names like producers' cooperatives, service cooperatives, and multi-purpose cooperatives. The producers' cooperatives were started during Derg period (1974-1991) under the auspicious of the Peasants' Associations. Peasants' Associations were larger bodies having wider area of operation to undertake collective agricultural activities on the Soviet model. Under PA, producers' cooperatives were organized to undertake multi-purpose activities to the farmers. Likewise, service cooperatives were also organized to undertake multi-purpose activities to the farmers. But both these types of cooperatives failed due to various reasons noted in this chapter. All the primary agricultural cooperatives were revised after 1991 and they were asked to re-register under the Cooperative Proclamation Number 147/1998. So at present all the primary agricultural cooperatives were reformed and working under the above proclamation.

Working of Primary Cooperatives

Primary agricultural cooperatives have the area of operation of few villages, which are called as *Kebeles*. All the farmers are expected to become members of these cooperatives. But due to the fear over the previous cooperatives and mismanagement during previous periods, many farmers have not come forward to become the members of these cooperatives. A rough estimate shows that only 25 per cent of the farmers have been covered by primary cooperatives in Ethiopia. Due to absence of federal structure, the primary cooperatives function on their own without any federal help. But recently, efforts have been taken to organize cooperative unions (by the international NGOs like VOCA, Self-help, etc), which form the federation of primary cooperatives.

Business Activities Undertaken by Primaries

Primary agricultural cooperatives in Ethiopia are not undertaking the function of the distribution of agricultural credit to the farmers. They are distributing only agricultural inputs like fertilizer and pesticides. Several primary cooperatives provide fertilizer credit and collect such credit after the harvest is over. Such loans are given on group basis. There is no over dues due to the group lending of fertilizer credit. Another activity undertaken by the primaries is the purchasing and selling of agricultural commodities especially food grains. Wherever cooperative unions are there, the primaries sell the grains through the cooperative unions. Wherever cooperative unions are not there, the primaries directly sell the grains.

Management

Elected management is a popular system of democratic management in Ethiopia. But yet the members and the office bearers are to be motivated and cooperatively educated. The general body is called as General Assembly in Ethiopia. The board of directors is called as Management Committee. Apart from the management committee other committees like audit committee, control committee, etc. function.

Profit Distribution

Primary cooperatives in Ethiopia distribute the net profit every year in the form of two major parts namely, dividend and reserves. Many cooperatives distribute dividend even up to 60 per cent of the net profit. There is need to build strong reserves and allocate net profit for other cooperative development purposes like cooperative education, welfare facilities, etc.

Saving and Credit Cooperatives (SACCOs)

There are two types of SACCOs that exist in Ethiopia namely, Rural SACCOs and Urban SACCOs. These cooperatives are engaged in the activities of savings and credit. The major deposits collected by them are savings and thrift deposit. Loans are distributed in small amounts for the purposes of undertaking small business, meeting consumer expenses, etc. In certain regions federations for these cooperatives have been organized in the form of SACCO Unions, and these unions help the primaries in mobilizing resources and undertaking loan operations. These cooperatives coordinate their activities with that of primary cooperatives.

Cooperative Unions

Cooperative unions are the real marketing cooperatives engaged in the marketing of agricultural commodities of primary cooperatives and farmers. These unions are considered to be the central societies and strong enough to make the agricultural cooperatives viable. If the cooperative unions are established throughout the country, a strong agricultural cooperative movement could be established in

Ethiopia. But a rough estimate shows that only 20 per cent of the primary cooperatives have established cooperative unions. The membership of cooperative unions is left to the primary cooperatives alone. On an average a cooperative union has 10 to 30 primaries affiliated to it. These unions collect the agricultural commodities from the primaries and sell them for a better price, after providing all marketing facilities. Many cooperative unions have constructed their own storage facilities to keep the produce and the inputs safely. Another major activity undertaken by the unions is the distribution of inputs like seed, fertilizer, and pesticides. Several unions have started importing fertilizers directly from foreign countries and that benefit has been transferred to the farmers in the form of low price for the inputs. Likewise, the unions have relieved the farmers from the exploitation of middlemen and they are able to provide 50 to 70 Birr per bag of grains (average price of grain per bag is around 300 Birr). This is a great achievement on the part of cooperative unions and many primaries have started organizing new cooperative unions with the help of international NGOs and the cooperative bureaus. There is a need to organize the federation of cooperative unions at regional levels and national levels. At present Ethiopia does not have any national level cooperative federations and very good scope is there for the organization of National and Regional Federation of Cooperative Unions, which can become the spokesman for cooperatives in Ethiopia.

Dairy Cooperatives

Introduction—Dairy Economy of Ethiopia

Ethiopia is an agricultural country and has the largest cattle population in Africa comprising 26 million cattle, 24 million sheeps, 17 million goats, 7 million equines, 1 million camels, and 52 million poultry (FAO, 1981). In 1984 there were about 8.33 million cows and heifers older than two years, of which 65 per cent were yielding milk. Milk production in Ethiopia grew by 1.7 per cent between 1965 and 1976 and by 1.1 per cent per year from 1976 to 1985. During 1981 milk produced in Ethiopia was 27 kg/person person. But it dropped to 17 kg/person during 1985. But it is still higher than the Sub-Saharan African average of 15.7 kg/person. By 1983 local cows produced 400 to 680 kg of milk per lactation period of less than 7 months.

Milk Production

Sour milk or yoghurt is produced in the traditional system by leaving the fresh milk to sour for few days. Soured milk keeps longer than raw milk, so this process is useful for storing milk during the days of Wednesday and Friday where Coptic Christians are forbidden to consume animal products. Sour milk not consumed at home is usually is sold to neighbours.

Sour milk can also be churned to make butter. The byproduct butter milk is rarely sold and it is fed to calves, consumed at home, or further processed. Ethiopian farmers prefer butter manufacturing and indigenous methods are followed.

Production Systems

Milk production system in Ethiopia is followed on the following pattern:

1. ***Pastoralism:*** Pastoralists are livestock owners who maintain natural grasslands in arid areas (lowlands) with their herds of camel, sheep, goat, and cattle. Pastoralists move from one place to another place searching for fresh grazing areas. Milk is the main source of food for pastoralists.
2. ***Agro pastoralists:*** They are the farmers who cultivate food crops for food and for sale. Their livestock are fed on grazing land and crop land after harvest. Livestock are used for draught, milk production, and savings.
3. ***Mixed Farming:*** Food or cash crop cultivation is the main activity. The farm size will be very small ranging from one to five hectares. Livestock are kept for draught, milk, and meat.

4. ***Intensive Dairy Farming:*** These farmers do dairy farming intensively and cultivate fodder crops exclusively. The dairy animals are not used for draught but manure is used for growing fodder. Milk is a major source of farm income. Labour intensity is high in this system.

5. ***Peri-urban Milk Production:*** This system is developed around cities that have high demand for milk. Milk is traded directly to the consumers of the city and is the major source of income to the farmers.

Measures to Improve Milk Production in Ethiopia

- ***Reduced mortality of stock:*** Efforts must be taken to protect cattle against the major diseases such as East Coast fever and tick-borne diseases.
- ***Lower calving intervals:*** These are necessary to increase the number of calves born and to reduce the period when cows are not producing milk.
- ***Improved calve rearing:*** This is necessary to ensure that a greater proportion of pure bred and cross bred are born and reared to reduce mortality.
- ***Upgrading indigenous stock:*** In the short run it will be beneficial to the farmers to improve the productivity of indigenous stock through cross-breeding and better management.
- ***Adequate levels of feeding:*** Efforts should be taken to reduce dry season shortage of feed. Such crops as maize, sorghum, and elephant grass must be used as feeding stuff.
- ***Commercial dairying:*** Commercial dairying through cooperatives with production and market orientation must be encouraged to make the dairy farming a successful venture.

Dairy Cooperatives in Ethiopia

There are two types of dairy cooperatives organized in Ethiopia, one by the producer cooperatives and the other by the service cooperatives. There are about 98 producer and service dairy cooperatives in Ethiopia. Exclusive dairy cooperatives were not organized in Ethiopia. Dairy Development Enterprise (DDE), a government enterprise, was having 14 dairy state farms under its control. These dairy farms supplied milk to Addis Ababa city.

Scope for Organizing Dairy Cooperatives in Ethiopia

The scope for organizing dairy cooperatives in Ethiopia is very high. The following factors favour the speedy organization of dairy cooperatives in Ethiopia:

- The high cattle population and dairy animals favor an atmosphere for increased production of milk and milk products through dairy cooperatives;
- The farmers are traditionally experienced in managing dairy farming and they can improve their conditions by organizing dairy cooperatives;
- With the economy moving fast, the income of the population is increasing, which may result in higher consumption of milk;
- Milk being an essential food for children, the scope is very high to increase milk production through dairy cooperatives;
- Enormous scope is there to have an export market. By means of setting processing units by dairy cooperatives, milk products can be exported to other countries;
- The atmosphere with the government is favorable for the organization of dairy cooperatives in Ethiopia;
- International help through NGOs can be available to organize diary cooperatives and dairy industries.

Scope for Organizing Sugar Cooperatives

- The country has good fertile soil and climate for the cultivation of sugarcane.
- Good rainfall is a positive factor.
- There is good demand for sugar within the country.

- An export opportunity for sugar is also bright.
- Government support can also be expected for licensing, capital formation, etc.
- Foreign private capital or cooperative capital can be invited to meet the financial needs of sugar cooperatives in Ethiopia.

Scope for Organizing Fisheries Cooperatives

Present Fishing Conditions in Ethiopia

- Ethiopia is landlocked country and hence, the fishing outlet is limited to lakes.
- Lakes form the major part of inland fishing in Ethiopia.
- River fishing is not popular in Ethiopia.
- Unlike other countries, the population is not divided as fishermen in Ethiopia.
- Fisheries cooperatives are practically non-existent in Ethiopia.
- There is no institutional protection in the form of bank financing, government subsidy, etc given to the fishery industry in Ethiopia.

Scope for Organizing Fisheries Cooperatives in Ethiopia

- The scope for organizing fisheries cooperatives in Ethiopia is limited to the lake areas.
- As the size of population depending on fishing is negligible in Ethiopia, the number of fisheries cooperatives that could be organized is limited.
- Fisheries cooperatives in the lake areas can be organized as an outlet of employment for the unemployed youth.
- Several NGOs have experimented in organizing fisheries cooperatives in lake areas and they are running successfully.
- As the priority for the government is on food security, government has greater concentration on the

promotion of agricultural and marketing cooperatives. Hence, the focus is not on fisheries cooperatives.

- The hold of the private traders is strong over fish catching and marketing, any organization of fisheries cooperatives has to face stiff resistance from the private traders.
- The government has to help in a big way for the organization of fisheries cooperatives in the form of providing long term capital, technical help, processing facilities, and marketing facilities. Without government initiatives, fisheries cooperatives on a popular scale cannot be organized in Ethiopia.

Scope for Organizing Forest Cooperatives

- Forest cooperatives have greater relevance to the highland people of Ethiopia.
- Through the organization of forest cooperatives, employment opportunities can be created to population.
- Afforestation measures can be undertaken through forest cooperatives.
- Soil erosion which is a major problem for Ethiopia can be handled properly by the forest cooperatives.
- Minor forest produces can be encouraged through forest cooperatives.
- Forest cooperative can also wider scope to export forest goods.

Scope for Organizing Industrial Cooperatives

- Ethiopia has an ancient civilization and the handicraft industry is very old and scope is high for organizing handicraft cooperatives.
- Industrial cooperatives can create employment opportunities for the educated and unemployed youth.
- Locally available agricultural raw materials provide enormous scope for the organization of industrial cooperatives.

- Handloom weaving is a popular industry in Ethiopia and industrial cooperatives can be organized in this sector.
- Sugar industry is a fast growing industry and sugar cooperatives can be organized on the model of India.
- International NGOs are helping to create self-employment for rural population in Ethiopia. Such ventures can be organized through industrial cooperatives.
- The federal government and regional governments are favourable to promote cooperatives in Ethiopia.

Scope for Organizing Labour Cooperatives

- Ethiopia has a growing population of unemployed farmers, who can be absorbed by labour cooperatives.
- By forming labour cooperatives, government contracts could be executed by labour cooperatives.
- Ethiopia has sizeable population of handicrafts workers, weavers and artisans who can be brought under the fold of labour cooperatives.
- In Ethiopia, construction industry is getting importance in urban areas, and the urban workers can be brought under labour cooperatives to improve their livelihood.

Scope for Organizing Irrigation Cooperatives

Ethiopia is a land locked country and irrigation cooperatives have been organized in lake areas. The purpose of forming such cooperatives is to distribute lands in lake areas for the unemployed youths and to provide sources of irrigation by erecting pump sets. In Ethiopia, irrigation cooperatives are not engaged in the construction of small dams, filter points, etc., like other countries. There is enormous scope for the organization of irrigation cooperatives in Ethiopia because the country has continuous rainfall for four months, which could be saved by irrigation cooperatives and can make the farmers to grow more than two crops a year. At present, irrigation cooperatives cover only lake areas. On the other hand, highland areas, river basins and low land areas have also immense scope for the organization of irrigation cooperatives. It is to be noted that in Ethiopia only 5 per cent of the agricultural lands are getting assured irrigation facilities. By encouraging the irrigation cooperatives this percentage could be increased and food production and agricultural production can be increased tremendously.

Scope for Organizing Other Innovative Cooperatives

Ethiopia has scope for organizing the existing type of cooperatives in cooperatively under developed regions and new or innovative cooperatives in all regions. Cooperatives like energy cooperatives, transport cooperatives, healthcare cooperatives, workers or technocrats cooperatives, value added or processing cooperatives such as tomato and fruits processing cooperatives, eucalyptus oil extracting cooperatives, industrial societies of paper manufacturing cooperatives, computer services cooperatives, and so on.

Self-learning Activity

Try to answer the following questions on your own.

1. What is the scope for organizing fisheries cooperatives in Ethiopia?
2. What is the scope for organizing new type of cooperatives like energy, wind mills?
3. What are the problems of irrigation cooperatives in Ethiopia?

Summary

- Problems of cooperatives, scope for organizing existing types of cooperatives and new types of cooperatives are explained in this chapter so as to enable to organize more relevant types of cooperatives to have vibrant and virile cooperative movement in the country.

References

150 Years of the Co-op (Special Supplement). 1994. *New Statesman and Society* *7*(June 17): i-xiv.

1960s: Trend Toward Fewer, Larger Farms Means Major Changes for Co-ops. 1999. *Rural Cooperatives* *66*(1): 28-37.

1980s: Mergers, Consolidations Change Look of U.S Cooperatives. 1999. *Rural Cooperatives* *66*(1): 48-55.

Abalkin, Leonid. 1988. Reviving the Cooperative Movement. *World Marxist Review* *31*(June): 53-59.

Andre Hirschfeld, "Some Thoughts on Cooperative Socialism, "Anthology of Cooperative Thought, Vol. III, 1977.

Andre Hirschfeld, "Some Thoughts on Cooperative Socialism, " Anthology of Cooperative Thought, Vol. III, 1977, p. 35.

Attwood, Donald. 1989. Does Competition Help Co-operation? *The Journal of Development Studies* *26*(October): 5-27.

Babcock, John. 1999. *Farmboy: Hard Work and Good Times on a Farm That Helped Change Northeast Agriculture.* Ithaca, NY: DeWitt Historical Society of Tompkins County.

Banerjee, Abhijit, Timothy Besley, and Timothy Guinnane. 1994. Thy Neighbour's Keeper: The Design of a Credit

Cooperative with Theory and a Test. *The Quarterly Journal of Economics 109* (May): 491-515.

Barnes, Donald, and Christopher Ondeck. 1997. *The Capper-Volstead Act: Opportunity Today and Tomorrow in Commemoration of the 75th Anniversary of the Capper-Volstead Act.* Report Presented at the National Council of Farmer Cooperatives' National Institute on Cooperative Education, Annual Conference, Pittsburgh, PA. Published Online by the University of Wisconsin Center for Cooperatives. Retrieved June 15, 2007, from www.uwcc.wisc.edu/info/capper.htm.

Bartlett, Will, John Cable, and Saul Estrin. 1992. Labour-managed Cooperatives and Private Firms in North Central Italy: An Empirical Comparison. *Industrial and Labour Relations Review 46*: 103-118.

Baumgardner, James. 1988. The Division of Labour, Local Markets, and Worker Organization. *Journal of Political Economy 96*(June): 509-527.

Ben-Ner, Avner. 1984. On the Stability of the Cooperative Type of Organization. *Journal of Comparative Economics 8*(3): 247-260.

Berman, Katrina, and Matthew Berman. 1989. An Empirical Test of the Theory of the Labour-managed Firm. *Journal of Comparative Economics 13*(June): 281-300.

Berry, Brian J. L. 1992. *America's Utopian Experiments: Communal Havens from Long-wave Crises.* Hanover, NH: Dartmouth College—University Press of New England.

Bhuyan, Sanjib. 1992. *Agricultural Cooperatives and Vertical Integration: A Theoretical Analysis.* Unpublished Master's Thesis (M.S.), University of Nebraska, Lincoln.

Birchall, Johnston. 1994. *Co-op: The people's business.* New York: St. Martin's Press.

Blanc, Francois, and Richard Matthewman. 1995. Cooperatives et gestion Communale en elevage: Un apercu comparatif entre pays en voie de developpement anglophones et francophones. [French] *Annals of Public and Cooperative Economics/Annales de l'Economie Publique Sociale et Cooperative 66*(September): 253-274.

Boehlje, M. 1996. Industrialization of Agriculture: What are the Implications? *Choices* (4): 30-33.

Bogetic, Zeljko, and Dennis Heffley. 1992. Market Syndicalism and Market Imbalances. *Journal of Comparative Economics 16*(December): 670-687.

Bonin, John, and Louis Putterman. 1993. Incentives and Monitoring in Cooperatives with Labour-proportionate Sharing Schemes. *Journal of Comparative Economics 17*(September): 663-686.

Bonin, John, Derek Jones, and Louis Putterman. 1993. Theoretical and Empirical Studies of Producer Cooperatives: Will ever the Twain Meet? *Journal of Economic Literature 31*(September): 1290-1320.

Bonn, John. 1984. Membership and Employment in an Egalitarian Cooperative. *Economica 51*(August): 295-305.

Bowen, E.R, The Cooperative Road to Abundance. New York: Henry Schuman, 1953, p. 144.

Bowles, Samuel, Herbert Gintis, and Bo Gustafsson. (Eds.). 1993. *Markets and Democracy: Participation, Accountability, and Efficiency*. Cambridge, UK: Cambridge University Press.

Bradley, Forrest. 1995. *Tapestry of Success: A History of Tennessee Farmers Cooperative and Its First 50 years of Cooperation*. LaVergne: Tennessee Farmers Cooperative.

Breimyer, Harold [Reviewer]. 1992. Farmers, Cooperatives, and USDA: A History of Agricultural Cooperative

Service [Book Review]. U.S. Department of Agriculture, 1991. *American Journal of Agricultural Economics 74*(August): 843-845.

Brown, Leslie [Reviewer]. 1989. Worker Cooperatives in America [Book Review]. University of California Press, 1984. *Canadian Review of Sociology and Anthropology 26*(August): 689-691.

Buccola, Steven, and Abdelbagi Subaei. 1985. Optimal Market Pools for Agricultural Cooperatives. *American Journal of Agricultural Economics 67*(February): 70-79.

Burger, Paul. 1997. *Market Area Modelling and Network Analysis of an Agricultural Cooperative System Using a Geographic Information System.* Unpublished Doctoral Thesis (Ed.D.), Oklahoma State University, Stillwater.

Carter, Neil [Reviewer]. 1989. Worker Cooperatives in Theory and Practice [Book Review]. Open University Press, 1988. *Political Quarterly 60*(April/June): 247-250.

Centre de Gestion des Cooperatives. 1996. *Profile of World Agricultural Cooperation.* Montreal: Ecole des Hautes Etudes Commerciales.

Certainly not in the same league (Cooperatives Seek Diversity). 1995. *Economist 335* (April 29): 76.

Chinchanker and Namjoshi, 'Cooperation and Welfare', Cooperation and Dynamics of Change, Bombay: Somaiya Publishing House, 1977.

Clark, Thomas R. 1999. The Limits of State Autonomy: The Medical Cooperatives of the Farm Security Administration, 1935-1946. *Journal of Policy History 11*(3): 257-282.

Clayre, Alasdair. 1980. *The Political Economy of Co-operation and Participation: A Third Sector.* New York: Oxford University Press.

Clyde Filley A.M, Cooperation in Agriculture, John Willey and Sons Inc, New York, 1929.

Cobia, David. (Ed.). 1989. *Cooperatives in Agriculture*. Englewood Cliffs, NJ: Prentice Hall.

Cook, Michael L. 1995. The Future of U.S. Agricultural Cooperatives: A Neo-institutional Approach. *American Journal of Agricultural Economics 77*(December): 1153-1159.

Cook, Michael L. 1997. *Cooperatives—Their Importance in the Future Food and Agricultural System: Proceedings of a January 1990 Symposium*. Washington, DC: National Council of Farmers Cooperatives and the Food and Agricultural Marketing Consortium.

Cook, Michael L., and Constantine Iliopoulos. 1999. Beginning to Inform the Theory of the Cooperative Firm: Emergence of the New Generation Cooperative. *The Finnish Journal of Business Economics 4*: 525-535.

Co-operate and Prosper (Mondragon). 1991. *Economist 311* (April 1): 61.

Cooperative Marketing Act: 60 years. 1986. *Farmer Cooperatives 53*(October): 4-19.

Craig, Ben, and John Pencavel. 1992. The Behaviour of Worker Cooperatives: The Plywood Companies of the Pacific Northwest. *American Economic Review 82*: 1083-1105.

Craig, Ben, and John Pencavel. 1993. The Objectives of Worker Cooperatives (Pacific Northwest). *Journal of Comparative Economics 17*(June): 288-308.

Craig, Ben, and John Pencavel. 1995. *Participation and Productivity: A Comparison of Worker Cooperatives and Conventional Firms in the Plywood Industry* (Brookings Papers on Economic Activity). (Microeconomics, 121-160, 173-174; Related Material: Discussion, 161-172)

Credit Union History. 1999. *Credit Union Management 22*(2): 21.

D'Aspremont, Claude, Alexis Jacquemin, and Jean Jaskold Gabszewicz. 1985. Cooperative Agreements and Conflicts of Interest. *European Economic Review 27* (February): 1-2.

Dasgupta, Siddhartha. 1997. *Cooperative Land Tenure Contracts Under Asymmetric Information.* Unpublished Doctoral Thesis (Ph.D.), Department of Agricultural Economics, Texas A&M University, College Station.

David W. Cobia, Cooperatives in Agriculture, Prentice Hall, New Jersy.

Digby, Margarat, the World Cooperative Movement, London: Hutchinson University Library, 1960.

Don, Yehuda, Nava Kahana, and Avi Weiss. 1992. Theoretical and Applied Aspects of Labour-managed Firms: Editors' Introduction. *Journal of Comparative Economics 16*(December): 567-572.

Dorrien, Gary. 1986. *The Democratic Socialist Vision.* Totowa, NJ: Rowman and Littlefield. Drabenstott, Mark. 1994. Industrialization: Steady Current or Tidal Wave? *Choices* (4): 4-8. Dunn, John. 1988. Cooperatives Best Hope for Farmers' Economic Survival: Senate Study. *Farmer Cooperatives 54* (January): 10-14.

Durant, Will, Story of Civilisation—the Life of Greece, New York: Simon and Schuster 1939.

Earle, John. 1985. Draining the Ostia Marshes: A Co-operative Achievement. *History Today 35*(July): 27-32.

Earnest Poisson, the Cooperative Republic, Manchester. The Cooperative Union Ltd., 1925.

Egerstrom, Lee, Pieter Bos, and Gert Van Dijk. (Eds.). 1996. *Seizing Control: The International Market Power of Cooperatives.* Rochester, MN: Lone Oak Press.

Egerstrom, Lee. 1994. *Make No Small Plans: A Cooperative Revival for Rural America*. Rochester, MN: Lone Oak Press.

Ellerman, David. 1984. Theory of Legal Structure: Worker Cooperatives. *Journal of Economic Issues 18* (September): 861-891.

Erba, Eric. 1996. *Comparisons of Costs and Efficiencies Between Cooperative, Proprietary, and Captive Fluid Milk Processors: A Neural Network Approach*. Ithaca, NY: Cornell University, Department of Agricultural, Resource and Managerial Economics.

Estrin, Saul [Reviewer]. 1984. The Economic Analysis of Producers' Cooperatives [Book Review]. St. Martin's Press, 1984. *Journal of Comparative Economics 9* (December): 462-464.

Estrin, Saul, and Jan Svejnar. 1993. Wage Determination in Labour-managed Firms Under Market-oriented Reforms: Estimates of Static and Dynamic Models. *Journal of Comparative Economics 17* (September): 687-700.

Fairbairn, Brett. 1989. *Building a Dream: The Co-operative Retailing System in Western Canada, 1928-1988*. Saskatoon, SK: Western Producer Prairie Books.

Filimonova, N., and I. Ermakova. 2005. Farmers' Dairy Cooperatives in the USA: Structure and Tendencies of Development. *Mezhdunarodnyi Sel'skokhozyaistvennyi Zhurnal* (3): 24-26.

Franz C Helm, The Economics of Cooperative Enterprises, The Cooperative College, Tanzxania and University of London Press, 1968.

Gartrell, David and Bernard Paille. 1997. Wage Cuts and the Fairness of Pay in a Worker-owned Plywood Cooperative. *Social Psychology Quarterly 60*(June): 103-117.

Gauthier, David. 1986. *Morals by Agreement*. Oxford, UK: Clarendon Press.

Gephart, Robert P. 2002. A Cooperative Approach to Local Economic Development. *Administrative Science Quarterly 47*(4): 736-739.

Gerber, Allen. (Ed.). 1996. *The Practical Approach to New Generation Cooperatives: An Exchange of Cooperative Experience from Renville, Minnesota.* St. Paul: Minnesota Association of Cooperatives.

Goddard, Ellen. 2002. Factors Underlying the Evolution of Farm-related Cooperatives in Alberta. *Canadian Journal of Agricultural Economics/Revue Canadienne D'Agroeconomie 50*(4): 473.

Goodman, David, and Michael Watts. (Eds.). 1997. *Globalising Food: Agrarian Questions and Global Restructuring.* New York: Routledge.

Gray, Thomas, and Charles Kraenzle. 1998. *Member Participation in Agricultural Cooperatives: A Regression and Scale Analysis.* Washington, DC: U.S. Department of Agriculture, Rural Development, Rural Business-Cooperative Service.

Guinnane, Timothy W. 2001. Cooperatives as Information Machines: German Rural Credit Cooperatives, 1883-1914. *The Journal of Economic History 61*: 366-389.

Guttman, Joel, and Adi Schnytzer. 1989. Strategic Work Interactions and the Kibbutz-kolkhoz Paradox. *Economic Journal 99* (September): 686-699.

Hakelius, Karin. 1996. *Cooperative Values: Farmers' Cooperatives in the Minds of the Farmers.* Doctoral Thesis, Swedish University of Agricultural Sciences, Department of Economics, Uppsala, Sweden.

Hamilton, Neil. 1994. Agriculture Without Farmers. *Successful Farming 92*(April): 28-29.

Hans Hedlund (Edr), Cooperation Revisited, Scandinavian Institute of African Studies, Uppasala, 1988.

Harris, Andrea, Brenda Stefanson, and Murray Fulton. 1996. New Generation Cooperatives and Cooperative Theory. *Journal of Cooperatives 11*: 13-28.

Harris, Andrea. 1998. *Agricultural Co-operatives: An Introduction and Start-up Guide*. Vernon, BC: Ministry of Agriculture and Food.

Harter, Lynn M., and Kathleen J. Krone. 2001. The Boundary-spanning Role of a Cooperative Support Organization: Managing the Paradox of Stability and Change in Non-traditional Organizations. *Journal of Applied Communication Research 29*(3): 248-277.

Haruna, Shoji. 1987. Random Input Price and the Theory of the Competitive Cooperative Firm. *Journal of Comparative Economics 11*(March): 81-95.

Haynes, Curtis, and Jessica Gordon Nembhard. 1999. Cooperative Economics: A Community Revitalization Strategy. *The Review of Black Political Economy 27*: 47-71.

Henehan, Brian, Bruce Anderson, Timothy Pezzolesi, and Robert Campbell. 1997. *Putting Co-operation to Work* (A Guidebook Developed for Cooperating for Sustainability: Achieving a Sustainable Agriculture Through Cooperation Teleconference). Ithaca, NY: Cornell University, Cooperative Enterprise Programme.

Henry, Stuart. 1985. Community Justice, Capitalist Society, and Human Agency: The Dialectics of Collective Law in the Cooperative. *Law and Society Review 19*(2): 303-327.

Herndon, Cary. 1984. *Vertical Integration by Regional Milk Cooperatives in the Southwest: Potentials and Problems*. Unpublished Doctoral Thesis (Ph.D.), Oklahoma State University, Stillwater.

Hindmoor, Andrew. 1999. Free Riding off Capitalism: Entrepreneurship and the Mondragon Experiment. *British Journal of Political Science 29*(1): 217-224.

Horowitz, Ira. 1991. On the effects of Cournot Rivalry Between Entrepreneurial and Cooperative Firms. *Journal of Comparative Economics 15*(March): 115-121.

Ichiishi, Tatsuro. 1990. A Contribution to the Macro Theory of Comparative Economic Systems. *Journal of Comparative Economics 14*(March): 15-32.

ILO, Cooperative Management and Administartion (Second Revised edn), Oxford and IBH Publishing Co. Pvt Ltd, New Delhi.

Ireland, Norman, and Peter Law. 1983. A Cournot-Nash Model of the Consumer Cooperative. *Southern Economic Journal 49* (January): 706-716.

Jentoft, Svein, and Anthony Davis. 1993. Self and Sacrifice: An Investigation of Small Boat Fisher Individualism and Its Implication for Producer Cooperatives. *Human Organization 52* (Winter): 356-367.

John Jacques (Edr), Manual on Cooperative Management, Cooperative Union, Holyoake House.

John Winfred and V.Kulandaiswamy, History of Cooperative Thought, Rainbow Publications, Coimbatore, India.

Jones, Derek, and Jan Svejnar. 1985. Participation, Profit Sharing, Worker Ownership and Efficiency in Italian Producer Cooperatives. *Economica 52*(November): 449-465.

Jones, Derek. 1985. The Economic Performance of Producer Co-operatives within Command Economies: Evidence for the Case of Poland. *Cambridge Journal of Economics 9* (June): 111-126.

Jones, Derek. 1987. The Productivity Effects of Worker Directors and Financial Participation by Employees in the Firm: The Case of British Retail Cooperatives. *Industrial and Labour Relations Review 41* (October): 79-92.

Kamat G.S, New Dimensions of Cooperative Management, Himalaya Publishing House, New Delhi.

Kang, Suk. 1988. Fair Distribution Rule in a Cooperative Enterprise. *Journal of Comparative Economics 12* (March): 89-92.

Kaswan, Jaques. 1992. *Projecting the Long-term Consequences of ESOP* vs *Co-op Conversion of a Firm on Employee Benefits and Company Cash* (Research Report 5). Davis: University of California at Davis, Center for Cooperatives.

Keillor, Steven J. 2000. *Cooperative Commonwealth: Co-ops in Rural Minnesota, 1859-1939.* St. Paul: Minnesota Historical Society Press. ISBN 0-87351-377-0.

Kempe.R.Hope, "Cooperative Socialism and the Cooperative Movement in Guyana" Review of International Cooperation, London: ICA, 1975.

Kiesling, Lynne. 1996. Institutional Choice Matters: The Poor Law and Implicit Labour Contracts in Victorian Lancashire. *Explorations in Economic History 33*: 65-85. (Related material: Discussion in 34: 56-76, January 1997).

Kimball, Miles. 1988. Farmers' Cooperatives as Behaviour Toward Risk. *American Economic Review 78* (March): 224-232.

Koller Fred E., 'Cooperatives in a Capitalistic Economy'. Agricultural Cooperation (Ed). Minnapolis: University of Minnesota Press, 1957.

Kreitner, Philip Colman. 1981. *The Theory of Economic Cooperation: U.S. New Generation Food Co-ops and the Cooperative Dilemma.* Doctoral Thesis (Ph.D.), University of Michigan, Ann Arbor, 1978. Ann Arbor, MI: University Microfilms International.

Krishnaswami O.R and V.Kulandaiswamy, Cooperation—Concept and Theory, Arudra Academy, Coimbatore, India, 2000.

Kulandaiswamy.V, Text Book of Cooperative Management, Arudra Academy, Coimbatore, India, 2002.

Kulkarni. K.R. in Theory and Practice of Cooperation in India and Abroad Vol I, Bombay: Cooperators' Book Depot, 1962.

Kurz, Mordecai. 1985. Cooperative Oligopoly Equilibrium. *European Economic Review 27*(February): 3-24.

Lacy, William, and Lawrence Busch. 1988. Biotechnology: Challenge and Opportunity for Agricultural Cooperatives. *Policy Studies Journal 17* (Fall): 203-214.

Laycock, David. 1989. Representative Economic Democracy and the Problem of Policy Influence: The Case of Canadian Co-operatives. *Canadian Journal of Political Science 22* (December): 765-792.

Lerman, Zvi, and Claudia Parliament. 1990. Comparative Performance of Cooperatives and Investor-owned Firms in U.S. Food Industries. *Agribusiness 6* (November): 527-540.

Lerman, Zvi, and Claudia Parliament. 1991. Size and Industry Effects in the Performance of Agricultural Cooperatives. *Agricultural Economics 6* (October): 15-29.

Lichtenstein, Jack. 1990. *Field to Fabric: The Story of American Cotton Growers*. Lubbock: Texas Tech University Press.

Lin, Justin Yifu. 1993. Exit Rights, Exit Costs, and Shirking in Agricultural Cooperatives: A Reply. *Journal of Comparative Economics 17* (June): 504-520.

Louis Smith, P.F., Evolution of Agricultural Cooperation.

Mahajan, VD., Ancient India, New Delhi, S. Chand and Co., 1970.

Malcolm Sargent, Agricultural Cooperation, Gower Publishing Co. Ltd, England, 1982.

Mansbridge, Jane. (Ed.). 1990. *Beyond Self-interest*. Chicago: University of Chicago Press.

Maslennikov.V, The Cooperative Movement in Asia and Africa, Progress Publishers, Mascow, 1983.

McLoughlin, Jane. 1989. Against the Tide. *New Statesman and Society 2* (April 28): 19-20.

Mellor, Mary, John Stirling, and Janet Hannah. 1988. *Worker Cooperatives in Theory and Practice*. Philadelphia: Open University Press.

Merrett, Christopher D., and Norman Walzer. 2003. *Cooperatives and Local Development: Theory and Applications for the 21st Century*. Armonk, NY: M.E. Sharpe. ISBN 0-7656-1123.

Mickiewicz, Tomasz. 1996. The Spatial Dimension of Transformation: Time Pattern and Ownership Factors on the Micro Level. *Europe-Asia Studies 48* (November): 1187-1202.

Milanovic, Branko. 1982. The Austrian Theory of the Cooperative Firm. *Journal of Comparative Economics 6* (December): 379-395.

Miller, David. 1981. Market Neutrality and the Failure of Co-operatives. *British Journal of Political Science 11*: 309-329. (Related material: Discussion in *13*: 125-128, January 1983)

Minnesota Association of Cooperatives. 1997. *Cooperatives Talk Minnesotan: Examining Cooperative Business*. St. Paul: Minnesota Association of Cooperatives.

Mitchell, Janet. 1990. Perfect Equilibrium and Intergenerational Conflict in a Model of Cooperative Enterprise Growth. *Journal of Economic Theory 51*(June): 48-76.

Molinas, Jose. 1998. The Impact of Inequality, Gender, External Assistance and Social Capital on Local-level Cooperation. *World Development 26*(3): 413-431.

Morgan, Zoe. 2006. Case Study—The Co-operative: Mutual Benefits of Staff Engagement. *Brand Strategy* (June): 50.

Munkner H.H and A.Shah, Creating a Favourable Climate and Conditions for Cooperative Development in Africa, ILO, Geneva, 1993.

Nakkiran.S, A Treatise on Cooperative Management, Rainbow Publications, Coimbatore, India, 2000.

National Council of Farmer Cooperatives. 1969. *Directory of Cooperatives of the United States.* Washington, DC: National Council of Farmer Cooperatives.

National Council of Farmer Cooperatives. 1995. *Journal of Cooperatives* (Entire Issue) 10.

Nor, Radziah. 1995. *Member Communication Methods used by Selected Agricultural Cooperatives in the Eastern North Central Region of the United States.* Unpublished Master's Thesis (M.S.), Ohio State University, Columbus.

P.E. Lambert, Studies in Social Philosophy of Cooperation, Manchester: Cooperative Union Ltd., 1963.

P.Y. Chinehankar and M.V. Namjoshi, Cooperation and the Dynamics of Charge, Bombay, Somaiya Publication Pvt, Ltd, 1977, p. 21.

Parliament, Claudia, Yacov Tsur, and David Zilberman. 1989. Cooperative Labour Allocation Under Uncertainty. *Journal of Comparative Economics 13* (December): 539-552.

Patrie, William. 1998. *Creating 'Co-op Fever': A Rural Developer's Guide to Forming Cooperatives* (RBS Service Report 54). Washington, DC: U.S. Department of Agriculture, Rural Business- Cooperative Service.

Paul Roy, Ewell, Cooperatives: Today and Tomorrow Illinois; The Interstate Printers and Publishers, 1964.

Payne, Malcolm [Reviewer]. 1998. The Myth of Mondragon: Cooperatives, Politics, and Working-Class Life in a Basque Town [Book Review]. *Human Relations 51*(9): 1179-1193.

Pencavel, John, and Ben Craig. 1994. The Empirical Performance of Orthodox Models of the Firm: Conventional Firms and Worker Cooperatives. *Journal of Political Economy 102*: 718-744.

Peterson, Christopher, and Bruce Anderson. 1996. Cooperative Strategy: Theory and Practice. *Agribusiness 12* (July/August): 371-383.

Ploughing for Profits. 1991. *Economist 320* (July 20): 84-85. Porter, Philip, and Gerald Scully. 1987. Economic Efficiency in Cooperatives. *Journal of Law and Economics 30* (October): 489-512.

Pritchard, William N. 1996. Shifts in Food Regimes, Regulation, and Producer Cooperatives: Insights from the Australian and US Dairy Industries. *Environment and Planning A 28*: 857-875.

Pritchard, William N. 1998. The Emerging Contours of the Third Food Regime: Evidence from Australian Dairy and Wheat Sectors. *Economic Geography 74*(1): 64-74.

Randall, Donna, and Mike O'Driscoll. 1997. Affective *vs.* Calculative Commitment: Human Resource Implications. *Journal of Social Psychology 137* (October): 606-617.

Rasmussen, Wayne. 1991. *Farmers, Cooperatives, and USDA: A History of Agricultural Cooperative Service* (Agricultural Information Bulletin #621). Washington, DC: U.S. Department of Agriculture.

Regan, Donald. 1980. *Utilitarianism and Co-operation.* Oxford, UK: Clarendon Press.

Reynolds, Bruce J. 2001. *A History of African-American Farmer Cooperatives, 1938-2000.* Washington, DC: U.S. Department of Agriculture, Rural Business-Cooperative Service.

Rhodes, James. 1983. The Large Agricultural Cooperative as a Competitor. *American Journal of Agricultural Economics 65*(December): 1090-1095. (Related Material: Discussion in 65: 1096-1098, December 1983).

Risto, Tainio. 1999. Strategic Change in the Evolution of Cooperatives. *Journal of Finnish Business Economics*: 484-490. Retrieved May 3, 2007, from www.pellervo.fi/finncoop/material/tainio.pdf.

Rooney, Patrick Michael. 1992. ESOPS, Producer Co-ops and Traditional Firms: Are they Different? *Journal of Economic Issues 26* (June): 593-603.

Rosow, Stephen, Naeem Inayatullah, and Mark Rupert. (Eds.). 1994. *The Global Economy as Political Space: Critical Perspectives on World Politics.* Boulder, CO: Lynne Rienner Publishers.

Rothburd, Carrie. 1986. Co-opted. *The Progressive 50* (May): 27-29. Royer, Jeffrey. 1987. *Cooperative Theory: New Approaches* (ACS Service Report 18). Washington, DC: U.S. Department of Agriculture, Agricultural Cooperative Service.

Russell, Raymond, and Robert Hanneman. 1992. Cooperatives and the Business Cycle: The Israeli Case. *Journal of Comparative Economics 16* (December): 701-715.

Sazama, Gerald W. 2000. Lessons from the History of Affordable Housing Cooperatives in the United States: A Case Study in American Affordable Housing Policy. *The American Journal of Economics and Sociology 59* (4): 573-608.

Schilthuis, Gijs. 2001. *Continuously Reinventing Cooperatives*. Marshall, MN: Southwest State University Center for Rural and Regional Studies.

Schroeder, Ted. 1991. *Multiproduct Scale and Scope Economies for Agricultural Cooperatives* (Staff Paper, 92-5). Manhattan: Kansas State University, Department of Agricultural Economics.

Sexton, Richard. 1984. Perspectives on the Development of the Economic Theory of Cooperatives. *Canadian Journal of Agricultural Economics 32* (July): 423-435.

Sommer, Robert, and Sandra Nelson. 1986. The use of Survey Results by Democratically Controlled Organizations. *Journal of Applied Behavioural Science 22*(2): 113-125.

Staber, Udo. 1992. Organizational Interdependence and Organizational Mortality in the Cooperative Sector: A Community Ecology Perspective. *Human Relations 45* (November): 1191-1212.

Staber, Udo. 1993. Worker Cooperatives and the Business Cycle: Are Cooperatives the Answer to Unemployment? *American Journal of Economics and Sociology 52* (April): 129-143.

Stanglin, Douglas. 1990. Front Row at the Revolution. *U.S. News and World Report 108* (March 26): 35-37.

Stans, Maurice. 1984. Running Dogs of Capitalism. *National Review 36* (December 14): 38. Staub, Ervin. 1984. *Development and Maintenance of Prosocial Behaviour: International Perspectives on Positive Morality.* New York: Plenum Press.

Tanzer, Andrew. 1996. Small is Beautiful. *Forbes 158* (September 23): 90-92. Torgerson, Randall. 1990. *Agricultural Cooperative Issues for the 1990s* (Working Paper Series, Number 5-A). Davis: University of California at Davis, Center for Cooperatives.

U.S. Department of Agriculture (USDA). 1997. *Co-ops 101: An Introduction to Cooperatives.* Washington, DC: USDA, Rural Business-Cooperative Service. USDA. 1998. *Cooperative Historical Statistics* (Cooperative Information Report: 1, Section 26, April). Washington, DC: USDA, Rural Business-Cooperative Service.

V.L. Mehta, Towards a Cooperative Socialist Common Wealth, Bombay: Maharashtra State Cooperative Union, 1965.

Van Ginkel, Rob. 1996. Cooperating Competitors: Texel Fishermen and Their Organizations (c.1870-1930). *Anthropological Quarterly 69* (April): 51-65.

Vercammen, James, and Murray Fulton. 1996. Non-linear Pricing Schemes for Co-operatives: The Equity/ Efficiency Trade-off. *Canadian Journal of Economics* (Special Issue) *29* (Pt. 1): S303-S307.

Wade, Robert. 1987. The Management of Common Property Resources: Collective Action as an Alternative to Privatization or State Regulation. *Cambridge Journal of Economics 11* (June): 95-106.

Wadsworth, James J. 1998. *Cooperative Restructuring, 1989-1998* (RBS Service Report 57). Washington, DC: U.S. Department of Agriculture, Rural Business-Cooperative Service.

Wagner, Ralph D. 2004. A history of the Farmington Plan. *Libraries and Culture 39* (4): 473-475.

Warman, Marc, Larry Stearns, and David Cobia. 1997. *Strategies for Survival by Cooperative Country Elevators: Revisited.* Washington, DC: U.S. Department of Agriculture.

Whatmore, Sarah, and Lorraine Thorne. 1997. Nourishing Networks: Alternative Geographies of Food. In *Globalising Food: Agrarian Questions and Global Restructuring*, ed. David Goodman and Michael Watts, 287-304. New York: Routledge.

Wilkins, Paul. 1980. *Marketing and Farm Supply Cooperatives Livestock Producer Membership and Use, 1980* (ACS Research Report 23). Washington, DC: U.S. Department of Agriculture, Agricultural Cooperative Service.

Williams, Ned. 1993. *The Co-op in Birmingham and the Black Country: 150 Years of Co-operation, 1844-1994.* Wolverhampton, UK: Uralia Press.

Williamson, Lionel, and Forrest Stegelin. 1989. *Successful Co-ops Don't Just Happen* (Staff Paper 262). Lexington: University of Kentucky, Department of Agricultural Economics.

Wills, Robert. 1985. Evaluating Price Enhancement by Processing Cooperatives. *American Journal of Agricultural Economics 67* (May): 183-192.

Wisconsin Center for Cooperatives, Cooperatives: A Tool for Community Economic Development, Madison.

Wyatt, Robert, Albert Kagan, and Darrel Davis. 1984. Cooperatives *vs.* Commercial Banks: The Uneasy Competition in Agri. Lending (Survey). *The Journal of Commercial Bank Lending 66* (April): 49-54.

Year in Cooperation: A Cooperative Development Magazine 2(2). 1996. St. Paul: Minnesota Association of Cooperatives.

Glossary of Cooperative Terms

Annual Meeting	General meeting which all members are entitled to attend and at which they are entitled to vote. A cooperative must hold an annual meeting each year, and no later than six months after the end of its fiscal year. The first general meeting must be held within four months of the cooperative's date of incorporation.
Articles or Incorporation	Official document required for incorporation; states the cooperative's name, purpose, share structure, directors and incorporators.
Board of Directors	Body elected by the members to direct the business, policy and operations of a co-op; all members could be on the board, but usually the membership is too large to meet to consider all decisions. See *Executive committee.*
Break-even Point	Level of sales or production needed to show neither income nor a loss.

Business Plan	Guide for managing the cooperative, setting its organizational structure, determining necessary shares capital, obtaining financing, identifying necessary facilities and equipment, and measuring progress.
By-laws	Statement of a cooperative's aims, objectives, and rules of operation. Must be approved by membership and may be amended as necessary. Proposed by-laws must be in accordance with the *Canada Cooperatives Act*. See *Certificate to Accompany By-laws.*
Capital	Total funds invested in a cooperative to enable it to conduct business.
Certificate of Incorporation	Legal document issued when incorporation has been approved. A cooperative legally comes into existence on the effective incorporation date stated on this certificate.
Consumer Cooperatives	Buy goods in bulk and sell them at competitive prices; examples are retail co-ops, direct charge co-ops, and buyers' clubs.
Co-operation Among Cooperatives	Cooperatives working together to strengthen and promote the Cooperative sector, and to avoid duplication of services. See *Cooperative principles.*
Cooperative	A legally incorporated organization that is developed, owned and controlled by and for its members. Established to provide members with goods or services, or to make joint use of available resources to improve members' social or economic conditions.

Cooperative Principles	Seven guidelines for cooperative philosophy and business practice; endorsed by The International Co-operative Alliance in 1966 and revised in 1995: (1) Voluntary and open membership; (2) Democratic member control; (3) Member economic participation; (4) Autonomy and independence; (5) Education, training and information; (6) Co-operation among cooperatives; and (7) Concern for community.
Democratic Control	One vote per member regardless of equity; members have a duty to participate in the cooperative's decision-making process. See *Cooperative principles.*
Education	Education of members and elected officials in cooperative principles and practices to ensure understanding of roles and responsibilities. See *Cooperative principles.*
Equity	The difference between the value of assets and liabilities.
Equity Capital	The investment in a cooperative that represents member ownership, usually expressed in common shares owned by members.
Executive Committee	The board of directors usually delegates some responsibilities, especially operations management issues, to an executive committee typically consisting of a president, vice president, secretary and/or treasurer. See *Board of directors.*

Financial Cooperatives	Provide a variety of financial services such as savings, investments and loans; examples include credit unions, insurance and trust cooperatives.
Forecasting	Predicting how many units of product or service will be sold in a given time frame, at what cost to the cooperative, and at what price to the buyer, in order to calculate the financial, material and human resources required to produce the goods or provide the service.
Incorporation	Legal formation of a cooperative; requires submission of an incorporation package (containing the Articles of Incorporation, a Notice of Registered Office, and a proposed set of by-laws) to the Registrar of Cooperatives. See *Articles and Certificate of Incorporation.*
Invested Share Capital	The money that shareholders members put up initially to start the cooperative.
Legislation	See the *Canada Cooperative Act* for current federal legislation and the Acts it replaced.
Limited Interest Shares	Shares are used to raise capital for a cooperative, rather than to generate a large return on investment for members. See *Cooperative principles.*
Market	The potential buyers of a product or service, determined by geographic, economic, social and other characteristics.

Market Analysis	The process of identifying potential consumers of a product or service, the size of the group, and the percentage of the market that could be captured, considering costs and competition.
Marketing Strategy	Strategy to make potential customers/ members aware of a cooperative's goods and services; includes promotion, publicity, advertising and sales.
Marketing Cooperatives	Cooperatives established to support members' efforts to sell their products; examples include agricultural cooperatives.
Member	An individual who has met the conditions of membership stated in the by-laws, and has been accepted as a member by the board of directors of a cooperative.
Membership	Membership in a cooperative must be voluntary and open, without discrimination, to anyone who can use its services. See *Cooperative principles.*
Operating Costs	Expenses incurred in conducting activities ordinary and necessary to the operation of a cooperative.
Patronage Refund	Net savings are reinvested in a cooperative or are returned to members as patronage dividends, which may be in the form of cash and/ or additional shares in the cooperative. See *Cooperative principles.*
Producer Cooperatives	Cooperatives owned by producers for their mutual benefit; examples include dairy, feeder, film, fishery, handicraft and worker (employment) cooperatives.

Refund	See *Patronage refund.*
Registrar of Cooperatives	Official appointed to oversee regulation and carry out regulatory duties set out in the *Canada Cooperative Act.* Maintains register of cooperatives. Collects, approves, issues and files legal documents related to the registration, incorporation and operation of cooperatives.
Registration	Official record in the province territory's legal registry that an organization has been incorporated as a cooperative.
Rochdale	A small group of people known as the Rochdale Pioneers established a retail cooperative in Rochdale, Lancashire, England in 1844. The policies and methods of developing and operating their cooperative enterprise became the foundation of current internationally-endorsed principles. See *Cooperative principles.*
Sales Forecast	A prediction of the number of units of product or service a cooperative will sell within a specified time period and at a given price.
Service Cooperatives	Provide needed services, generally at improved quality, price and availability; examples include health care, child care, cablevision, farm machinery, housing and transportation cooperatives.
Share	One of the equal parts into which a cooperative's capital is divided.

Start-up	The initial period of operation of a co-op or other business or service, usually the period before the enterprise begins receiving income.
Start-up Capital	The total amount of money, resources and property that a cooperative needs to begin operating and to support it until income is received.
Statement of Income	A summary report of all forms of income generated over a specific period including sales, tax credits, dividends and receivables.
Target Market	A very specific group of potential customers, usually defined by one or more of: age, lifestyle, gender, socio-economic position, income, geography, needs and interests, etc.
Types of Cooperatives	Five categories when classified by function. See *Consumer, Financial, Marketing, Producer* and *Service cooperatives.*
Variable Costs	Expenses that vary with the volume of goods or service provided by a cooperative.
Worker Cooperatives	See *Employment cooperatives.*
Working Capital	The difference between current assets and current liabilities.

Index

D

G

H

I

J

K

L

T

U

V

W

❑❑❑